American Modernism

OTHER TITLES IN THE
GREENHAVEN PRESS COMPANION TO LITERARY
MOVEMENTS AND GENRES SERIES:

American Romanticism
Greek Drama
Victorian Literature

Joseph Stella, *Steel Mill*, 1919-1920
National Museum of American Art,
Washington, D.C.

THE GREENHAVEN PRESS COMPANION TO
Literary Movements and Genres

American Modernism

Scott Barbour, *Book Editor*

David L. Bender, *Publisher*

Bruno Leone, *Executive Editor*

Bonnie Szumski, *Editorial Director*

David M. Haugen, *Managing Editor*

Greenhaven Press, Inc., San Diego, California

Every effort has been made to trace the owners of copy-
righted material. The articles in this volume may have
been edited for content, length, and/or reading level. The
titles have been changed to enhance the editorial purpose.
Those interested in locating the original source will find
the complete citation on the first page of each article.

Library of Congress Cataloging-in-Publication Data

American modernism / Scott Barbour, book editor.
          p.   cm. — (Literary movements and genres)
     Includes bibliographical references (p.   ) and index.
     ISBN 0-7377-0200-1 (pbk. : alk. paper). —
  ISBN 0-7377-0201-X (lib. : alk. paper)
     1. American literature—20th century—History and
criticism. 2. Modernism (Literature)—United States.
I. Barbour, Scott, 1963–   . II. Series.
PS228.M63A49   2000
810.9'112—dc21   99-25707
                                                        CIP

Cover photo: National Museum of American Art,
         Washington/Art Resource

CONTENTS

Foreword   9

Introduction   11

A History and Overview of American Modernism   13

Chapter 1: Defining American Modernism

1. **The Characteristics of Modernism** *by Irving Howe*   28
   Modernists sought to overturn the prevailing literary styles
   and cultural beliefs. Their work was therefore characterized by subjectivity, moral relativism, and historical
   discontinuity.

2. **American Modernism Is Distinct from European
   Modernism** *by Julian Symons*   36
   American modernists rejected the intellectual tack of European modernists and instead produced works in a simple, colloquial style.

3. **The Use of Concrete Words and Images in
   American Modernism** *by Floyd C. Watkins*   44
   American modernists avoided abstract concepts and in-
   stead presented concrete facts in an objective manner.
   Their rejection of empty rhetoric and false sentiment was
   a reflection of their post-World War I disillusionment.

4. **Modernism Expresses Both Historical
   Discontinuity and a Sense of Tradition**
   by Richard Ellmann and Charles Feidelson Jr.   51
   While modernists broke with the past, they also explored
   history and their place in the literary tradition.

Chapter 2: The New Poetry

1. **The American Poetic Renaissance: New Freedoms
   in Subject and Form** *by Louise Bogan*   56
   Beginning with the foundation of *Poetry* magazine in 1912,
   American poetry underwent permanent change. The style
   changed from traditional poetic meter to conversational
   speech patterns, and the thematic content became more
   realistic and dark.

2. **The Tenets of Imagism: Directness, Conciseness, and Musical Rhythm** *by Richard Gray*　　64
The Imagists headed the resurgence in American poetry from 1912 to 1917. Imagist poets stressed the direct treatment of subject matter, a lack of superfluous words, and the use of musical rhythm instead of traditional poetic meter.

3. **T.S. Eliot's *The Waste Land:* The Chief Example of Modernist Poetry** *by David Perkins*　　72
T.S. Eliot's poem *The Waste Land* is the definitive work of modernist poetry. The poem's formal discontinuity, symbolism, mythological references, and allusions all contribute to Eliot's vision of the sterility of modern life.

4. **The Influence of World War I on American Modernist Poetry** *by Babette Deutsch*　　82
Following World War I, American poets relied on satire to express their grief, their despair, and their disgust with an increasingly urban and technological society that seemed to lack meaning.

Chapter 3: American Writers of the 1920s and 1930s

1. **The Lost Generation: Writers in a Time of Transition** *by Malcolm Cowley*　　91
Members of the lost generation—young American writers following World War I—shared certain experiences that set them apart from their predecessors. These writers were lost because they lacked a sense of connection to their country's traditions and because they were not prepared to cope with the societal changes they encountered.

2. **The American Expatriates Fled a Repressive Society** *by Donald Pizer*　　98
The American writers who called Paris their home between the two world wars sought freedom from American society's repressive sexual mores and social conventions.

3. **F. Scott Fitzgerald Captured the Spirit of His Generation** *by Malcolm Bradbury*　　104
Fitzgerald involved himself in the excessive lifestyle of his generation and produced fiction that presented the conflicts between idealism and the unpleasant realities of modern life. This process required the use of techniques of modernism, including symbolism and a sense of temporal discontinuity.

4. **Ernest Hemingway Used a Precise Style to Depict the Individual in Crisis** *by Alfred Kazin*　　112
Hemingway's exact, evocative style was one of the most significant facets of the modernist movement in fiction.

This style enabled Hemingway to vividly depict his heroes confronting the tragedy of war and anarchy.

5. **The Stream-of-Consciousness Technique in American Modernist Fiction**
   by Frederick J. Hoffman   120
   Authors employing stream of consciousness attempt to convey the unconscious and semiconscious thought processes of their characters. William Faulkner effectively uses this approach in his novel *The Sound and the Fury.* He tells the story from four points of view, varying the vocabulary and style to reveal the different states of consciousness of the four characters.

Chapter 4: Regional Movements: Renaissance in Harlem and the South

1. **The Harlem Renaissance: A Florescence of Creativity** *by Amritjit Singh*   127
   While white authors such as T.S. Eliot and Ernest Hemingway were forging new literary ground, African-American writers in Harlem and other U.S. cities were involved in their own artistic flowering. Countee Cullen, James Weldon Johnson, Jean Toomer, and others expressed the new racial pride of the 1920s.

2. **The Fugitives, the Agrarians, and the Southern Renaissance** *by Alexander Karanikas*   141
   The Agrarian movement—consisting of John Crowe Ransom, Allen Tate, Robert Penn Warren, and several other men—was central to the renaissance in southern literature that began in the 1920s. The Agrarians, earlier known as the Fugitives, rejected some aspects of traditional southern culture but nonetheless sought to preserve the southern way of life.

Chapter 5: Evaluating American Modernists and Their Contribution

1. **American Modernists Revolted Against Genteel Tradition** *by Malcolm Cowley*   155
   American writers of the 1920s rejected the genteel tradition that had emerged in America following the Civil War. They eschewed puritanism, optimism, and English literary forms in favor of sensuality, realism, and original American styles of writing.

2. **American Modernists Were Defenders of Genteel Tradition** *by Marcus Klein*   162
   American modernists did not rebel against genteel tradition. Instead, they attempted to preserve that tradition in the face of rapid urbanization and a mass immigration of

foreigners who threatened to dispossess them of their privileged social status.

3. **Modernism Is an Exclusively White, Western Movement** *by Houston A. Baker Jr.*   171
Modernist writers—including American authors such as F. Scott Fitzgerald, T.S. Eliot, and Eugene O'Neill—deal with themes and perspectives alien to black Americans. While modernists concerned themselves with preserving their wealth and contentment, African Americans were concerned with basic survival.

4. **American Modernists Were Intellectually Shallow** *by Ernest Earnest*   178
While the American modernist writers were revolutionary for their time, they failed to produce a useful legacy. Because they dwelt mostly on superficial, ephemeral issues, their work pales in comparison to that of their predecessors, such as Edgar Allen Poe, Herman Melville, and Nathaniel Hawthorne.

5. **American Modernists Strove to Improve American Society** *by C. Barry Chabot*   188
Modernism is usually believed to be concerned with aesthetic issues, such as new forms and styles of poetry and fiction. However, American modernists also sought, through their writing, to restore economic equality and a sense of community to American society.

Chronology   194

For Further Research   197

Index   201

FOREWORD

The study of literature most often involves focusing on an individual work and uncovering its themes, stylistic conventions, and historical relevance. It is also enlightening to examine multiple works by a single author, identifying similarities and differences among texts and tracing the author's development as an artist.

While the study of individual works and authors is instructive, however, examining groups of authors who shared certain cultural or historical experiences adds a further richness to the study of literature. By focusing on literary movements and genres, readers gain a greater appreciation of influence of historical events and social circumstances on the development of particular literary forms and themes. For example, in the early twentieth century, rapid technological and industrial advances, mass urban migration, World War I, and other events contributed to the emergence of a movement known as American modernism. The dramatic social changes, and the uncertainty they created, were reflected in an increased use of free verse in poetry, the stream-of-consciousness technique in fiction, and a general sense of historical discontinuity and crisis of faith in most of the literature of the era. By focusing on these commonalities, readers attain a more comprehensive picture of the complex interplay of social, economic, political, aesthetic, and philosophical forces and ideas that create the tenor of any era. In the nineteenth-century American romanticism movement, for example, authors shared many ideas concerning the preeminence of the self-reliant individual, the infusion of nature with spiritual significance, and the potential of persons to achieve transcendence via communion with nature. However, despite their commonalities, American romantics often differed significantly in their thematic and stylistic approaches. Walt Whitman celebrated the communal nature of America's open democratic society, while Ralph Waldo

Emerson expressed the need for individuals to pursue their own fulfillment regardless of their fellow citizens. Herman Melville wrote novels in a largely naturalistic style whereas Nathaniel Hawthorne's novels were gothic and allegorical.

Another valuable reason to investigate literary movements and genres lies in their potential to clarify the process of literary evolution. By examining groups of authors, literary trends across time become evident. The reader learns, for instance, how English romanticism was transformed as it crossed the Atlantic to America. The poetry of Lord Byron, William Wordsworth, and John Keats celebrated the restorative potential of rural scenes. The American romantics, writing later in the century, shared their English counterparts' faith in nature; but American authors were more likely to present an ambiguous view of nature as a source of liberation as well as the dwelling place of personal demons. The whale in Melville's *Moby-Dick* and the forests in Hawthorne's novels and stories bear little resemblance to the benign pastoral scenes in Wordsworth's lyric poems.

Each volume in Greenhaven Press's Companions to Literary Movements and Genres series begins with an introductory essay that places the topic in a historical and literary context. The essays that follow are carefully chosen and edited for ease of comprehension. These essays are arranged into clearly defined chapters that are outlined in a concise annotated table of contents. Finally, a thorough chronology maps out crucial literary milestones of the movement or genre as well as significant social and historical events. Readers will benefit from the structure and coherence that these features lend to material that is often challenging. With Greenhaven's Literary Movements and Genres in hand, readers will be better able to comprehend and appreciate the major literary works and their impact on society.

INTRODUCTION

When attempting to pinpoint the genesis of the modernist movement in literature, critics often cite English novelist Virginia Woolf's remark that "on or about December, 1910, human character changed." This statement humorously and succinctly expresses the futility of attempting to identify the exact start date of a phenomenon that evolved as the result of various social, cultural, and literary forces. Perhaps more importantly, it hints at the enormity of change that the modernist movement represented.

Modernism, as its name implies, was a response to modernization. It was the literature that sprang up in the wake of the transition of Western nations, including the United States, from pre-industrial to modernized societies during the late nineteenth and early twentieth centuries. By 1910, rapid industrial growth and technological advancement had transformed America from a primarily agricultural society to an overwhelmingly industrial one. Massive migration to the urban centers, combined with waves of immigration from Europe and Asia, had swelled the cities with burgeoning populations. The new industrial base of the nation had created an increasingly commercialized culture in which an abundance of new products were vigorously advertised for public consumption.

American authors of the early twentieth century were acutely sensitive to the cultural transformation occurring around them, and they responded in disparate ways. Some applauded the nation's technological progress while others criticized its materialistic culture. Some sought meaning in the imagination or in history while others searched for truth in the concrete world of the immediate present. Some developed allegiances to their particular regions while others fled the continent. An example of two differing responses to modernization is evident in the work of the poets Carl Sandburg and T.S. Eliot. In his *Chicago Poems*, Sandburg celebrated the new bustling metropolis. In *The Waste Land*, on

11

the other hand, Eliot depicted the modern city as a spiritually debased and dehumanizing environment. This is merely one example of the divergent paths taken by American authors during the modernist era.

The differences between individual modernist authors add to the difficulty of defining modernism. Modernism can be defined as an era, a time period from about 1905 to about 1929. It can also be defined in terms of its content—its struggle to make sense of a chaotic, modernizing world. However, the one element that all modernist authors shared was their dedication to using language in new ways. Modernist authors believed that the traditional literary forms and styles were inadequate to reflect the realities of the modern world, so they experimented with new structures and means of expression. Sandburg and Eliot, although they differed in their attitudes toward urbanization, are linked as American modernists because both poets relied on new modes of writing in an attempt to capture the spirit of the modern scene.

The transition from the pre-industrial period to the modern era in America thus produced not only new social institutions and economic structures; it brought forth a new literary aesthetic, a permanent change to the literary tradition of the nation. Although critics debate the quality of much of the literature of this era, few deny the lasting impact of the formal and stylistic developments wrought by modernist authors. No American poet (or any poet in English) writing after 1922 is free of the influence of Eliot's *The Waste Land.* Similarly, no fiction writer escapes the effects of the "Hemingway style." Eliot, Hemingway, and their contemporaries altered the course of American literature. The nature and history of this change are described in the essays compiled in *American Modernism,* a volume in Greenhaven Press's Companions to Literary Movements and Genres series. It is the editors' hope that this anthology will aid the reader in understanding the new literature that emerged during the modernist era in American literature.

A HISTORY AND OVERVIEW OF AMERICAN MODERNISM

American literary modernism was a movement in American literature that occurred roughly between 1910 and 1940. Although the exact start and end dates of the movement are debated, most critics of the era's literature focus primarily on two bodies of work: the poetry written between 1912 and 1917 (when the U.S. entered World War I) and the poetry and fiction of the 1920s (the postwar period). In some ways these two periods are distinct; however, they are both equally modernist.

More important than the exact dates of the movement are the characteristics of the literature bearing the label American modernism. Briefly put, American modernist literature is characterized by a reevaluation of traditional styles, forms, and subject matter and a new emphasis on experimentation. Some of the most salient features of American modernism are a direct presentation of experience, economical use of language, symbolism, and an informal, colloquial style. In poetry, American modernists eschewed traditional forms, rhyme schemes, and meter in favor of original, nonrhyming forms and musical or conversational rhythms.

In addition to formal and stylistic features, American modernism is distinguished by particular thematic elements. Especially in the postwar period, the works of American modernists express a sense of disillusionment with American society and culture. Some modernists were critical of America's increasingly mechanized, commercial, and capitalistic nature. In fact, many American modernists were extremely cynical and pessimistic about the state of American society and of Western culture generally. The works of these authors, including T.S. Eliot, Ezra Pound, and Ernest Hemingway, portray individuals and a society in the midst of a spiritual crisis and a modern world (especially a modern city) in which human life has lost its meaning.

The works of American modernists reflect a sense that the world has undergone a transformation from a stable, ordered past to a chaotic, technological, mechanized modern era in which the basic underlying beliefs and assumptions have been brought into question. One element of the literature of the period is therefore a sense of discontinuity. This discontinuity is both a formal and thematic characteristic of the literature. For example, in much of the poetry and fiction of the period, chronological time has been broken up—that is, the sequence of events is jumbled. In addition, much of the poetry consists not of structured narrative but of juxtaposed and fragmented images and symbols. These formal characteristics of the literature reflect the authors' sense of a broken connection with the past and confusion, chaos, and a crisis of faith in the present.

AMERICAN LITERARY MODERNISM IN CONTEXT

In order to better understand American literary modernism, it is necessary to view the movement in the context of international developments. Modernism was an international movement. American modernism was not distinct from European modernism. In fact, some of the most prominent American modernists lived and wrote in Europe, and many were heavily influenced by European artists. For example, poets such as T.S. Eliot and Ezra Pound were influenced by the French symbolist poets of the nineteenth century. Therefore the term American modernism refers not to a separate movement, or even a submovement; it simply refers to the American authors who were part of the international modernist movement. In some ways these authors resembled their European counterparts; in other ways they did not.

The international literary modernism movement was itself simply the literary strain of a larger movement taking place in all the arts. Ross Murfin and Supryia M. Ray, authors of *The Bedford Glossary of Critical and Literary Terms*, characterize modernism as

> a revolutionary movement encompassing all of the creative arts that had its roots in the 1890s (the fin de siecle [end of the century]), a transitional period during which artists and writers sought to liberate themselves from the constraints and polite conventions we associate with Victorianism.[1]

As this definition makes clear, modernism was marked by a spirit of revolt—specifically, revolt against formal and thematic conventions characteristic of the Victorian era. Many social and cultural factors contributed to this artistic revolution. Modernism can be seen as a reflection of, or reaction to, modernization and the Industrial Revolution. Dramatic social and cultural changes took place in the industrial western nations of late nineteenth and early twentieth centuries. In America, one of the greatest changes was the nation's shift from a predominately rural, agricultural society to an urban, industrial one. As Richard Gray, a literature professor at the University of Essex in the United Kingdom, notes, the populations of cities swelled during this period:

> As early as 1880 . . . , over half the population of the Eastern United States lived in towns of more than 4,000 people; while places like New York, Philadelphia, and Boston, which had once been provincial market-places, were turning into urban, metropolitan centres.[2]

This trend toward technological and industrial development, and the urban population explosion that accompanied it, accelerated in the early decades of the twentieth century.

This rapid societal change, combined with the increasing mechanization and commercialization of the culture, contributed to the sense of discontinuity, temporal and spatial fragmentation, and chaos found in the art and literature of the modernist era. In addition, whereas the Romanticism of the Victorian era had focused on nature and rural settings, modernist literature, as a result of the massive urbanization of society, more often focused on the city and its inhabitants.

Intellectual developments also helped to produce the modernist movement—especially the work of Charles Darwin, Karl Marx, Sigmund Freud, and Albert Einstein. Alan Shucard, Fred Moramarco, and William Sullivan, authors of the book *Modern American Poetry, 1865–1950*, describe the contribution that each of these thinkers made to unsettling people's underlying assumptions about human beings, their relationships with one another, and the universe in which they live:

> From Darwin came the idea that the emergence of human forms was a natural, not supernatural, event that occurred over millions of years, the result of random forces and natural selection. Chance, not divine will, seemed the governing principle of what appeared to be an increasingly accidental universe. From Marx came a view of human society as perpetually engaged in class struggle. In Freud's work the inner world of humanity was depicted as dominated by uncon-

scious drives and motives, accessible only through dreams and deep exploratory analysis. And from Einstein came the revolutionary principle that time and space, the psychic and physical environment of humanity, were relative, not absolute, entities, subject to continuing alteration and redefinition as the mysteries of the cosmos unfolded.[5]

German philosopher Friedrich Nietzsche added to this atmosphere of intellectual upheaval by questioning the legitimacy of Christian morality. All of these thinkers contributed to the general sense that the old ideas and belief systems that had previously lent stability and order to the universe and human relations no longer applied and that, consequently, a new type of art was needed to accurately capture the new understanding of reality.

THE INFLUENCE OF THE VISUAL ARTS

The various social, cultural, and intellectual developments of the late nineteenth and early twentieth centuries first made themselves felt in the visual arts. European Impressionists such as Claude Monet had begun to revolutionize painting as early as the 1870s. In general, the Impressionists, as well as post-Impressionists like Vincent Van Gogh, Pablo Picasso, Marcel Duchamp, and Wassily Kandinsky, abandoned the traditional artistic approach of creating realistic representations of their subjects. Instead, they relied on stylistic techniques, including the use of bold colors and expressive brush strokes, to convey the emotion evoked by the subjects of their paintings, whether rural landscapes, urban scenes, or nudes. In the paintings of the Impressionists, Alan Shucard and his colleagues explain, "the previously static and orthodox landscape is shattered into a fluid array of dots, colors, and vigorous brush strokes that create a sense of the transitory and shifting environment of the modern world."[4]

Two exhibits of the visual arts are often cited as key moments in the history of modernism. The first was a 1905 exhibit at the Autumn Salon in Paris. This show featured the work of the Fauvists, a school of artists led by Henri Matisse and inspired by Vincent Van Gogh, Paul Gauguin, and Paul Cézanne. The Fauvists used vivid colors in an expressive, violent manner to create dynamic paintings. The name Fauvist was derived from the word "fauve," which is French for "wild beast." The group received this name after an art critic attending the 1905 show saw a traditional sculpture among

these paintings and stated that it looked like it was surrounded by "les fauves."

The second, and more significant, exhibit was a 1913
show in New York, which was named the Armory Show because it took place in the Sixty-ninth Regiment Armory. This
show brought the work of the avant-garde European
artists—including the Fauvists but also the Cubists and Expressionists—to American soil for the first time. Prominent
among the new works was Marcel Duchamp's Cubist work
Nude Descending a Staircase, an expressive painting in
which the subject has been distorted and fragmented virtu-
ally beyond recognition.

The Armory Show was a significant moment in the history of American modernism because it allowed American
writers, who felt an immediate affinity with the European
artists, to recognize themselves as part of an international
movement of experimental artists struggling to make sense
of the modern world. Shucard and his colleagues describe
the impact of the Armory show on the international community of modernist artists:

> The Armory Show created a sense of the international com-
> munity of artists who shared an awareness of the revolution-
> ary and distinctive newness of twentieth-century life and cul-
> ture. The parochialism of nationality and regionalism was
> superseded by images of the rapidly changing urban, indus-
> trial, and fragmented twentieth-century world. This world
> could be expressed only in radically new images that de-
> parted from the formally structured, natural or supernatural
> images of the art of previous times. The new art was an art of
> motion, speed, urbanity, machinery, and the accelerated pace
> of life. Duchamp's *Nude* was an appropriately representative
> piece for the exhibit because it presented the human form as
> a succession of lines and planes in motion, a quintessential
> expression of the wedding of human and machine.[5]

Among American writers, the Armory Show had its most
profound effect on poets. Poet William Carlos Williams, who
attended the Armory Show, later recalled seeing Duchamp's
Nude Descending the Staircase: "I laughed out loud when I
first saw it, happily, with relief."[6] Richard Gray explains the
significance of Williams's laughter:

> The relief Williams, and others, felt was the relief of liberation:
> here, at last, was something that would help to free them from
> tradition, the tyranny of conventional, representational art.[7]

Thus the Armory Show served to embolden and liberate
American authors to pursue their experimentation in new

forms, styles, and subject matter in order to effectively express their vision of a changing world.

The Armory Show closely coincided with another major event that helped produce a modernist movement in American literature: the creation of *Poetry* magazine by Harriet Monroe in Chicago in 1912. Although American fiction writers had been producing works with modernist characteristics prior to 1912—most notably Theodore Dreiser, Henry James, Upton Sinclair, and Gertrude Stein—collectively their work owed more to the tenets of naturalism than the forces of modernism. Naturalists such as Dreiser and Sinclair had presented realistic, objective observations of American life— including its unpleasant realities. While James and Stein were more modernist than their counterparts, modernist fiction did not fully develop until the postwar period.

Prior to World War I poetry took the lead in modernist literature. Although poets throughout America had been engaged in experimentation prior to 1912, the arrival of *Poetry* helped to create a sense that they were part of a larger poetic renaissance. Many literary critics argue that this event marked the beginning of the literary modernist movement in America. It is also commonly agreed that in poetry, Americans outpaced the Europeans in creating new styles and forms.

The "New Poetry," as it was called, was largely a revolt against the Romanticism of the previous decades. In general, the poets sought to free themselves from the constraints of conventional poetic forms and styles—especially those inherited from England. More specifically, they rejected poetic diction and regular meter in favor of colloquial words and phrases, often attempting to recreate distinctively American speech. They eschewed rhyme schemes in favor of non-rhyming free verse. Instead of focusing on abstract concepts like nature, truth, or beauty, as the Romantic poets had done, they attempted to express the emotion of everyday, concrete objects and experience. Rather than expressing their internal emotional states, they attempted to describe the external world.

The effect of this sudden explosion of poetic experimentation was a sense of excitement among the poets of the era. One of the chief participants in the poetic renaissance, Amy Lowell, describes the nature of the poetry and the spirit of the period in the following passage written in 1923:

In the first place, it was an effort to free the individual from
the expression of the herd; in the second, it had for its object
the breaking down of mere temperamental barriers. . . . The
poetry of the two preceding decades had been almost entirely
concerned with recording personal emotions, but recording
them in a perfectly stereotyped way. The new poetry found
that emotions were not confined to the conjugation of the
verb to love, and whether it said "I love" or "Behold the earth
and all that is thereon," if it followed its natural inclination, it
would say it quite differently from the way its fathers had said
it. The truth is that this new poetry, whether written by men
or women, was in essence masculine, virile, very much alive.
Where the nineties had warbled, it was prone to shout.[8]

Along with Lowell, some of the prominent poets of this era
were T.S. Eliot, Ezra Pound, Vachel Lindsay, Edgar Lee Masters, Robert Frost, Carl Sandburg, H.D. (Hilda Doolittle),
William Carlos Williams, Edward Arlington Robinson, and
Alfred Kreymborg.

Between 1912 and 1917, the modernist movement in poetry was far from unified. Various schools and submovements arose and competed with one another for promi-
nence. Ezra Pound, an American poet who had moved to
London in 1908, was a chief figure in many of these movements. The first and most important poetic movement was
Imagism, which received its name from Pound. The Imagists
adhered to three tenets: direct treatment of the subject, concise use of language, and musical rhythms rather than traditional poetic meter. By using language precisely, the Imagists hoped to create an image that would capture the
emotion produced by the object or subject being described.

Pound's poem "At a Station in the Metro" is frequently
cited as an example of Imagist poetry. The poem, which is
only two lines long, is Pound's attempt to capture the experience of being struck by the beauty of faces in the crowd at a
subway station in Paris.

> The apparition of these faces in the crowd;
> Petals on a wet, black bough.

As Shucard and his colleagues point out, by comparing the
faces to petals, Pound suggests the sense that human life is
fragile and beautiful. Although "the poem resists para-
phrase," they continue, "its images are haunting and carry
something of the force of a painting of the same objects. The
language is used exactly as brush strokes."[9] Along with
Pound, the Imagist movement included such poets as H.D.

(Hilda Doolittle), Amy Lowell, and William Carlos Williams.

In addition to Imagism, movements of this era included the Others, Vorticism, Dadaism, and Futurism. Most of these movements were relatively small and short-lived. Some, including Dadaism and Futurism, were primarily present in the European visual arts and only marginally in American poetry. However, the various movements led to the creation of many small magazines that competed with *Poetry*, including *Others*, *Blast*, and the *Little Review*. Taken all together, the disparate movements and their magazines contributed to the atmosphere of creative energy, artistic experimentation, and intellectual fervor that characterized the American poetic renaissance prior to the war.

American poets continued to create experimental works during the 1920s. However, the disagreements and divergent strands that had been present in the movement prior to the war intensified in the postwar period. A glance at three of the most prominent poets of the period—T.S. Eliot, William Carlos Williams, and Wallace Stevens—provides a partial view of the different approaches to both form and content following the war.

T.S. Eliot, an extremely influential critic as well as poet, was one of the most significant figures of the entire modernist movement in the arts. His poem *The Waste Land* (1922) is considered the quintessential modernist poem and is commonly listed along with James Joyce's novel *Ulysses* as one of the two seminal modernist texts. In *The Waste Land*, Eliot continued the poetic experimentation of the prewar era—including a sense of discontinuity, fragmentation, an emphasis on urban rather than rural settings, use of colloquial language, and heavy use of symbolism. However, while Eliot's poetry was representative of modernism to a large degree, Eliot was in many ways a traditionalist. For all his formal experimentation, he remained firm in his conviction that poets should have a deep understanding of poetic tradition and its relationship with the present. For this reason, his poetry is often pedantic and academic. For example, *The Waste Land* contains numerous references and allusions to classical myths and scholarly texts. When it was originally published, the poem contained extensive footnotes to help the reader make sense of these obscure references.

In contrast to Eliot, William Carlos Williams called for a more sincere, straightforward, and distinctively American poetry. Williams was appalled by *The Waste Land*, which he considered to be excessively self-conscious and scholarly. In his autobiography he wrote that the poem "wiped out our world as if an atom bomb had been dropped upon it."[10] In opposition to the intellectual poetry of Eliot, Williams declared, "No ideas but in things." By this dictum he meant that poets should avoid complex structures and abstract concepts and should instead accurately describe reality and allow the meaning and emotion of objects to speak for themselves. This philosophy became the basis of a new poetry movement: Objectivism.

In contrast to Williams, who focused on "things," another important poet of the era, Wallace Stevens, focused on ideas. Stevens concerned himself primarily with the relationship between the external world and the individual imagination. Stevens believed that the poet, through the act of perceiving, imagining, and creating poetry, transforms reality and invests it with meaning. As explained by Richard Gray:

> In a way, Stevens argues, our world is always an imagined one because our senses start to arrange things almost as soon as they perceive them, and whenever we think about experience we begin to structure it according to some law—such as the scientific law of cause and effect. We start to "read" and interpret the world in the same manner that, instinctively, we read and interpret a written text. For Stevens, however, the supreme example of this shaping, structuring capacity, is the artistic imagination: those acts of the mind whereby people attempt quite consciously to give significance to life—to devise some moral or aesthetic order, however fragile or provisional, which can give coherence and a sense of purpose to things. This kind of order was what Stevens called a "supreme fiction", and for him, . . . the prime creator of such fictions was the poet.[11]

Stevens's conception of the imagination is illustrated in his poem "The Man with the Blue Guitar." As Shucard and his colleagues point out, in this poem the blue guitar represents the imagination and the musician is the artist or poet. The artist does not recreate reality exactly but transforms it through the imaginative process: "Things as they are / Are changed upon the blue guitar." Therefore, the narrator of the poem says, "I cannot bring a world quite round, / Although I patch it as I can."[12]

Eliot, Williams, and Stevens thus represent three divergent strands of American poetry in the postwar period. Although these poets are at odds in many ways, they are all considered modernist because of their rejection of the formal and stylistic conventions of the Romantic era and their emphasis on experimentation. Other poets of the era also made distinctive contributions to the movement in poetry, including Ezra Pound, John Crowe Ransom, Allen Tate, and Hart Crane.

THE FICTION OF THE TWENTIES

As previously noted, poetry took the lead in the modernist movement prior to World War I. In the 1920s, fiction caught up with poetry as American authors produced some of the greatest novels and short stories in American history. Speaking of the novel, professor and critic Malcolm Bradbury writes, "At first it was the poets who were most notable. . . . Fiction was somewhat slower to respond to the new experimental spirit, and the modern movement did not really fully flower in the novel until after the First World War and into the 1920s, which would produce one of the great ages of the American novel."[13] Some of the most notable works of American fiction published in the 1920s include F. Scott Fitzgerald's *The Great Gatsby* (1925), Ernest Hemingway's *The Sun Also Rises* (1926), and William Faulkner's *The Sound and the Fury* (1929). (Sherwood Anderson's *Winesburg, Ohio* barely missed the twenties, having been published in 1919.) In addition to these classics, the decade saw a plethora of other great works: Conrad Aiken's *Blue Voyage* (1926), e.e. cummings's *The Enormous Room* (1922), John Dos Passos's *Three Soldiers* (1921) and *Manhattan Transfer* (1925), Ellen Glasgow's *Barren Ground* (1925), Hemingway's *In Our Time* (1922), Sinclair Lewis's *Main Street* (1920) and *Babbitt* (1922), Edith Wharton's *The Age of Innocence* (1920), and others.

The nature of the modernist movement in America changed somewhat following World War I. One major change was a shift in mood; the sense of exhilaration that had accompanied the poetic renaissance gave way to a much more somber attitude. The Great War, which resulted in 10 million deaths, was extremely demoralizing to American authors. Various factors made this war particularly devastating: the massive loss of life, the mechanized nature of the warfare, and the political realities that emerged from the war—especially the triumph of communism in Russia and the failure of Woodrow Wilson's League of Nations, an international peace organization similar to today's United Nations. Critic Richard Ruland and Malcolm Bradbury describe the effect of the war on American writers:

> The First World War had a tragic impact on aesthetic sensibility, especially among the young American writers or would-be writers who served in Europe, either as combatants or as members of the various ambulance corps. It imprinted itself across the writing of the 1920s and had much to do with the atmosphere of Spenglerian gloom and decadent anxiety which haunted that period. F. Scott Fitzgerald's Amory Blaine, in *This Side of Paradise* (1920), missed the war, as his creator just did, but has "grown up to find all gods dead, all wars fought, all faiths in man shaken." For many American writers, the war marked a cutoff point from the past, an ultimate symbol for the dawn of modernity.[14]

In effect, the war injected American modernism with a renewed sense of disillusionment, chaos, and nihilism without reducing the modernists' dedication to aesthetic experimentation.

The sense of desolation wrought by World War I was reflected in the poetry of the era, as illustrated by the following lines from Eliot's *The Waste Land*:

> Unreal City,
> Under the brown fog of a winter dawn,
> A crowd flowed over London Bridge, so many,
> I had not thought death had undone so many.

However, as Bradbury suggests, the war had its greatest impact on the younger generation of fiction writers, including Fitzgerald and Hemingway, whom Gertrude Stein dubbed the "lost generation." This generation of authors produced works that were extremely critical of U.S. society and culture. Many of them fled America and joined a growing group of expatriate artists and writers living in Paris. In leaving America, the expatriates sought to free themselves from sexual constraints and social conventions that they considered excessively moralistic and Puritanical. They were also repelled by a perceived lack of cultural and artistic sophistication in the United States.

Though the various fiction writers of the 1920s were of a generation, they made disparate contributions to the modernist movement. Hemingway is known for his sparse prose style that reflects the emotional and spiritual numbness of his protagonists, who have been traumatized by war and other dehumanizing forces of the modern world. Fitzgerald in *Gatsby* used symbolism to explore the limits of the Amer-

ican Dream. Faulkner constructed an ornate style and fragmented structures to probe the conflict between defeated
southern traditions and the rise of the New South. Sinclair
Lewis used satire to criticize small-town American moralism, conformity, and commercialism. Dos Passos in *Manhattan Transfer* relied on collage and montage to portray the
mechanized life of the modern city.[15] While these authors,
and others of the era, created works using various techniques and examining different themes, they are all considered modernists because they, like their poet counterparts,
rejected forms and styles inherited from the previous generations. Summing up the contribution of the fiction writers of
the twenties, Ruland and Bradbury write that the achievement made during that decade

> represents one of the most remarkable periods of American
> literary history, and its hunger for new styles, new forms,
> new attitudes to human nature and human history, new
> modes of artistic self-discovery, generated an atmosphere of
> innovation perhaps even more powerful than what had been
> happening in the new poetry. It often began in expatriate
> withdrawal to Europe or in bohemian separation from a cul-
> ture that was seen as Puritanic, materialistic and fundamen-
> tally hostile to art, but it took European experiments and as-
> similated some of the cultural despair and the sense of
> psychic and historical crisis we recognize as part of what was
> coming to be called the Modern temper. . . . [These writers]
> expressed the novelty of the new and often European forms
> and their relation to their own culture, as it experienced the
> rape of an older American innocence. . . . If American poetry
> had found a new way to utter the meaning of the nation, so
> too had the American novel.[16]

THE HARLEM RENAISSANCE AND THE SOUTHERN AGRARIANS

While white authors such as Hemingway and Fitzgerald were
producing their masterpieces, African-American writers in
Harlem and other U.S. cities were experiencing their own literary movement. Various social, economic, and cultural factors—including the mass migration of southern blacks to
cities in the North—combined in the 1920s to produce the
Harlem Renaissance. Some critics debate the validity of the
phrase Harlem Renaissance. Others insist that the movement
should not be discussed in the context of modernism because
the literature it produced did not share the characteristics of
modernist prose and poetry. However, few deny that in the
1920s Harlem and other U.S. cities experienced an outpour-

ing of art and literature expressing a new sense of racial pride. Charles S. Johnson, one of the main organizers and leaders of the renaissance, describes the sense of liberation experienced by black writers of the era. They were, he says,

> less self-conscious and less interested in proving that they were just like white people; . . . they seemed to care less about what white people thought, or were likely to think, than about themselves and what they had to say.[17]

Some of the leading figures of the Harlem Renaissance were Countee Cullen, Zora Neale Hurston, Langston Hughes, and Claude McKay.

Meanwhile, also in the 1920s, at Vanderbilt University in Nashville, Tennessee, a group of writers, poets, and literary critics were forming their own movement. Initially calling themselves the Fugitives, then the Agrarians, these scholars sought to preserve aspects of the southern way of life against the threat of industrialization. Among the most prominent members of the Agrarian movement were John Crowe Ransom, Allen Tate, and Robert Penn Warren. Their work culminated in the publication of a collection of essays entitled *I'll Take My Stand* in 1930. Thomas Daniel Young characterizes this book as a

> cry of outrage at the attempts of man to deify the machine, at the amount of time and energy devoted to emphasizing the inevitability of a technocratic society, and at the concerted attacks on man's basic humanity.[18]

Due to their regional focus and their emphasis on preserving tradition, the Agrarians are often considered only marginally related to the modernist movement. However, like the Harlem Renaissance, the southern Agrarian movement was a response to the dramatic social changes brought on by the processes of industrialization and modernization.

The disparate strands and submovements of the American modernist era produced a rich body of literature. The regional movements imbued American letters with a sense of place, while the expatriates provided a unique perspective on U.S. culture. The New Poetry introduced a spirit of liberation and energetic exploration, while the fiction writers reflected the conflicts that arose as the country underwent momentous change. All of the various forms, styles, and themes that emerged in American writing during the modernist era left a lasting imprint on the literature and culture of the United States and the entire western world.

NOTES

1. Ross Murfin and Supryia M. Ray, *The Bedford Glossary of Critical and Literary Terms*. New York: Bedford Books, 1997, p. 220.

2. Richard Gray, *American Poetry of the Twentieth Century*. New York: Longman, 1990, p. 29.

3. Alan Shucard, Fred Moramarco, and William Sullivan, *Modern American Poetry, 1865–1950*. Boston: Twayne Publishers, 1989, pp. 65–66.

4. Shucard et al., *Modern American Poetry, 1865–1950*, p. 68.

5. Shucard et al., *Modern American Poetry, 1865–1950*, pp. 69–70.

6. Quoted in Gray, *American Poetry of the Twentieth Century*, p. 43.

7. Gray, *American Poetry of the Twentieth Century*, p. 43.

8. Amy Lowell, "Two Generations in American Poetry," *New Republic*, December 5, 1923. Reprinted in *Critical Essays on American Modernism*. Ed. Michael J. Hoffman and Patrick D. Murphy. New York: G.K. Hall, 1992, p. 47.

9. Shucard et al., *Modern American Poetry, 1865–1950*, p. 71.

10. Quoted in David Perkins, *A History of Modern Poetry: From the 1890s to the High Modernist Mode*. Cambridge, MA: Harvard University Press, 1976, p. 549.

11. Gray, *American Poetry of the Twentieth Century*, pp. 89–90.

12. This discussion of "Man with the Blue Guitar" is informed by Shucard et al., *Modern American Poetry, 1865–1950*, pp. 146–47.

13. Malcolm Bradbury, *The Modern American Novel*. New York: Penguin Books, 1993, p. 55.

14. Richard Ruland and Malcolm Bradbury, *From Puritanism to Postmodernism: A History of American Literature*. New York: Viking, 1991, p. 273.

15. This summary of the authors' contributions is informed by Bradbury, *The Modern American Novel* and Ruland and Bradbury, *From Puritanism to Postmodernism: A History of American Literature*.

16. Ruland and Bradbury, *From Puritanism to Postmodernism: A History of American Literature*, pp. 314–15.

17. Charles S. Johnson, "The Negro Renaissance and Its Significance," In *The New Negro Thirty Years Afterward*. Washington, DC: Howard University Press, 1955. Reprinted in David Levering Lewis, ed., *The Portable Harlem Renaissance Reader*. New York: Viking, 1994, p. 215.

18. Thomas Daniel Young, *Waking Their Neighbors Up: The Nashville Agrarians Rediscovered*. Athens: University of Georgia Press, 1982, p. 59.

CHAPTER 1

Defining American Modernism

American
Modernism

The Characteristics of Modernism

Irving Howe

Irving Howe is a well-known literary critic and the author of several books on American literature. The following selection was excerpted from the introduction to his anthology entitled The Idea of the Modern in Literature and the Arts. *Howe writes that modernism was a revolt against the established literary tradition, societal norms, and cultural order. As such, its characteristics included an emphasis on subjective experience, a dynamic style, historical discontinuity, and moral relativism.*

In the past hundred years we have had a special kind of literature. We call it modern and distinguish it from the merely contemporary; for where the contemporary refers to time, the modern refers to sensibility and style, and where the contemporary is a term of neutral reference, the modern is a term of critical placement and judgment. Modernist literature seems now to be coming to an end, though we can by no means be certain and there are critics who would argue that, given the nature of our society, the modern period cannot come to an end.

The kind of literature called modern is almost always difficult to comprehend: that is a sign of its modernity. To the established guardians of culture, the modern writer seems wilfully inaccessible. He works with unfamiliar forms; he chooses subjects that disturb the audience and threaten its most cherished sentiments; he provokes traditionalist critics to such epithets as "unwholesome," "coterie," and "decadent."

A REVOLT AGAINST THE PREVALENT STYLE

The modern must be defined in terms of what it is not: the embodiment of a tacit polemic, an inclusive negative. Mod-

Excerpted from Irving Howe, Introduction, *The Idea of the Modern in Literature and the Arts* (New York: Horizon Press, 1967). Copyright ©1967 by Irving Howe. Reprinted by permission of the Estate of Irving Howe.

ern writers find that they begin to work at a moment when the culture is marked by a prevalent style of perception and feeling; and their modernity consists in a revolt against this prevalent style, an unyielding rage against the official order. But modernism does not establish a prevalent style of its own; or if it does, it denies itself, thereby ceasing to be modern. This presents it with a dilemma which in principle may be beyond solution but in practice leads to formal inventiveness and resourceful dialectic—*the dilemma that modernism must always struggle but never quite triumph, and then, after a time, must struggle in order not to triumph.*

Modernism need never come to an end, or at least we do not really know, as yet, how it can or will reach its end. The history of previous literary periods is relevant but probably not decisive here, since modernism, despite the precursors one can find in the past, is, I think, a novelty in the development of Western culture. What we do know, however, is that modernism can fall upon days of exhaustion, when it appears to be marking time and waiting for new avenues of release.

At certain points in the development of a culture, usually points of dismay and restlessness, writers find themselves affronting their audience, and not from decision or whim but from some deep moral and psychological necessity. Such writers may not even be aware that they are challenging crucial assumptions of their day, yet their impact is revolutionary; and once this is recognized by sympathetic critics and a coterie audience, the *avant garde* has begun to emerge as a self-conscious and combative group Paul Goodman writes:

> . . . there are these works that are indignantly rejected, and called not genuine art, but insult, outrage, *blague, fumiste,*[1] wilfully incomprehensible. . . . And what is puzzling is not that they are isolated pieces, but some artists persistently produce such pieces and there are schools of such "not genuine" artists. What are they doing? In this case, the feeling of the audience is sound—it is always sound—there *is* insult, wilful incomprehensibility, experiment; and yet the judgment of the audience is wrong—it is often wrong—for this is a genuine art.

Why does this clash arise? Because the modern writer can no longer accept the claims of the world. If he tries to acquiesce in the norms of the audience, he finds himself depressed and outraged. The usual morality seems counterfeit; taste, a genteel indulgence; tradition, a wearisome fetter.

1. fib, joke

It becomes a condition of being a writer that he rebel, not merely and sometimes not at all against received opinions, but against the received ways of doing the writer's work.

A modernist culture soon learns to respect, even to cherish, signs of its division. It sees doubt as a form of health. It hunts for ethical norms through underground journeys, experiments with sensation, and a mocking suspension of accredited values. Upon the passport of the Wisdom of The Ages, it stamps in bold red letters: *Not Transferable.* It cultivates, in Thomas Mann's phrase, "a sympathy for the abyss." It strips man of his systems of belief and his ideal claims, and then proposes the one uniquely modern style of salvation: a salvation by, of, and for the self. In modernist culture, the object perceived seems always on the verge of being swallowed up by the perceiving agent, and the act of perception in danger of being exalted to the substance of reality. *I see, therefore I am.*

SUBJECTIVITY AND HISTORICAL IMPASSE

Subjectivity becomes the typical condition of the modernist outlook. In its early stages, when it does not trouble to disguise its filial dependence on the romantic poets, modernism declares itself as an inflation of the self, a transcendental and orgiastic aggrandizement of matter and event in behalf of personal vitality. In the middle stages, the self begins to recoil from externality and devotes itself, almost as if it were the world's body, to a minute examination of its own inner dynamics: freedom, compulsion, caprice. In the late stages, there occurs an emptying-out of the self, a revulsion from the wearisomeness of individuality and psychological gain. (Three writers as exemplars of these stages: Walt Whitman, Virginia Woolf, Samuel Beckett.) Modernism thereby keeps approaching—sometimes even penetrating—the limits of solipsism, the view expressed by the German poet Gottfried Benn when he writes that "there is no outer reality, there is only human consciousness, constantly building, modifying, rebuilding new worlds out of its own creativity."

Behind this extreme subjectivity lurks an equally extreme sense of historical impasse, the assumption that something about the experience of our ages is unique, a catastrophe without precedent. The German novelist Herman Hesse speaks about "a whole generation caught . . . between two ages, two modes of life, with the consequence that it loses all power to understand itself and has no standards, no security, no simple acquiescence." Above all, no simple acquiescence.

Whether all of this is true matters not nearly so much as the fact that modernist writers, artists, and composers— James Joyce, Franz Kafka, Pablo Picasso, Arnold Schoenberg—have apparently worked on the tacit assumption that it is true. The modernist sensibility posits a blockage, if not an end, to history: an apocalyptic *cul de sac* in which both teleological ends and secular progress are called into question, perhaps become obsolete. Man is mired—you can take your choice—in the mass, in the machine, in the city, in his loss of faith, in the hopelessness of a life without anterior intention or terminal value. By this late date, these disasters seem in our imaginations to have merged into one.

"On or about December 1910 human nature changed." Through this vivid hyperbole, Virginia Woolf meant to suggest that there is a frightening discontinuity between the traditional past and the shaken present; that the line of history has been bent, perhaps broken. Modernist literature goes on the tacit assumption that human nature has indeed changed, probably a few decades before the date given by Mrs. Woolf; or, as Stephen Spender remarks, that the circumstances under which we live, forever being transformed by nature, have been so radically altered that people feel human nature to have changed and thereby behave as though it has. Commenting on this notion, Spender makes a keen distinction between the "Voltairean I" of earlier writers and the "I" of the moderns:

> The "Voltairean I" of George Bernard Shaw, H.G. Wells and others acts upon events. The "modern I" of [Arthur] Rimbaud, Joyce, [Marcel] Proust, [T.S.] Eliot's *Prufrock* is acted upon by events. . . . The faith of the Voltairean egoists is that they will direct the powers of the surrounding world from evil into better courses through the exercise of the superior social or cultural intelligence of the creative genius, the writer-prophet. The faith of the moderns is that by allowing their sensibility to be acted upon by the modern experience as suffering, they will produce partly as the result of unconscious processes, and partly through the exercise of critical consciousness, the idioms and forms of new art.

CULTURE AT WAR WITH ITSELF

The consequences are extreme: a break-up of the traditional unity and continuity of Western culture, so that the decorums of its past no longer count for very much in determining its present, and a loosening of those ties that, in one or another way, had bound it to the institutions of society over the centuries. Not their enemies but art and literature themselves assault the *gemütlichkeit*[2] of autonomy, the classical balances and resolutions of the past. Culture now goes to war against itself, partly in order to salvage its purpose, and the result is that it can no longer present itself with a Goethian serenity and wholeness. At one extreme, there is a violent disparagement of culture (the late Rimbaud), and at the other, a quasi-religion of culture (the late Joyce).

In much modernist literature, one finds a bitter impatience with the whole apparatus of cognition and the limiting assumption of rationality. The mind comes to be seen as an enemy of vital human powers. Culture becomes disenchanted with itself, sick over its endless refinements. There is a hunger to break past the bourgeois proprieties and self-containment of culture, toward a form of absolute personal speech, a literature deprived of ceremony and stripped to revelation. In the work of Thomas Mann, both what is rejected and what is desired are put forward with a high, ironic consciousness: the abandoned ceremony and the corrosive revelation.

But if a major impulse in modernist literature is a choking nausea before the idea of culture, there is another in which the writer takes upon himself the enormous ambition not to remake the world (by now seen as hopelessly recalcitrant and alien) but to reinvent the terms of reality. I have already quoted Benn's remark that "there is only human consciousness . . . rebuilding new worlds out of its own creativity." In a similar vein, the painter Paul Klee once said that his wish was "not to reflect the visible, but to *make* visible." And Charles-Pierre Baudelaire wrote, "The whole visible universe is but an array of images and signs to which the imagination gives a place and relative value. . . ." At first glance, this sentence reads like something an English romantic poet or even a good American transcendentalist might have said; but in the context of Baudelaire's experience as a poet—that experience which led him to say that "every man who refuses to accept the conditions of life sells his soul"—it comes to seem the report of a desire to create,

2. cordiality

or perhaps re-create, the very grounds of being, through a permanent revolution of sensibility and style, by means of which art could raise itself to the level of white or (more likely) black magic. Rationalistic psychoanalysts might regard this ambition as a substitute gratification of the most desperate kind, a grandiose mask for inner weakness; but for the great figures of literary modernism it is the very essence of their task.

A DYNAMISM OF QUESTIONS

We approach here another dilemma of modernism, which may also in principle be beyond solution but in practice lead to great inventiveness—that, as the Marxist critic Georg Lukacs has charged, *modernism despairs of human history, abandons the idea of a linear historical development, falls back upon notions of a universal* condition humaine[3] *or a rhythm of eternal recurrence, yet within its own realm is committed to ceaseless change, turmoil and recreation.* The more history comes to be seen as static (in the Marxist idiom: a locomotive stalled in an inescapable present), the more art must take on a relentless dynamism.

It is quite as if Georg Hegel's "cunning of reason," so long a motor-force of progress in history, were now expelled from its exalted place and locked into the exile of culture. E.H. Gombrich speaks of philosophies of historical progress as containing "a strong Aristotelian ingredient insofar as they look upon progress as an evolution of inherent potentialities which will follow a predictable course and must reach a predictable summit." Modernist versions of literature do assign to themselves "an evolution of inherent potentialities": there is always the hope for still another breakthrough, always the necessary and prepared-for dialectical leap into still another innovation, always an immanent if by no means gradual progress in the life of a form. But these do not follow "a predictable course," nor can they reach "a predictable summit"—since the very idea of "predictable," or the very goal of "summit," violates the modernist faith in surprise, its belief in sensibility and style. And if history is indeed stalled in the sluggishness of the mass and the imperiousness of the machine, then culture must all the more serve as the agent of a life-enhancing turmoil.

3. human condition

The figure chosen to embody and advance this turmoil, remarks Gombrich, is the Genius, an early individualistic precursor of the *avant-garde* creative hero. If there is then "a conflict between a genius and his public," declares Hegel in a sentence which thousands of critics, writers and publicists will echo through the years, "it must be the public that is to blame . . . the only obligation the artist can have is to follow truth and his genius." Close to romantic theory at this point, modernism soon ceases to believe in the availability of "truth" or the disclosures of "genius." The dynamism to which it then commits itself—and here it breaks sharply from the romantics—becomes not merely an absolute without end but sometimes an absolute without discernible ends.

It is a dynamism of asking and learning not to reply. The past was devoted to answers; the modern period confines itself to questions. And after a certain point, the essence of modernism reveals itself in the persuasion that the true question, the one alone worth asking, cannot and need not be answered; it need only be asked over and over again, forever in new ways. It is as if the very idea of a question were redefined: no longer an interrogation but now a mode of axiomatic value. We represent ourselves, we establish our authenticity, by the questions we allow to torment us. "All of [Fyodor] Dostoevsky's heroes question themselves as to the meaning of life," writes Albert Camus. "In this they are modern: they do not fear ridicule. What distinguishes modern sensibility from classical sensibility is that the latter thrives on moral problems and the former on metaphysical problems."

A modernist culture is committed to the view that the human lot is inescapably problematic. Problems, to be sure, have been noticed at all times, but in a modernist culture the problematic as a style of existence and inquiry becomes imperious: men learn to find comfort in their wounds. Friedrich Nietzsche says: "Truth has never yet hung on the arm of an absolute." The problematic is adhered to, not merely because we live in a time of uncertainty when traditional beliefs and absolute standards, having long disintegrated, give way to the makeshifts of relativism—that is by now an old, old story. The problematic is adhered to because it comes to be considered good, proper, and even beautiful that men should live in discomfort. Again Nietzsche:

> Objection evasion, joyous distrust, and love of irony are signs
> of health; everything absolute belongs to pathology.

THE POWER OF SINCERITY

One consequence of this devotion to the problematic, not always a happy consequence, is that in modernist literature there is a turn from truth to sincerity, from the search for objective law to a desire for authentic response. The first involves an effort to apprehend the nature of the universe, and can lead to metaphysics, suicide, revolution, and God; the second involves an effort to discover our demons within, and makes no claim upon the world other than the right to publicize the aggressions of candor. Sincerity becomes the last-ditch defense for men without belief, and in its name absolutes can be toppled, morality dispersed, and intellectual systems dissolved. But a special kind of sincerity: where for the romantics it was often taken to be a rapid motion into truth, breaking past the cumbersomeness of intellect, now for the modernists it becomes a virtue in itself, regardless of whether it can lead to truth or whether truth can be found. Sincerity of feeling and exact faithfulness of language— which often means a language of fragments, violence, and exasperation—becomes a ruling passion. In the terrible freedom it allows the modernist writer, sincerity shatters the hypocrisies of bourgeois order; in the lawlessness of its abandonment, it can become a force of darkness and brutality.

Disdainful of certainties, disengaged from the eternal or any of its surrogates, fixated upon the minute particulars of subjective experience, the modernist writer regards settled assumptions as a mask of death and literature as an agent of metaphysical revolt. Restlessness becomes the sign of sentience, anxiety the premise of responsibility, peace the flag of surrender—and the typewriter the Promethean rock.

American Modernism Is Distinct from European Modernism

Julian Symons

In the following excerpt, Julian Symons contends that American modernists rejected European styles and forms and created work that was uniquely American. Citing the works of Edgar Lee Masters, William Carlos Williams, and Sherwood Anderson, Symons argues that American authors, unlike Europeans, were anti-intellectual and wrote in relaxed styles and forms. Symons is a British literary critic, social historian, poet, and crime novelist. This reading is taken from his book *Makers of the New: The Revolution in Literature, 1912–1939.*

If America was a literary desert in the early years of the twentieth century green shoots showed in several places during its second decade, shoots that sprouted into plants and flowers of a distinctively national kind. Suddenly . . . poetry was everywhere, Boston as well as Chicago reverberated with it, and there was a demand that this poetry—and imaginative prose as well—should owe as little as possible to Europe, be both American and new.

What, in a literary sense, did the words mean? In prose they represented a rejection of what was cosmopolitan, consciously sophisticated, stylish—Edith Wharton, Ellen Glasgow, James Branch Cabell—in favour of Theodore Dreiser, Sherwood Anderson, Sinclair Lewis, writers who were unmistakably national, owed nothing to Europe. Almost everything of literary interest, H.L. Mencken said, now originated in Chicago. *Poetry*[1] lived in Chicago, the *Little Review* was born there, to Chicago came writers like Anderson, Carl

1. a magazine founded by Harriet Monroe in 1912

Sandburg and Edgar Lee Masters, happy to accept the label *provincial* fixed on their prose and poetry. A number of energetic literary journalists were ready to give the new American writing columns of praise in the *Chicago Tribune* and elsewhere. Literary activity bubbled away furiously in the city, rather differently from Boston where the fire under the pot was stoked chiefly by Amy Lowell. Her money, her powerful physical presence, the readings of her own work at which she instructed the audience to clap or hiss but *do* something, the magisterial manner in which she paraded and praised her six chosen poets in *Tendencies in Modern American Poetry*, combined to make readers pay attention when she said the country was on the eve of an artistic and poetic renaissance. . . . New York's Greenwich Village was full of aspiring poets, novelists and painters, although its most representative magazine, *The Masses*, edited by Max Eastman from 1912 to 1917, was primarily political. The city's literary magazine in the period was *Others*, founded in 1915 by Alfred Kreymborg. . . .

The national quality of this new writing, its rejection of European models as irrelevant to American life and landscape, and the anti-intellectualism that became its hallmark, can be seen clearly in the work of two poets and a prose writer: Edgar Lee Masters, William Carlos Williams and Sherwood Anderson. Others in the period, including Sandburg and Vachel Lindsay, could equally well be used to exemplify the need that was felt to produce work owing no debt to Europe in theme or language.

A UNIQUELY AMERICAN POET

The poems in Edgar Lee Masters's *Spoon River Anthology* appeared from week to week in *Reedy's Mirror,* run by the liberal journalist William Marion Reedy. Masters was a lawyer living in Chicago who had produced several books of poems and a verse play about the Emperor Maximilian of Mexico without success when, in his middle forties, the Spoon River poems rocketed him to fame. As collected in volume form, they consisted of epitaphs for some two hundred and fifty inhabitants of a small town in the Midwest. All were in free verse, a kind of writing he had encountered first in the pages of *Poetry,* and they represented a break from all of his earlier poetry. It is unlikely that Masters thought of himself as a verbal pioneer, yet even today the best of these poems seem markedly original, and the relaxed form of these short pieces, able to accommodate varying lengths of line and changes of tone within a single poem, was perfectly suited to the material. The epitaphs are by turn savage, sentimental, realistic, ironic, pawkily funny, the best of them vivid character sketches. Often the images are crude, as in Robert Fulton Tanner's likening of life to a gigantic rat-trap or the Widow McFarlane's comparison of it to a loom with an unseen pattern, but such crudeness does not much mar the final effect. The range of characters is large—con men, doctors, judges, bank president, lawyers, local poets, tradesmen, artisans. Frank Drummer tries to memorise the *Encyclopaedia Britannica* before being hanged, Sam Hookey runs away to join the circus and is eaten by Brutus the lion, but most of the lives are humdrum. Violent events, murders, suicides, abortions, are recorded with a flatness more effective than any possible rhetoric. If there is a prevailing tone it is that of Mrs Williams the milliner, meditating on adultery and divorce:

Well now, let me ask you:
If all of the children, born here in Spoon River,
Had been reared by the County, somewhere on a farm;
And the fathers and mothers had been given their freedom
To live and enjoy, change mates if they wished,
Do you think that Spoon River
Had been any the worse?

The combination of such flatness with intensity of feeling gave *Spoon River Anthology* its unique, and uniquely American, flavour. In theory it is possible to think of a British equivalent, but no British poet of the time could have written with Masters's awkward simplicity, his rawness, his combination of affection and hatred. Masters was never able to understand the reason for the success of the collection, nor to repeat it.

The popularity of what had first been weekly space-fillers was immediate and overwhelming when the space-fillers appeared as a volume. Masters found himself hailed as a great American poet. 'It has been insisted over and over again', Lowell said, 'that here was the great American poet, this verse was at last absolutely of America, that not since [Walt] Whitman had anything so national appeared in print.' Masters, along with Sandburg, was labelled a revolutionary poet, although the word had no political or literary application to either. The only 'revolutionary' thing about them was the crudeness of their language, which for a brief period helped to energise American poetry. For a brief period only. *Domesday Book* (1922) and *The New Spoon River* (1924), in which Masters used again the biographical approach of the original collection, are almost entirely unsuccessful, and most of Sandburg's later work offers less vivid and energetic variations on his poetry before 1920. Both men, as they became established literary figures, lost the intensity and energy that had made their poems memorable.

THE HOMETOWN NOVEL

If Masters, and Sandburg in his *Chicago Poems* (1916) and *Cornhuskers* two years later, were wholly American poets, Sherwood Anderson was their prose counterpart. The appearance in 1919 of *Winesburg, Ohio*, 'A Group of Tales of Ohio Small Town Life', brought Anderson instant celebrity. He was in his early forties, a small-town boy like Sandburg and Masters, who in 1912 had abandoned wife, family and job as paint-factory manager, and made his way to Chicago to live the literary life. He contributed to the first number of the *Little Review,* was part of the city's rather genteel literary bohemia, but remained little known until the publication of *Winesburg.*

Anderson is little read today, and it is difficult now to understand why Hart Crane said that *Winesburg* was a book that Americans should read on their knees, Irving Howe felt it opened a new world for him, or the youthful Lionel Trilling found everything Anderson wrote a revelation. It is equally hard to appreciate the force of the remark made by the critic Ernest Boyd when he said Anderson's writing represented the 'revolt against the great illusion of American civilization, the illusion of optimism'. At this distance of time, and from across the Atlantic, Winesburg looks very much like Spoon River done into prose. The model was the small town of Clyde where Anderson had spent his childhood, and the short sketches are joined only by the presence of the young local reporter George Willard. The incidents, mostly too slight to be called stories, deal with 'characters', the drunken doctor with very few patients who expects to be crucified, the closet homosexual teacher driven out of town, the girl in the family way, the sex-obsessed clergyman. Some of these themes were thought shocking, as readers were shocked by Masters's rapes, seductions and murders, but the sensational element in the stories was only a minor element in their success. Anderson said that in these stories he had made his own loose literary form, but in fact they have no form at all. The style is obviously indebted to Mark Twain rather than William Dean Howells, Anderson was in the over-simple definition a Redskin and not a Paleface, but his homespun manner also has a mock simplicity reminding us that he was much excited by Gertrude Stein's early writings, combined with a mock energy apparent in phrases like 'All over his body Jesse Bentley was alive' or the sentence telling us that Tom Foster when drunk 'was like an innocent young buck of the forest that has eaten of some maddening weed'. Anderson felt a mystical identification with the America of his youth where, as he said in a letter, men alone in the fields and the forest 'got a sense of bigness outside them-selves that has now in some way been lost' and 'mystery whispered in the grass, played in the branches of trees over-head, was caught up and blown across the American line in clouds of dust at evening on the prairies'. Such phrases would have made T.S. Eliot and Ezra Pound shudder.

Lowell and Kreymborg, Masters and Anderson and many others: modernism in America was fashionable, and com-mercially successful. It was a different kind of thing from the modernism practiced and advocated on the other side of the Atlantic. James Joyce, Eliot and Sinclair Lewis, even Pound, were 'difficult' writers, all in greater or less degree with a contempt for populism, the 'ordinary man', the 'mob'. Many American writers, however, felt they belonged to that very mob and were delighted to discover how easy it was to be a poet or a story writer. American modernists had no truck with what most would have found the unpleasant or unin-telligible ideas of T.E. Hulme.[2] They did not particularly want to link modernism in art with any kind of development in society, but if pressed to do so would have pronounced it democratic. Just as Lowell had cried out that she too was an Imagiste,[3] so a hundred young men and women felt all they had to do was to rake up a few memories of childhood and youth and put them down in the simplest possible prose like Sherwood Anderson's, or set down their thoughts and emo-

2. a philosopher and art critic who led the modernist movement in Britain   3. a mem-ber of the Imagisme (Imagism) movement in poetry

tions in unrhymed lines written in vaguely modern language, to be prose writer or poet. . . .

WILLIAM CARLOS WILLIAMS: "NO IDEAS BUT IN THINGS"

The most categorical demands for a specifically American literature, and the most complete rejection of intellectual, or European, modernism, came now and in the following years from William Carlos Williams. . . . For some years he was evidently unsure of what kind of poetry he wished to write. Although he only gradually freed himself from the English poetic locutions and manners he had been taught at school and college, Williams was from youth, and almost instinctively, inclined to dislike and distrust the literature of Europe. . . .

Publication of *The Waste Land* [a poem by T.S. Eliot] changed Williams's instinctive distrust of a modern movement based on European culture into outright opposition. The poem's appearance, he said later, had set him back twenty years. Eliot had returned poetry to the classroom just when poets in America were moving towards a new art form rooted in their own home ground. Eliot could have become 'our adviser, our hero', and what had he done instead? Walked out on his native traditions. When Williams saw the *Criterion*[4] he recognised that there was no place in it for him 'or anything I stood for'.

Eliot's poem had at least the benefit for Williams that it clarified his feelings about the kind of poems he wanted to write. They would be in a language and rhythms specifically American, and of course with no whiff of classroom scholarship. He determined also to have nothing to do with symbolism or metaphor. It was not until the publication in the forties of his long poem *Paterson* that he voiced what was to become a famous dictum, 'No ideas but in things', but it was implied in his poetry from *Spring and All* (1923) onwards. . . .

To say there are *no ideas but in things:* is that a sensible remark? It is one that contradicts any intellectual conception of the world, for ideas are evidently not things, although they may be *about* things. Ideas are abstractions, what is abstract belongs to the intellect, and as one of Williams's severest critics said, Williams was not just anti-intellectual, but did not know what the intellect was. *No ideas but in things,* when applied to the writing of poems, involves the consideration of

4. a magazine edited by Eliot

the 'thing' as a thing-in-itself, something having an existence outside anything else in the world. And that was in fact this poet's intention, a desire to see in any individual poem 'the world contracted to a recognisable image'. The poet regards this image and puts it down on paper, but Williams's assumption is that it exists without him. The poem would not exist without the poet writing it, that is true, but what he records has, according to Williams, an independent existence, and the recording should be testimony to that.

The result is poems much simpler than the metaphysical attitude from which they spring, very often poems about trees, flowers, insects, common objects. 'The Red Wheelbarrow' is considered here because it was well regarded both by Williams and by critics, and because it is very short:

> so much depends
> upon
>
> a red wheel
> barrow
>
> glazed with rain
> water
>
> beside the white
> chickens

The poem is rather like a naive painting,[5] it creates a crudely simple picture. 'Creates a picture', however, is a phrase that would not do for a follower of Williams. He would say this was not *a picture*, with the artificiality implied in that word, but a poem given over wholly to wheelbarrow, rainwater, chickens, perhaps quoting Williams's own assertion in relation to his similar 'Chicory and Daisies' that the poet 'gives his poem over to the flower and its plant themselves', concerned to 'borrow no particle from right or left'. . . .

OBJECTIVISM: THE POEM AS OBJECT

For Williams the Object was a subject for poetry simply by *being there:* the red wheelbarrow was unique like everything else in the world, and the poet's awareness of it was neither subjective nor objective but both at once, so that for the time of the poem he both became and observed the red wheelbarrow. To copy nature, Williams said, was a spineless activity, the important thing was to *become* nature 'and so in-

5. a painting produced by a self-taught artist

vent an object which is an extension of the process', the poem being the object.

Williams's likeness to Stein is apparent in his insistence on using simple words, and viewing things as a child might. No complex thought or observation is permissible, the effect in Stein being one of repetition, in Williams an appearance of complete banality or foolishness. 'January!/The beginning of all things' one poem begins, another 'When I was younger/it was plain to me/I must make something of my-self', a third 'In brilliant gas light/I turn the kitchen spigot/and watch the water plash/into the clean white sink'. There are many similar passages. In some of them the poet keeps his eye on the Object (the kitchen spigot, the water, the sink), in others it strays into social observation or moral reflection. The effects obtained were certainly very different from those of European modernists. At best they may be thought trivial, at worst null.

It would be wrong to deny that such poems are express-ing *something* through their bareness, their mock or real simplicity, their sense of colour, awareness of flowers, fruit, trees, animals, their struggling inexpressive awkwardness and determined lack of sophistication. 'Aw, shucks,' many of them seem to be saying, 'I'm just putting down things the way I see them, and if you write them down true, what else is there to say?' It is very much the spirit in which Stein wrote at the beginning of the first draft of *The Making of Americans:* 'It has always seemed to me a rare privilege that of being an American, a real American and yet one whose tradition it has taken scarcely sixty years to create.'

No doubt Williams thought it a rare privilege too, and as the years passed he gathered disciples, became the patron saint of a movement called Objectivism, and codified his dis-trust of European sophistication into a creed which con-demned for modern use any and every formal poetic struc-ture because it belonged to a British, not an American tradition. Americans had to begin, he said, by understanding that they spoke a distinct and separate language, which was not English.

The Use of Concrete Words and Images in American Modernism

Floyd C. Watkins

Floyd C. Watkins maintains that the American modernist writers of the early twentieth century favored
objective description of facts over empty rhetoric
and discussions of abstract concepts. According to
Watkins, writers were disillusioned by the way
language was distorted to promote World War I.
In response, they focused on concrete imagery to
evoke genuine emotion rather than false sentiment.
Watkins is the author of several books on American
literature, including *Then & Now: The Personal Past
in the Poetry of Robert Penn Warren*, *In Time and
Place: Some Origins of American Fiction*, and *The
Flesh and the Word: Eliot, Hemingway, Faulkner*,
from which this selection is excerpted.

Most great writers of the early twentieth century wrote
about object, fact, and person and rejected abstractions of all
kinds. This is often true of a good writer, but in no other age
have men of letters been more devoted to the empirical fact
and more wary of statements of meanings. Men of letters
were not alone in their emphasis on the world which could
be observed by the five senses. Especially from about World
War I until the end of the 1920s, historian, semanticist, psy-
chologist, philosopher, and scientist distrusted general statements and trusted the facts. Few doubted that data had
meaning which transcended the factual ways of representation; most had little faith in the ability of the mind and language to describe transcendence. Many writers did not deny
the possibility of the existence of mind and spirit, but they
refused to contemplate the meanings in words. Many authors and the characters they created believed that words

might destroy meanings for a person of sensibility. Abstract words were a shallow pose. William Faulkner described the death of language [in 1955]: "now what we hear is a cacophony of terror and conciliation and compromise babbling only the mouth-sounds, the loud and empty words which we have emasculated of all meaning whatever—freedom, democracy, and patriotism."

Writers in later decades turned from the hardness of fact and flesh in the early century toward abstract, moralistic, didactic discursiveness. Authors and their characters more and more discussed patriotism, morals, and religion. The change was greater in language and technique than in belief. Indeed, Ernest Hemingway in some ways possibly believed less and less as he preached more and more. To know what in the writer and what in the times caused this trend would be to understand much of the history of our age and to comprehend what old age does to many artists. But we cannot know the exact roles of all the causes. The point is that the trend did occur. . . .

The general movement from objectiveness to abstraction, from the flesh to the word, is apparent in almost every major writer of the twentieth century. The extremes may be more noticeable in the greater writers. Indeed, an author such as T.S. Eliot—certainly one of the eminent men of letters in the twentieth century—tended as a young man to write more concretely with hard objects and few generalizations. Yet Eliot's very accomplishment may have led him to philosophical discursiveness as he and his time grew older. The young poet who had been most attached to the empirical world, who had most completely refused to state his meanings, became an older man of letters who wished to be theological and philosophical. The positions of a poet in youth and in old age may contradict each other, but the development from one to another may not be surprising. Early in the century Eliot set his direction, and writers great and small followed. The dedication to concreteness may have been particularly American, perhaps in revolt against the era of slogans during World War I. Certainly the tendencies were characteristic of the most notable American winners of the Nobel Prize—Eliot, Faulkner, and Hemingway. Even if the manifestations of the change are greatly different in the three, the changes in style are similar and significant. The best works of Eliot, Hemingway, and Faulkner between 1910 and 1935 were almost uniformly impersonal; the writer took himself out of his work and made almost no statements of intent or meaning; he presented his characters through their own thinking or in the stark simplicity of objective narrative or dramatic fiction and poetry. He distrusted a vocabulary of religion, morality, or patriotism. Characters who spoke of abstract values were hypocrites; those who had values did not speak of them; to speak was to negate.

REJECTING SPECIOUS RHETORIC

This objective and impersonal literature was in many ways a reaction to an age of verbomania and logorrhea. Slogans, glorified statements, magniloquent claims of virtue and victory idealized and sentimentalized the War and in the process ruined the language. Woodrow Wilson's florid rhetoric first stirred the country and then turned banal and stale. . . . Lionel Trilling has written that Wilson is Hemingway's Widow Douglas—"the pious, the respectable, the morally plausible." In 1919 Robert Frost decided that the President talked "like a fraud," and later he described him as "the whole world's mistake. . . . He missed a mark that wasn't there in nature or human nature." After the world was not saved for democracy and the war had not ended all wars, those who had been swayed [by] Wilson's rhetoric . . . turned cynical, avoided the old specious rhetoric, and developed contempt for Wilson's ideals.

The user of empty words became one of the most common kinds of characters in literature written after Wilson and the sentimental patriots had deadened the language. The talker—orator, politician, or intellectual—declined to villain. John Crowe Ransom advised young girls vigorously twirling their skirts and "travelling the sward" to listen to "teachers old and contrary/Without believing a word." J. Ward Moorehouse in John Dos Passos's *U.S.A.* builds his career and financial and political empire on the false and shallow words of advertising. The wonder of Fitzgerald's Great Gatsby is that he has retained mystery partly in his silence amid those whose noise is an indication of insincerity. In contrast, at his parties there were "enthusiastic meetings between women who never knew each other's names."

In *Pale Horse, Pale Rider*, a short novel about a young couple in love during World War I, Katherine Anne Porter contrasts the almost wordless sincerity of Adam and Miranda with the false vocabulary of a shallow patriot. One scene depicts the two main styles or languages of our time. Watching "a long, dreary play," Adam and Miranda hold hands; their "steady and noncommittal" eyes meet once, "but only once"; Adam watches "the monotonous play with a strange shining excitement, his face quite fixed and still." Before the third act, the curtain rises and reveals "a Liberty Bond salesman" standing before "an American flag improperly and disrespectfully exposed, nailed at each upper corner." Adam and Miranda do not hold hands as they listen to

> the same old moldy speech with the same old dusty backdrop. Miranda tried not to listen, but she heard. These vile Huns—glorious Belleau Wood—our keyword is Sacrifice—Martyred Belgium—give till it hurts—our noble boys Over There—Big Berthas—the death of civilization—the Boche—

As this "local dollar-a-year man" approaches "the home stretch" of his speech, as Adam puts it, the young couple hear only the worn fragments of rhetoric:

> these dead have not died in vain—the war, the war, the WAR to end WAR, war for Democracy, for humanity, a safe world forever and ever—and to prove our faith in Democracy to each other, and to the world, let everybody get together and buy Liberty Bonds and do without sugar and wool socks—was that it? Miranda asked herself, Say that over, I didn't catch the last line. Did you mention Adam? If you didn't I'm not interested.

Such professional patriotism succumbed when it reached the battlefront, but it left a sour taste in the mouth of the soldier and of the writer after the war.

DISTRUST OF WORDS

The particularity, sensuousness, and restraint of twentieth-century literature begins with an unprecedented distrust of rhetoric. Edith Wharton pondered "how the meaning had evaporated out of lots of our old words, as if the general smash-up had broken their stoppers." It was as if people suddenly grew old in their attitudes toward language. "You live with words a long time," Jack Burden says in Robert Penn Warren's *All the King's Men.* "Then all at once you are old, and there are the things and the words don't matter any more." Beliefs may be entangled with things and facts—incarnated perhaps—and words which do not refer directly to experience of the senses consequently become false. The good do, and liars talk. "It is not hard to love men for the things they endure," a Civil War soldier says in Warren's same novel, "and for the words they do not speak." Mere words are distrusted because they are spoken by those who do not know the facts or have real feeling. Even the professional user of words—the man of letters—was skeptical of language. Ezra Pound defined the good writer as one who "uses the smallest possible number of words."

When silence is impossible for characters who feel truly and deeply, they speak factually, briefly, cryptically. Often the tone of voice used becomes colder and more scientific when the content is emotional and profound. Characters in a novel by C.P. Snow talk about the most emotional and romantic matters in a "flat, sensible, methodical voice" and in "the dry, analytic language of the day." In World War II among the students at Devon School in John Knowles's *A Separate Peace,* "Exposing a sincere emotion nakedly ... was the next thing to suicide." Much of this kind of inhibition results from the temper of the time, but perhaps Americans are usually more restrained in expressing feelings than most peoples. "The characteristic attitude of American poets," David Bulwer Lutyens has written, "is similar to that of Americans generally—a suspicion of abstraction."

Words during modern war become "a normal part of the mechanism of deceit," [according to C.K. Ogden and I.A. Richards], and "the emotional aspects of modern thought" become "a veritable orgy of verbomania." Partly in reaction to the cheapening of language, Eliot, Hemingway, Faulkner and many other good writers of the time began to strive toward what C.K. Ogden and I.A. Richards called "a gesture language." More than ever before, poets were aware that the word was not the thing and that even rather concrete words might suggest different things to different persons. "A genuine poet, in his moments of genuine poetry," writes R.G. Collinwood, "never mentions by name the emotions he is expressing." The poet's distrust of general statement was shared by philosopher and scientist. T.E. Hulme wrote,

> It is essential to prove that beauty may be in small, dry things.
> The great aim is accurate, precise and definite description.
> The first thing is to recognize how extraordinarily difficult this is.

For primitive peoples, an anthropologist [Bronislaw Malinowski] argued, narrative speech had been "primarily a mode of social action rather than a mere reflection of thought." Primitive language "is a mode of action and not an instrument of reflection." Here ethnologist and semanticist describe exactly the language and style which Ernest Hemingway and many other writers wished to achieve. "It does not matter what men say in words," Alfred North Whitehead wrote in *Science and the Modern World*, "so long as their activities are controlled by settled instincts. The words may ultimately destroy the instincts. But until this has occurred, words do not count."

Whitehead links medieval decorative sculpture—and the poetry of Geoffrey Chaucer, William Wordsworth, Walt Whitman, and Frost—with the processes of science: "The simple immediate facts are the topics of interest, and these reappear in the thought of science as the 'irreducible stubborn facts.'" He could also have cited Eliot's objective correlative[1] and the one eighth of an iceberg which rose out of the water in Hemingway's prose.[2] The immediate fact and the avoidance of the generalization was also the aim of Ezra Pound and the imagists. Their objectives were "Direct treatment of the 'thing' whether subjective or objective" and "To use absolutely no word that does not contribute to the presentation." Abstraction was regarded as a cause of the declines of civilizations. At this time Joseph Wood Krutch viewed history as a series of collapses which mankind can survive only "because naïver creatures, incapable of understanding the problems and hence not feeling the need to solve them, have appeared somewhere upon the face of the globe."

The dedication of Eliot, Hemingway, and Faulkner to the fact, the thing, and the image represents the proclivities of nearly all good writers in the early years of the twentieth century. Arthur Mizener has written,

> The ordering form of Mr. Eliot's verse derives immediately from Ezra Pound's imagism. Pound's imagism is only one manifestation of an almost mystical theory of perception which is one of the remarkable phenomena of our time. From Henry James's "represent" through James Joyce's "epiphanies" and Mr. Eliot's "objective correlative" to Hemingway's "the way it was," our writers have been dominated by a belief that every pattern of feelings has its pattern of objects and events, so that if the writer can set down the pattern of objects in exactly the right relations, without irrelevances

1. Eliot's theory that a specific emotion can be expressed by means of a formula consisting of objects, names, and other concrete elements   2. Hemingway believed writers should use words sparingly, e.g., describe the visible one eighth of the iceberg in a way that implies the seven eighths that lies under water.

or distortions, they will evoke in the reader the pattern of feelings. Whatever the limitations of this view—and we have hardly considered seriously yet what they may be—it suited Mr. Eliot's talent, with its great powers of visual and aural perception.

If the style of the writer was attempting to create the beauty of "small dry things," obnoxious and despicable and futile characters in the literature of the twenties might be ignorant of the "small dry things" and therefore incapable of speaking except in discursive generalities and abstractions. Such characters were seldom given extensive roles. The most prominent bore of this kind is probably Dawson Fairchild in Faulkner's *Mosquitoes*. Others are Robert Cohn and Gino in Hemingway, and, to some extent, the old man in Eliot's "Gerontion." More typical characters are those who intellectualize and abstract but still think—though they seldom speak—in beautifully concrete imagery, which reflects their desire if not their ability to appreciate the beauty of "small dry things." Prufrock, Quentin Compson, and Darl Bundren speak this kind of language—images of desire rather than of the known and loved.

Modernism Expresses Both Historical Discontinuity and a Sense of Tradition

Richard Ellmann and Charles Feidelson Jr.

Richard Ellmann and Charles Feidelson Jr. are coeditors of the book *The Modern Tradition: Backgrounds of Modern Literature.* In the following selection, excerpted from their introduction to that book, they write that modernism represents both a break with the past and a connection to history. While modernism is by definition opposed to tradition, modernists explored their relationship to the past in their writing. Ellmann was an American literary critic and scholar who specialized in the life and works of James Joyce, William Butler Yeats, Oscar Wilde, and other modern British and Irish writers. Feidelson wrote and edited several books on American literature.

We have grown accustomed to speak offhandedly of "modern literature," of the "modern temper," and even of "the modern," but until recently we have not made much effort to analyze the meaning of this term that we find so useful. We have postponed the task of defining it for the same reason we feel it to be important—it refers to something intimate and elusive, not objective and easily analyzed. The modern is not like the reassuring landscape of the past, open and invadable everywhere. It is at once more immediate and more obscure: a blur of book titles, a mood of impatience with anachronisms, a diffuse feeling of difference. Or it is a voice to which we intuitively respond, a language that gives new valences to words long enrolled in the dictionary, including "modern" itself.

Intellectual and cultural historians and historians of art

seem to have been more inquisitive in this respect than students of modern literature. Criticism has certainly not neglected the literature of the twentieth century, but most of the comprehensive studies have not been very analytic, and most of the analytic studies have not been very comprehensive. The last volume of the *Oxford History of English Literature,* an extreme example, makes no attempt at general definition—indeed, offers no broad consideration of the period at all—but consists of separate essays on *Eight Modern Writers.* Yet it is clear that "modern" amounts to more than a chronological description. The term designates a distinctive kind of imagination—themes and forms, conditions and modes of creation, that are interrelated and comprise an imaginative whole. One characteristic of works we call modern is that they positively insist on a general frame of reference within and beyond themselves. They claim modernity; they profess modernism. That is what we vaguely acknowledge when we invoke the word to describe them. However difficult to objectify, therefore, the modern awaits definition, and there is reason to think that the study of modern literature will increasingly become a study of the modern in general. Criticism is growing bolder in method and more philosophic in purpose, responding to the breadth of intention that we perceive in modern writing.

An Untraditional Tradition

Moreover, we no longer completely identify the modern with the contemporary—the immediate literary world in which we live without much hope of defining it. Harry Levin's recent essay, "What Was Modernism?", makes explicit what everyone has begun to realize, that the great age of the century's literature, the age of Yeats, Joyce, Eliot, and Lawrence, of Proust, Valéry, and Gide, of Mann, Rilke, and Kafka, has already passed into history. Looking back upon that age historically, we are able to see it in historical depth. We become aware of what we must call a "modern tradition," which reaches well back into the romantic era and even beyond. And the more we extend our perspective in time, the less inclined we are to see this tradition as narrowly literary. What comes to mind is rather something broadly imaginative, a large spiritual enterprise including philosophic, social, and scientific thought, and aesthetic and literary theories and manifestoes, as well as poems, novels, dramas.

If we can postulate a modern tradition, we must add that it is a paradoxically untraditional tradition. Modernism strongly implies some sort of historical discontinuity, either a liberation from inherited patterns or, at another extreme, deprivation and disinheritance. In an essay on "The Modern Element in Modern Literature," Lionel Trilling singles out a radically anti-cultural bias as the most important attribute of the modern imagination. Committed to everything in human experience that militates against custom, abstract order, and even reason itself, modern literature has elevated individual existence over social man, unconscious feeling over self-conscious perception, passion and will over intellection and systematic morals, dynamic vision over the static image, dense actuality over practical reality. In these and other ways, it has made the most of its break with the past, its in-born challenge to established culture. Concurrently, it has been what Henry James called an "imagination of disaster." Interwoven with the access of knowledge, the experimental verve, and the personal urgency of the modern masters is, as Trilling also finds, a sense of loss, alienation, and despair. These are the two faces, positive and negative, of the modern as the anti-traditional: freedom and deprivation, a living present and a dead past.

Yet the concept of a modern tradition is not simply the invention of historically minded critics. The modernists have been as much imbued with a feeling for their historical role, their relation to the past, as with a feeling of historical discontinuity. They have had a sense of an ancestral line, even if it is often an underground stream. Their suspicion of old forms has made them search for kinsmen in old rebellions. Or, striving to locate their disinheritance in the course of history, they have constantly been searching for and never quite finding their starting-point—the end of Victorianism, the beginning of romanticism, the mid-seventeenth century, the end of the Middle Ages. The paradoxical task of the modern imagination, whether liberated or alienated, has been to stand both inside and outside itself, to articulate its own formlessness, to encompass its own extravagant possibilities.

That undertaking is what Stephen Spender, in *The Struggle of the Modern,* formulates as "the vision of a whole situation." The modern, according to Spender, finds its character by confronting the past and including this confrontation within itself as part of a single total experience. It is more than a cultivation of immediacy, of free or fragmented awareness; it is the embodiment in current imagery of a situation always larger than the present, and as such it is also a containment of the resources and perils of the present by rediscovery of a relevant past. In this sense, modernism is synthetic in its very indeterminacy. Modern writers, working often without established models and bent on originality, have at the same time been classicists, custodians of language, communicators, traditionalists in their fashion.

CHAPTER 2

The New Poetry

American
Modernism

The American Poetic Renaissance: New Freedoms in Subject and Form

Louise Bogan

In the following excerpt, Louise Bogan traces the emergence of the modernist movement in American poetry, which is often referred to as the American poetic Renaissance. She places the starting point of this movement at the creation of *Poetry* magazine in 1912—a date that is widely agreed on by literary historians. According to Bogan, the new poetry was characterized by a freedom of form and style, including free verse and conversational language, as well as an exploration of themes that had previously not been treated in poetry, such as the realities of small-town life and urban industrialization. Bogan (1897–1970) was an American poet and literary critic.

The year 1912 has come to be recognized as the year in which a truly organized movement toward a new American poetry began. It was in October 1912 that Harriet Monroe began to publish, in Chicago, a little magazine entirely devoted to what the editor meticulously called, from the first, "the art of poetry." *Poetry: A Magazine of Verse,* whose role was to become historic, in its first number presented material of a mixed sort, but still of a predominantly conventional style. ... This first number of *Poetry* published, along with the conventional verse of Arthur Davison Ficke and William Vaughan Moody, an exquisite lyric by a woman, Helen Dudley, and two poems by Ezra Pound.

ENTER EZRA POUND

It is at this point that Pound enters the arena as a strong, eccentric, untiring, and seemingly inexhaustible motive force

Excerpted from Louise Bogan, *Achievement in American Poetry, 1900–1950* (Chicago: Henry Regnery, 1951).

in poetry. In 1912 he was already for some years a resident of London, having left the United States "for good" in 1908, after a short and stormy attempt to adjust himself to an American academic career. Born in Idaho in 1885, he had been educated in the East. Precocious, he entered the University of Pennsylvania at fifteen and soon shifted to the status of special student, in order to follow his strong bent toward comparative literature. He spent some time in Venice, after his departure from America, in great poverty—a poverty which, however, did not prevent him from having his first collection of poems *A Lume Spento* published in a limited edition of 100. He speaks, in the *Pisan Cantos* of his starving isolation at this period; of his despairing urge, at one point, to throw the entire small lot of this first book into the Grand Canal. He went on to London, where a few friendships soon launched him in a group of artists and writers; and his *Personae* and *Exultations*, both published in 1909, received remarkably good notices in the English press. Pound's interest in comparative literature (a subject which then received little attention in academic curricula) and especially in the medieval literature of Provence, was reflected in a prose study, *The Spirit of Romance*, which appeared in 1910; by 1912 Pound had published two further books of poems: *Canzoni* (1911) and *Ripostes* (1912). *Provença* had appeared in 1910.

One of Pound's two poems, in *Poetry*'s first number, was dedicated to Whistler—on the occasion of the Whistler show at the Tate Gallery in September 1912. It deserves quotation:

You also, our first great,
Had tried all ways;
Tasted and pried and worked in many fashions,
And this much gives me heart to play the game.

· · · · · · · · · · ·

You had your searches, your uncertainties,
And this is good to know—for us, I mean,
Who bear the brunt of our America
And try to wrench her impulse into art.

You were not always sure, not always set
To hiding night or tuning "symphonies";
Had not one style from birth, but tried and pried
And stretched and tampered with the media.

You and Abe Lincoln from that mass of dolts
Show us there's a chance at least of winning through.

A more awkwardly written poem cannot be imagined. At

twenty-seven Pound had yet to learn much that he was about to preach concerning form, emphasis, and tone. Yet in this fumbling utterance, a good deal of Pound's authentic side— as well as much of his nonauthentic—comes through. Here is the fanatical artist, the born iconoclast, the American "village atheist." The passion for great men is also apparent— along with the two sides of a nascent messianic drive: the side that must "bear," and the side that must "redeem." The style, moreover, is broken from the regular beat of the iamb[1] to the trochaic[2] beat of common conversational speech; and a struggle between rather affected literary procedure and the advance of natural words in their natural order, goes on before our eyes.

Miss Monroe seems first to have heard of Pound as an Englishman; her delight at finding him an American is un- bounded, and she proudly states that Mr. Pound "authorizes the statement that at present such of his poetic work as re- ceives magazine publication in America will appear exclu- sively in *Poetry*." This promise was soon broken (Pound ap- peared in *The Smart Set* as early as 1913); but Pound stayed on for years in another capacity: "[acting] as foreign corre- spondent of *Poetry*, keeping its readers informed of the pre- sent interests of the art in England, France and elsewhere."

THE IMAGIST MOVEMENT

The first "imagist" poem to appear in America came out promptly in *Poetry*'s second issue. This was "Choricos" by the young poet Richard Aldington, later the husband of H.D. (Hilda Doolittle). "*The Imagistes*," Miss Monroe explained, "[is] a group of ardent Hellenists[3] who are pursuing interest- ing experiments in *vers libre*,[4] trying to attain in English cer- tain subtleties of cadence of the kind which Mallarmé[5] and his followers have studied in French."

The link with the French symbolist poets is thus made, at the outset of the imagist movement; but it is still uncertain exactly what influences molded the early work of the group. Pound had known Miss Doolittle at the University of Penn- sylvania, when her father was a professor of astronomy. There he had also met William Carlos Williams, a young medical student. Pound's own early poetic style, directly de-

---

1. a metrical foot consisting of an unstressed syllable followed by a stressed syllable
2. a stressed followed by an unstressed syllable   3. specialists in the language and cul- ture of ancient Greece   4. free verse   5. Stéphane, a French poet

rived from Robert Browning, was loaded with imitation-archaic language, effective at some moments but irritatingly artificial at others. Miss Doolittle now lived in London, and Pound's circle of London acquaintance included the antiromantic "philosopher" of the arts, T. E. Hulme. Hulme's influence seems to be undeniable, in view of the fact that Pound published Hulme's *Works*, five free-verse poems, as an addendum to *Ripostes*, a volume dedicated to W.C. Williams. Also involved in the imagist situation was a growing interest in Oriental verse forms, stemming in part from Judith Gautier's translation of Chinese poetry into French. Pound, having been made literary executor of the American orientalist, Ernest Fenollosa, who died in 1908, had access to an extremely valuable collection of notes on, and translations of, Chinese and Japanese poetry and drama after 1913. The influence of the French symbolists, at this moment, was slight; whole areas of symbolist tendency and meaning were left unexplored until a later day. But from 1912 on, imagist tone and coloring begins to appear in Pound's own verse. *Ripostes* announces the beginning of a more restrained and less theatrical writer. The inversions disappear; the language is freed from exclamations and exhortations in the second person singular; and a new coolness and colorlessness of surface allow Pound to deal with contemporary material.

CHANGING POETRY FOR GOOD

Pound and his friends had learned from contemporary French poets and critics that vers libre demanded as much critical responsibility, on the part of the poet himself, as poetry written in form; that free verse should be kept, by every possible technical means, from monotony and flaccidity. The lack of regular meter and of rhyme should not result merely in pieces of disguised prose. This early insistence on the formal elements of free verse is interesting, in the light of future developments. The early contribution of Pound and the imagists to the establishment, in free verse, of responsible poetic standards cannot be overestimated. Pound's continual experiment with the freer forms, from 1912 to 1916 (when the volume *Lustra* was published) finally resulted in a formal vers libre in English which was at once flexible and severe, capable of dignity and poignance, afflicted with neither flabbiness nor rigidity. The imagists' admirable condensation, their attention to the matter in hand, their com-

plete lack of literary dilution and confusion brought into immediate notice a clarity compared to which current "magazine verse" seemed both soft and shabby. By the time that
formal metrics were again brought into use—by Pound
working with Eliot in the "Mauberly" period (1920)—the
years of free verse experimentation had changed conventional English poetic procedures for good. The former insis-
tent iambic beat was varied; the high pitch of poetic tone had
been, as it were, lowered; a healthy fusion between light and
serious verse had taken place. Poetry in English was again
free to be applied to any human situation, broadening out
then into the freedom characteristic of high cultures: where
everything is open to the play of mind and spirit; where
there are no forbidden subjects and no proscribed methods;
where poetry, again become a natural human art, is no
longer a parlor decoration.

ESTABLISHING NEW GROUND

The first years of *Poetry* were exciting ones. Not only did
Pound send Yeats, at the beginning of Yeats' later style, to
Miss Monroe, but he also introduced her to Rabindranath
Tagore's translations from the Bengali. Meanwhile, it seemed
that every hidden American quality, as well as certain American peculiarities, began to find a poetic voice. New poetic
ground was established with unbelievable rapidity. . . .

Edgar Lee Masters . . . was . . . given a method by free verse
which coincided with his own nature and the nature of his
material. Masters spent his youth and young manhood struggling with conventional poetic form. He was a man of forty-
five in 1914—a Chicago lawyer who had written and published poems and plays under pseudonyms—when he began
to write and to publish in *Reedy's Mirror* his memories of the
Illinois town in which he had spent his childhood and youth.
These free-verse notations, when published in 1915 under
the title *Spoon River Anthology* swung open [a] door upon
neglected facts of American life: the interplay of materialism
and idealism in a Midwestern town. The keynote of the poems, written in the first person in the form of self-epitaphs,
is frustration—of a kind that Sherwood Anderson was soon
to describe in more detail and with a softer pathos. The detail here is sharp, the accent lies upon the waste of human
vitality and human aspirations, and this is undoubtedly an
accent weighted with remembered suffering. But the tone of

the short verses is not entirely grim. Masters was able to lift the situation into a kind of nobility by contrasting misused energy with a kind of smothered gallantry. It is not entirely without a hint of nostalgia that he looks back upon these thin, baffled, sour lives kept from full knowledge of themselves and others by false allegiances, ignorance, and bigotry; and by the fear and deception resultant upon the rigidity of moral standards. A fiber of energy runs through these portraits; they are neither mawkish nor cynical.

Many readers responded to the truth and the succinct method of *Spoon River*. In spite of a minority that condemned it as "sensational" the book became the first best seller of the "poetic Renaissance." Masters never succeeded in equaling either the power or the appeal of this book in his later writing; and a shadow of bitterness and of rather small-minded iconoclasm clouds his many subsequent books. *Spoon River*, however, bears the mark of the difficulties that shaped it—difficulties which made it important for more than its own day.

[Another] Midwestern talent . . . was that of Carl Sandburg. Born in 1878 in Galesburg, Illinois, of Swedish immigrant parentage, he spent his youth as an untrained worker in many haphazard jobs, served in Puerto Rico during the Spanish-American War, and later entered Lombard college in Galesburg. On leaving college, he became a salesman and newspaperman in Chicago. In 1904 he had printed a pamphlet of twenty-two poems. Ten years later "Chicago Poems," a free-verse group, appeared in *Poetry*. Here realism in the Whitman vein was tempered with a kind of Scandinavian mysticism. Sandburg added to the effects of the free-verse realists by writing in common speech, in coarse vernacular, in current slang. . . . Sandburg also broadened the field by his descriptions of scenes of industry: of the packing houses, the mills, and the factories at the outskirts of the cities, by which the cities were fed and of which the cities were somewhat ashamed. And this industrial grime, stench, grinding, shriek, and clatter is celebrated by Sandburg, as well as described. . . .

ROBERT FROST: UNIVERSAL TRUTHS IN ORDINARY EVENTS

New freedoms in subject and treatment continued to widen the American poetic horizon. Americans were beginning to produce their own brand of impressionism. But this impressionism lacked background; it had not grown by slow stages, but had burst into being overnight. A shift of sensibility had been marked by a change in form, but both form and sensibility were still free-floating—without definite roots. A young and growing art must have some liaison with convention. Some feeling for rule and order must exist. If the American poetic Renaissance had succeeded only in establishing a set of American experimentalists, without an accompanying group of formalists, its successes would have been shallow, indeterminate, and fleeting. We have seen to what an extent the imagists insisted on purity of direction and economy of means; their struggle to keep these ends important was, in fact, just beginning. At this time an American poet came into view whose form, although conventional, was original enough to further widen and diversify the American poetic scene. He was Robert Frost, whose first book of poems, *A Boy's Will*, was published in London in 1913.

Frost, born in San Francisco in 1875, was brought back as a boy to his family's native New England by his widowed mother. He graduated from high school in the industrial city of Lawrence, Massachusetts, and, after his marriage in 1895, entered Harvard College for a stay of two years. His early poetry found no favor with magazine editors, and he determined, after spending his young manhood as a teacher and farmer in New Hampshire, to try his luck in England. Once in England, he made friends among the poets who called themselves "Georgian." He also met Pound, who felt "reality" in him.

Frost's early poems have a simple, unforced lyric charm; they seem to have been written as naturally and effortlessly as breathing. Frost, also from the first, [was] less literary and closer to the soil than his fellow New Englander. Frost is "a countryman." He has a deep love for natural things, for things of field and pasture, for bird, flower, weed, and tree; and for the motions and rhythms attendant upon man's age-old cultivation of the land—the rhythm of sowing and reaping in recurring seedtime and harvest. Frost also sees with great clearness the wayward and frustrating elements which run counter to nature's abundance and man's efforts on nature's behalf and on his own. His sympathy with the stray, the unused, and the overlooked gives his best poetry poignance and pathos. What he cannot bear to contemplate at length are the evidences that veins of evil run deeply through the natural scene.

North of Boston, published in England with success in 1914, achieved American acclaim the following year. The poems in *North of Boston* are for the most part written in isolated dramatic scenes, or else in the dramatic monologue Browning had done so much to develop. In these episodes Frost broke through all stock ideas concerning New England country living into the tragedy and eccentric comedy of a countryside still bound to obsolete and degenerating custom. He described a dying region's ingrown life; its joys and fears; its stubborn strength still opposed to decay; its terrors and stratagems; its common sense and its groundwork of human dignity. Here is a countryside still lit by lamps and lanterns, still measured by the slow pace of a man's walk or a horse's run. Here is Yankee talk made an integral part of the drama. To use a speech so close to patois, without slipping over into the dangers of actual dialect, was in itself an achievement. Frost was able, moreover, to keep his incidents dramatic, although his material is continually working against this intensification toward a lower level, that of the sentimental-colloquial. . . .

Frost's later work never completely realized the tragic power that *North of Boston* promised. . . . But it is difficult to imagine the American poetry of our time without the figure of Frost being deeply involved in it from the start. His early themes were indeed real, with a reality for which American expression was starved, and lacking which it would not have achieved, in the following restless years, full balance. Frost's use of understatement and of ellipsis, both emotional and stylistic, helped to bring the lyric and the short dramatic poem written in English onto a level where they could deal easily with everyday matters; and the younger poets learned from him. His moments of vision, expressed on this level, take on an added poignance; the ordinary event is given an unexpected turn, the universal flashes through.

The Tenets of Imagism: Directness, Conciseness, and Musical Rhythm

Richard Gray

Imagism, the primary school of American poetry from 1912 to 1917, led the resurgence in poetry that marked the beginning of the American modernist movement in literature. Richard Gray, a literature professor at the University of Essex in the United Kingdom, outlines the philosophy of the imagist poets: direct treatment of the subject, economy of words, and the use of musical rhythm rather than traditional poetic meter. Gray describes the work of H.D. (Hilda Doolittle) in order to illustrate these concepts.

'The *point de repère* usually and conveniently taken as the starting-point of modern poetry', declared T.S. Eliot, 'is the group denominated 'imagists' in London about 1910'. Actually, the beginnings of the Imagist movement can be traced to an earlier date than this, and to the feeling common among young writers in the first few years of the twentieth century that poets were for the most part playing for safety and sentimentality. 'The common verse . . . from 1890', remarked Ezra Pound with characteristic brusqueness, 'was a horrible agglomerate compost, not minted, most of it not even baked, all legato, a doughy mess of third-hand Keats, Wordsworth, heaven knows what, fourth-hand Elizabethan sonority blunted, half-melted, lumpy'. In reaction against all this, a group began to gather around T.E. Hulme and F.S. Flint in London dedicated, among other things, to the aim of reproducing 'the peculiar quality of feeling which is induced by the flat spaces and wide horizons of the virgin-prairie'— and to the belief that 'poetic ideas are best expressed by the rendering of concrete objects'. They were joined, in April 1909, by the young expatriate Pound whose own ideas about poetry had been outlined in a letter to William Carlos Williams approximately six months earlier:

1. To paint the thing as I see it.
2. Beauty.
3. Freedom from didacticism.
4. It is only good manners if you repeat a few other men to at least do it better or more briefly.

Some while after this, in 1911, Pound renewed acquaintances with Hilda Doolittle, newly arrived from the United States and already calling herself H.D. By now, Pound was looking around for good poetry to send to Harriet Monroe[1] in Chicago and found it both in the work of H.D. and in that of a young British writer, Richard Aldington. He was in the habit of meeting H.D. and Aldington in a tea shop in Kensington, to discuss their verse with them; and it was at one such meeting in 1912 that he informed them, apparently to their surprise, that they were Imagistes. H.D., Pound insisted, was even to sign herself 'H.D. Imagiste', and in writing to Harriet Monroe about her he forced the point home. 'I've had luck again', Pound exulted:

> and am sending you some *modern* stuff by an American. I say modern, for it is in the laconic speech of the Imagistes, even if the subject is classic. This is the sort of American stuff that I can show here and in Paris without its being ridiculed. Objective—no slither; direct—no excessive use of adjectives, no metaphors that won't permit examination. It's straight talk, straight as the Greek!

Pound did not explain it, but evidently the French version of the word was chosen to suggest a connection with modern French poetry. Whatever the reason, he and his colleagues eventually thought better of it and reverted to the English word: the new group of poets were to be called Imagists. . . .

THE RULES OF IMAGISM

What matters about Imagism is not so much the movement itself as the beliefs it articulated. It provided a focus: not a practical focus but an ideological one. It served to crystallise certain tendencies, certain notions about the nature of poetic experiment, which had been developing in a rather piecemeal fashion over the previous decade—to organise, to define, and so to promote them. The nature of these tendencies can be glimpsed in two essays about Imagism published in

1. the founder of *Poetry* magazine

Poetry in 1913, one written by Pound and the other by F.S. Flint. Pound's essay begins with this:

> An Image is that which presents an intellectual and emotional complex in an instant of time . . .
> It is the presentation of such a 'complex' instantaneously which gives that sense of sudden liberation; that sense of freedom from time limits and space limits; that sense of sudden growth, which we experience in the presence of the greatest works of art.
> It is better to produce one Image in a lifetime than to produce voluminous works.

Flint's essay, in turn, announces three 'rules' that all Imagists, and by implication all good poets, were to follow:

1. Direct treatment of the 'thing' whether subjective or objective.
2. To use absolutely no word that did (*sic*) not contribute to the presentation.
3. As regarding rhythm: to compose in sequence of the musical phrase not in sequence of the metronome.

'The point of Imagisme', Pound wrote in 1914, 'is that it does not use images as ornaments. The image itself is the speech. The image is the word beyond formulated language'. This statement, corresponding to his own opening remarks in the *Poetry* essay and to the first of Flint's 'rules', suggests the primary Imagist objective: to avoid rhetoric and moralising, to stick closely to the object or experience being described and hardly ever, if at all, to move from this to *explicit* generalisation. Poetry, the feeling was, had for too long relied upon expansive verbal gestures, the ethereal and the abstract. It had to be brought back to fine particulars. The poet might very well (as the philosopher of the Imagist movement, T. E. Hulme put it) 'glide through an abstract process', but he had to make it seem inevitable, a natural result of his meditation on particulars; and, in any event, it would be far better if he left it to the reader to intuit those abstractions, to gather up what is commonly called the 'meaning' of the poem, from the resonance, the reverberations of the image. Several things could be said about this primary tenet of Imagism. In the first place, it reveals the links between Romanticism, Symbolism, and Imagism. Whatever the differences between these movements (and there are, of course, many) all three had this in common: a belief in the primacy of a condensed, intense, and above all intuitive form of communication, in imaginative rather than rational discourse.

In the second, it exposes some of the specifically American roots of Imagist thinking: for this observation of the concrete that Pound and Flint talk about, that allows the observer to catch the wonder, the aura that surrounds simple, particular things is a stance towards reality that characterises many earlier American writers—people like Ralph Waldo Emerson, say, or Walt Whitman. And, in the third place, the *representative* nature of Imagism is clear when we note how omnipresent this belief in the concrete is in twentieth-century American poetry. There are the obvious examples like Robert Frost, whose own brand of subtle, playful pragmatism is expressed in lines like, 'The fact is the sweetest dream that labour knows', or William Carlos Williams who, in one of his most famous and repeated statements, insisted that there should be 'No ideas but in things.' But—and this is the crucial point—we need not necessarily confine ourselves to such immediate and self-evident cases. Even Hart Crane, who is surely one of the most unworldly and mystical of modern American writers, wanted to anchor his mysticism in mundane experience. His favourite metaphor for the speculative flight was, in fact, the bridge: something that crosses another element (water), reaches towards heaven, yet keeps both feet firmly planted on earth. He would never have dreamed of simply rejecting the ordinary as earlier followers of the Ideal had done; and the fact that he would not have done so testifies to the strength, the almost incalculable impact of an idea to which Pound, Flint, and their companions were among the first (in this century at least) to give memorable expression.

'Use no superfluous word', insisted Pound in his 1913 *Poetry* essay, 'no adjective, which does not reveal something'. This, the second of Flint's 'rules', was perhaps what Amy Lowell had in mind when she said that the Imagist principles 'are not new; they have fallen into desuetude. They are the essentials of all great poetry'. Be that as it may, this 'ridding the field of verbiage' became one of the central activities in modern American poetry. 'Cut and cut again whatever you write', William Carlos Williams advised Denise Levertov '—while you leave by your art no trace of your cutting—and the final utterance will remain packed with what you have to say'. 'The test of the artist', he added later, 'is to be able to revise without showing a seam. . . . It is quite often no more than knowing what to *cut*'. Williams demonstrated an almost ferocious enthusiasm in following such advice; and so too did poets as otherwise different, from Williams and each other, as Carl Sandburg and Wallace Stevens. Superficially, at least, the diction of Sandburg or of Stevens bears little resemblance to that of Williams; yet fundamentally their concern—or, one might say, their obsession—is the same. Sandburg's robust colloquialism and Stevens's precious, meticulous language, both issue out of a preoccupation with functional speech: which is to say, a speech that achieves a maximum effect with the minimum possible resources. 'Precision, economy of statement, logic employed to means that are disinterested, drawing and identifying . . . liberate the imagination', said Marianne Moore. Her statement of faith was echoed by scores of other American poets, many of whom had no direct connection with Imagism—and, in fact, would have stoutly resisted the suggestion that they had any sympathy with its principles.

And then there is the third 'rule' promulgated by Flint and expanded upon by Pound in this fashion:

> Don't chop your stuff into separate *iambs*. Don't make
> each line stop dead at the end, and then begin every next
> line with a heave. Let the beginning of the next line catch
> the rise of the rhythm wave, unless you want a definite
> longish pause.
> In short, behave as a musician, a good musician,
> when dealing with the phase of your art which has exact
> parallels in music. The same laws govern, and you are
> bound by no others.

'Rhythm MUST have meaning', Pound wrote to Harriet Monroe. 'It can't be merely a careless dash off, with no grip and no real hold to the words and sense, a tumty tum tumty tum tum ta'. The *vers libre*[2] of the Imagists was one aspect of their work to which contemporary critics took particular exception. John Livingstone Lowes, for example, claimed to see no difference between Amy Lowell's free verse and George Meredith's prose: to which Lowell herself replied, '. . . there is no difference. . . . Whether a thing is written as prose or verse is immaterial'. Pound would not have put things as categorically as Lowell. As he saw it, poetry should be at least *'as well written as prose'* but there *was* a difference: because in poetry, he believed, words are infused with something more than their prose meaning—with a musical quality that gives them a further dimension, an additional substance and

2. free verse

thrust. 'To break the iamb, that was the first heave', as he put it in the *Cantos:* the poet should first shake off the tyranny of predetermined verse forms. Having done this, however, his aim should not be mere looseness or licence, the 'fluid, fruity, facile stuff' of an Amy Lowell, but movements and melodies intrinsic to the occasion: tough, sinuous, sharply etched rhythms that described the contours of an individual experience—a hidden but nevertheless clearly audible music that captured the pace, poise, and tone of the personal voice. In this sense, Imagism was building on the innovations, not only of an obvious *vers libriste* like Walt Whitman, but of idiosyncratic rhythmists like Edgar Allan Poe and Emily Dickinson. And to this extent, the Imagist belief in a flexible verse form (which was in turn the symptom of a broader commitment to an open, unpremeditated structure) was to find expression, both in the language experiments of e.e. cummings, Theodore Roethke, and Marianne Moore, and in the less extreme but no less original, musical shapes of John Crowe Ransom, Robinson Jeffers, and Hart Crane.

H.D.: An Exemplary Imagist

Among the poems included in [a] 1915 Imagist anthology was 'Oread' by H.D. Cited by Pound as the supreme example of an Imagist poem, it is besides a perfect illustration of what Richard Aldington referred to as the 'accurate mystery' of H.D.'s work. For both these reasons (and because it is, in any case, characteristically terse), it is well worth quoting in its entirety:

> Whirl up, sea—
> Whirl your pointed pines,
> Splash your great pines
> On our rocks,
> Hurl your green pine over us,
> Cover us with your pools of fir.

Perhaps the first thing that strikes a reader about a poem like this is the absence of certain familiar elements. There are no similes, no symbols, no generalised reflections or didacticism, no rhymes, no regular metre, no narrative. One might well ask what there is, then; and the answer would be a great deal. There is a pellucid clarity of diction, and a rhythm that is organic, intrinsic to the mood of the poem; there is a vivid economy of language, in which each word seems to have been carefully chiselled out of other contexts, and there is a subtle technique of intensification by repetition—no phrase is remarkable in itself, perhaps, but there is a sense of rapt incantation, an enthralled dwelling on particular cadences that gives a hermetic quality, a prophetic power, to the whole. It is the entire poem that is experienced, not a striking line, a felicitous comparison, or an ingenious rhyme; the poem has become the unit of meaning and not the word, so each single word can remain stark, simple, and unpretentious. In 'Oread', the image that constitutes the poem becomes not merely a medium for describing a sensation but the sensation itself. The sea *is* the pinewood, the pinewood *is* the sea, the wind surrounds and inhabits both; and the Greek mountain-nymph of the title comprehends and becomes identified with all three elements. There is a dynamic and unified complex, an ecstatic fusion of natural and human energies; and the image represents the point of fusion, 'the precise instant' (to quote Pound) 'when a thing outward and objective transforms itself, or darts into a thing inward and subjective'.

'Oread' is typical of H.D.'s work in many ways. . . .

All through her life, she retained an intense belief in the religious possibilities of art—or, to be more exact, in the mystical nature of the creative process, the act of turning experience into words. 'Writing . . . trains one to a sort of yogi or majic (*sic*) power', she insisted, 'it is a sort of contemplation, it is living on another plane'. In her eyes, poetry tended to become an equivalent of prayer. It was a way of communicating with another world, of using the idiom of what she termed once 'passionate grave thought' to enter into a higher level of consciousness. Her great war trilogy makes this especially clear. Written in London during the Second World War the three books that comprise the trilogy—*The Walls Do Not Fall, Tribute to the Angels,* and *The Flowering of the Rod*—represent a search for 'ancient wisdom', the still, generative centre at the heart of the contemporary turbulence. '*We are voyagers*', she declares:

> *discoverers*
> *of the not-known*
> *the unrecorded;*
> *we have no map;*
> *possibly we will reach heaven,*
> *haven.*

Firm in the belief that 'every concrete object / has abstract value', she attempts to fathom the mystery of personality, to re-create her own identity—in a sense, to write herself by reinventing her life in the process of remembering and re-hearsing it. . . .

She depends on what Pound called the ideogrammic method—which involves, essentially, a rapid association of images. Images are, in H.D.'s own words, 'superimposed on one another like a stack of photographic negatives': one image or perception leads into another and the reader's imagination is actively engaged, making the connections, discovering the point of intersection. Instead of a story, in which events occur in time, or a process of logical argument, there is a juxtaposing or overlaying of different images and impressions; and their inter-action, the energy that passes between them, constitutes the 'argument' of the poem. In her trilogy, H.D. characteristically uses an image to describe this Imagistic technique—of the many colours which, at their point of intersecting, become one colour:

> And the point in the spectrum
> where all lights become one,
> is white and white is not no-colour
> as we were told as children
> but all-colour;
> where the flames mingle
> and the wings meet, when we gain
> the arc of perfection,
> we are satisfied, we are happy,
> we begin again;

In this sense, Robert Duncan is entirely right to suggest that H.D.'s trilogy stands, along with Pound's *Cantos* and William Carlos Williams's long poem *Paterson*, as 'a major work of the Imagist genius in full'.

T.S. Eliot's *The Waste Land:* The Chief Example of Modernist Poetry

David Perkins

T.S. Eliot's poem *The Waste Land*, first published in 1922, is widely considered the most significant work of modernist poetry and is often cited as one of the two most important works of modernist literature, along with James Joyce's novel *Ulysses*. In the following excerpt, David Perkins describes the characteristics of the poem that make it the primary example of modernist poetry: an emphasis on the realities of city life; the use of symbols, myth, and allusion; a fragmented structure; and themes depicting the social isolation and spiritual sickness of modern urban life. As a professor of English and American literature at Harvard University, Perkins wrote the two-volume book *A History of Modern Poetry*.

Several of the poems T.S. Eliot published before *The Waste Land* were minor masterpieces. . . . Each of these poems was arrestingly "modern" in its own way, and each was imitated. But they were not so widely imitated as one might now suppose, and the main reason was the rapidity with which Eliot developed. Their impact was lost in that of *The Waste Land*. In Ezra Pound's eyes *The Waste Land* was "the justification of our modern experiment, since 1900." In the eyes of more conservative poets and critics it was a "mad medley." For many a "new" poet in America it was a "piece of tripe" (the phrase is Amy Lowell's), parasitic on past styles, uprooted, formless, academic, anti-democratic, and defeatist. But for adolescent future poets it possessed to an unrivaled degree the prestige of the modern. Not that they understood it bet-

Reprinted by permission of the publisher from *A History of Modern Poetry: From the 1890s to the High Modernist Mode*, by David Perkins (Cambridge, MA: Harvard University Press). Copyright ©1976 by the President and Fellows of Harvard College.

ter than other readers, but they admired its technical boldness and defiance, the more so since it defied not only conservative taste but also the free-verse and Imagist conventions of the school that was then loudest in protesting its
own modernity.

LIFE IN THE CITY

Because *The Waste Land* had a unique influence on the development of modern poetry it must be dwelt on here. . . .
The earlier poetry was important, but *The Waste Land* im-
mensely more so. Our purpose in discussing this much-
scrutinized poem is not to offer another interpretation, com-
mentary, or evaluation but to indicate why it came to be
viewed as the chief example of the modern in poetry, so
much so that Eliot was seen as the counterpart in poetry to
James Joyce, Pablo Picasso, Igor Stravinski, and to other major creators of the Modernist revolution in their respective
arts. One reason was Eliot's use of the modern city as setting.
Precedents could be found in English, American, and French
poetry of the last seventy-five years, notably in Charles-
Pierre Baudelaire, and in some twentieth-century poetry,
such as Carl Sandburg's *Chicago Poems* (1916), not to mention Eliot's *Prufrock and Other Observations* (1917). Nevertheless, no previous poem gave so vivid an impression of the
contemporary, urban metropolis. In some sequences *The
Waste Land* resembled an avant-garde documentary film; it
explored the city and the lives of its inhabitants by juxtaposing images, scenes, fragments of conversation, and the like.
The technique resembled cinematic montage,[1] which was
developed at about the same time, though Eliot did not learn
his methods from films. We are present at a session with a
fortune-teller, we are later in the boudoir of a wealthy, hys-
terical woman, then in a pub at closing time, and then beside
a pub in Lower Thames Street, where we hear

> The pleasant whining of a mandoline
> And a clatter and a chatter from within
> Where fishmen lounge at noon: where the walls
> Of Magnus Martyr hold
> Inexplicable splendour of Ionian white and gold.

Some of these sights are not unpleasant:

> The barges drift
> With the turning tide

1. the use of a rapid succession of images to present an association of ideas

Red sails
Wide
To leeward, swing on the heavy spar.

Others explore the literary uses of the disagreeable:

A rat crept softly through the vegetation
Dragging its slimy belly on the bank
While I was fishing in the dull canal
On a winter evening round behind the gashouse.

And some are not ugly but dolorous—for example, the half-visionary scene of the white-collar workers on their way to their jobs in the morning. They have come by train from the suburbs and walk from the railroad station across London Bridge to the financial district:

Under the brown fog of a winter dawn,
A crowd flowed over London Bridge, so many,
I had not thought death had undone so many.
Sighs, short and infrequent, were exhaled,
And each man fixed his eyes before his feet.

Eliot's achievement was not simply to present the city but to endow such scenes with imaginative intensity and suggestion; his images fuse, as he put it, "the sordidly realistic and the phantasmagoric." (He first learned, he said, the possibility of this fusion from Baudelaire.) The crowd flowing over London Bridge is a scene in contemporary London and in Dante's Limbo. (There are even verbal echoes of Dante.) Thus generalized and potentiated, Eliot's naturalistic report and interpretation of life in the city (which was also an interpretation of the life of man per se) was the most accessible and compelling aspect of the poem for its first readers. In a favorable review written in 1922 on commission for *The Dial,* Edmund Wilson warmed especially to this aspect of the poem: "All about us we are aware of nameless millions performing barren office routines, wearing down their souls in interminable labours of which the products never bring them profit—people whose pleasures are so sordid and so feeble that they seem almost sadder than their pains.". . .

Quasi-naturalistic scenes of modern life dominate (though not exclusively) the first three of the poem's five parts. The fifth part includes, however, a long passage of a directly visionary kind, which presents the speaker walking with others, or with all mankind, amid dry and stony mountains, a wasteland. The passage recalls an earlier one in the first part of the poem, where also the speaker or speakers are gazing on the "stony rubbish" of a desert,

> where the sun beats
> And the dead tree gives no shelter, the cricket no relief,
> And the dry stone no sound of water.

When two things are given at the same time readers will associate them together if possible. It was easy to suppose, especially in view of the title, that the imagery of the city and that of the desert were intended to interpret each other, that the modern city was compared to an arid, sterile waste. By the logic of this metaphor, water became a symbol for whatever would save or rescue. If this seems obvious, it also begins to indicate why the poem perplexed almost all its early readers, including admirers: to an extraordinary degree it relied on symbols and their interrelations to convey its meanings. It was not the mere activation of symbols that puzzled. But even in the most densely symbolic works to which English and American readers were up to then accustomed—Samuel Coleridge's "Ancient Mariner" or Herman Melville's *Moby Dick* or Henry James' *The Golden Bowl*—symbolism had been an element in a design that one apprehended primarily through other elements, especially plot and character.

LACK OF PLOT OR CHARACTER

The Waste Land struck readers as aggressively modern and bewildering because of what they did not find as well as what they found. It had no plot. There was no poet speaker to be identified with, as there was when reading William Wordsworth, Shelley, Walt Whitman, Alfred Tennyson, William Butler Yeats, or almost any other familiar poet of the last hundred and fifty years. Despite a strange footnote at the end of the poem about the role of Tiresias, the poem could not be taken as a dramatic monologue. Certainly it was not verse drama, though it contained quasidramatic vignettes.

My point is not simply that the poem could not be fitted into any known genre but that there seemed to be nothing—no narrative, meditation, flow of lyric emotion, characterization—which one could follow, thus "understanding" the poem. It began in a chantlike rhythm, the speakers seeming to lament the return of life in the spring:

> Winter kept us warm, covering
> Earth in forgetful snow, feeding
> A little life with dried tubers.

This was sustained for seven lines, and seemed to be continuing in the eighth line with "Summer surprised us." But suddenly an altogether different voice was heard, that of a woman named Marie, who reminisced conversationally. After eleven lines this passage also ended suddenly, and one was, with no transition, elsewhere, listening to a completely different, faintly biblical voice; the speaker seemed to be gazing on a desert:

What are the roots that clutch, what branches grow
Out of this stony rubbish?

Thus in the first thirty lines of the poem there were three different, apparently unrelated blocks of poetry, with dissimilar speakers, rhythms, images, and associations; and the poem continued in the same pell-mell flow of heterogenous fragments.

A POEM ORGANIZED LIKE MUSIC

If readers were familiar with French symbolist poetry or with the recent poetry of Pound or with cubist painting or with stream-of-consciousness and depth psychology or with experiments in "point of view" in the modern novel, they felt they had a clue to the procedures of the poem. Not that the poem was closely similar to any of these prototypes, but they made it seem less unfamiliar. If the poem juxtaposed discontinuous fragments, the method, one might argue, released implications with a swiftness, density, and complex interaction no traditional technique could achieve. Or perhaps the fragments were not as separable as they seemed but evoked each other by irrational and subconscious associations. In either case, one thus asserted the profound meaningfulness, conscious or not, of the fragments—and especially of their multiple interrelations.

Even if single passages and juxtapositions could be explained and enjoyed on these or analogous grounds, there remained the question of the governing form of the whole. Admirers were challenged to account for their feeling of coherence in a poem without continuity of setting, style, speaking voice, or plot. The poem, they presently said, was organized like music. Of course no literary work can much resemble a musical composition, not even a composition of the later nineteenth century. The main use of the analogy was negative: it kept readers from looking for types of form and meaning they were not going to find. "Music" did not mean in this connection the sounds and rhythms but the sequence of emotions the poem created. In the sequence was a logic, it was asserted; the different phases of emotion inter-related to make a complex whole. Since an organization of emotion could only be felt, not shown, the point could not be elaborated; but it was supported by a special feature of the poem—the repetition in separate contexts of the same or easily associated scenes, images, and allusions. Recurrent passages, for example, describe a desert. The fortune-teller warns her client to fear death by water; the poem returns three times in separate allusions to Ariel's song describing the drowned Alonso in Shakespeare's *The Tempest;* it alludes also to the death by drowning of Ophelia in *Hamlet;* the fourth section of the poem pictures a drowned Phoenician floating in the sea.

Such recurring images and symbols could easily be de-scribed as "themes"; in the context of post-Wagnerian[2] mu-sic they could be called leitmotifs. Thus it was possible to claim that *The Waste Land* was a poetic form on a new prin-ciple and that the principle was not simply the musical se-quence and interrelations of emotions but the repetition and gradual interweaving of leitmotifs. As they return in a new context, they bring with them suggestions and associations from former contexts and become progressively denser nodes of connotation and feeling. At the same time, they fur-ther link the diverse passages and parts together. The liter-ary use of the leitmotif was not unique to *The Waste Land,* but more than any other single source the poem called the attention of English-speaking readers to it. . . .

ELIOT'S USE AND CREATION OF SYMBOLS

As they collect associations in different contexts, the leitmo-tifs gradually become symbols. Generally speaking, a writer may obtain an imagery of symbolic power in two different ways. Either he uses symbols previously established in liter-ature, myth, occult lore, liturgy, and the like; or he trans-forms images into symbols within the context of his own work. Both methods are usually present. Fire was associated with lust long before *The Waste Land;* the poem cites the Buddha's Fire Sermon and Augustine's *Confessions.* The symbolism of seasonal death and rebirth is age-old. But Eliot also created symbols by the incremental return to the same or closely similar images, as we see if we follow the associ-

2. after Richard Wagner, a German opera composer, 1813–1883

ations that gradually gather in the poem around the imagery of water. Water is longed for if the protagonists are in a desert, yet feared lest they drown in it, and yet also—through allusions to Ariel's song—to drown may mean to be transformed in a process that is, as Ariel speaks of it, uncanny and ominous yet also strangely reassuring. Water is associated with sexual desire, and this throws still another implication into the fortune-teller's warning, "fear death by water." Assimilating such associations, we understand the mingled longing, fascination, and fear that water excites in the protagonists throughout the poem.

Death by drowning, furthermore, is one mode of the imagery of death and burial that also recurs throughout the poem. In the context of *The Waste Land* death does not mean only the extinction of life; the aimless, anxiety-ridden life of men and women in this urban wasteland is a living death. The Sibyl of the epigraph speaks for all the protagonists when, being asked, "Sibyl, what do you want?" she replies, "I want to die." But though she does not know it, her words may refer to death in a third sense, which haunts many of the protagonists of the poem, in which to die may mean to suffer a "sea-change," to receive a new being. Fearing death by water, the men and women in *The Waste Land* may fear their only hope.

THE "MYTHICAL METHOD"

In addition to quasi-naturalistic presentation and symbolism, *The Waste Land* conveyed meaning through a third dimension, the mythical. In the footnotes he included with the first publication of *The Waste Land* as a book, Eliot called particular attention to this:

> Not only the title, but the plan and a good deal of the incidental symbolism . . . were suggested by Miss Jessie L. Weston's book on the Grail legend: *From Ritual to Romance*. . . . To another work of anthropology I am indebted in general, one which has influenced our generation profoundly; I mean [Sir James Frazer's] *The Golden Bough*. . . . Anyone who is acquainted with these works will immediately recognize in the poem certain references to vegetation ceremonies.

In *The Golden Bough* Frazer sought to demonstrate that apparently different myths may be traced back to the same underlying and original one. The myth Eliot especially had in mind is that which Frazer calls the myth of the dying and reviving god, especially as this myth was seized by Weston to interpret the medieval romances of the quest for the Holy Grail. According to Frazer, primitive men explained the annual death and resurrection of vegetation as "effects of the waxing or waning strength of divine beings, of gods and goddesses," as effects of "the marriage, the death, and the rebirth or revival of the gods." He also argued that the king was regarded as an incarnation of the fertility of the land; if he weakens or dies, the land becomes waste and returns again to fertility only when the king is healed or resurrected, either in his own person or in a successor. The ancient fertility myths were incorporated within Christianity—the vegetation king or deity was identified with the God of Christian faith—and, according to Miss Weston, the medieval romances of the Holy Grail blended these fertility myths surviving in the folk imagination with Christian materials. She called special attention to the figure of the Fisher King in many of the Grail romances (the fish, she said, is an ancient symbol of life); his land is arid and its people and animals are sterile because the king is (in different versions) dead, ailing, or impotent. If a questing knight can make his way through dangers to the Chapel Perilous, and there pass further trials, the king will be healed or restored. It is impossible in a few words to do justice to the complexity of Frazer's or Weston's argument or of Eliot's use of these sources. The point is that the poem alludes repeatedly to primitive vegetation myths and associates them with the Grail legends and the story of Jesus. In the underlying myth of the poem the land is a dry, wintry desert because the king is impotent or dead; if he is healed or resurrected spring will return, bringing the waters of life. The myth coalesces with the quasi-naturalistic description of the modern, urban world, which is the dry, sterile land. . . .

ALLUSION

When *The Waste Land* was published its mythical dimension did not excite as much interest as we might suppose. Eliot's references to myth seemed only additional examples of his allusiveness, and his use of allusions in the poem caused so much controversy that little attention was paid to his use of myth as a separate method or technique. Allusions in his early poems, *Prufrock and Other Observations* (1917), had been relatively few and easy to follow. . . . In *The Waste Land* they were fully developed:

London Bridge is falling down falling down falling down
Poi s'ascose nel foco che gli affina
Quando fiam uti chelidon—O swallow swallow.

A few such cruxes might have passed as tolerable eccentricities, but there were not a few. The poem of 433 lines quoted or referred to at least thirty-seven other works of art, literature, or music—and to some of them several times. They were not necessarily familiar works; they included not only the Bible and Shakespeare, Virgil, Wagner, and Ovid but Baudelaire's "Les Sept Vieillards," Thomas Middleton's *A Game of Chess* and *Women Beware Women,* John Webster's *The Devil's Law Case,* the Buddha's Fire Sermon, Day's *Parliament of Bees,* Paul Verlaine's *Parsifal,* Gérard de Nerval's "El Desdichado," and so forth—and some of these back-to-back allusions were by means of quotations in Greek, Latin, German, French, Italian, and Sanskrit. . . .

THE WOUNDED HUMAN SPIRIT

Before Eliot made his impact on a whole generation, poets and readers were less likely to assume that modern poetry would be difficult. . . . Whether the poem is actually difficult depends on what one seeks to understand. Particular cruxes of interpretation cannot be decided but the vision of human nature and life is powerfully conveyed. Meanings are ambiguous, emotions ambivalent; the fragments do not make an ordered whole. But precisely this, the poem illustrates, is the human condition, or part of it. Men and women emerge and disappear; our encounters with them are brief and wholly external, for we apprehend them only as bits of speech overheard or gestures spotlighted. But this is the mode and extent of human contact in general, as the poem represents it. The protagonists in the poem are isolated from each other or they make part of a faceless crowd. When they speak there is no dialogue, for the other person, if one is present, does not reply. Whether we assume that the poem renders the stream of consciousness within a mind or that it presents modern civilization and culture by objective methods—it does both at the same time, but in many passages not quite either—it suggests that below the conscious levels of the mind and the ways of civilized life are the subconscious and primitive and that images from these spheres abide or well up suddenly, perhaps with deep significance. The personal and historical past lingers in fragmentary memories and visible reminders, which sharpen our sense of our present condition but suggest no way out of it. The individual mind and the civilization are on the edge of crack-up. Before the impending collapse there is passive waiting but no suggestion of will or even of wish. (At most the protagonists muse vaguely on what might be wished.) At the conclusion of the poem a total disintegration is suggested in a jumble (or apparent jumble) of literary quotations.

Exhibiting what men and women see, hear, say, and feel, the poem conveys in one vignette after another the sickness of the human spirit. But also in its web of vignettes and allusions the poem involves many of the current hypotheses about the cause of this modern sickness, theories then common in intellectual circles. It did not argue about the impact of historical events or social institutions on the human psyche; it did not speculate concerning the effect of new anthropological, psychological, and scientific lore; but it was plainly relevant to such familiar generalizations that sought to explain how the human spirit had been wounded in modern times. Comparative religion and mythology, depth psychology, the World War, industrialized work, and urbanized life were concretely reflected in the poem, and so were the effects to which they were often said to have contributed— the weakening of identity and will, of religious faith and moral confidence, the feelings of apathy, loneliness, helplessness, rootlessness, and fear. Yet the panoramic range and inclusiveness of the poem, which only Eliot's fragmentary and elliptical juxtapositions could have achieved so powerfully in a brief work, held in one vision not only contemporary London and Europe but also human life stretching far back into time. The condition of man seen in the poem was felt to be contemporary and perennial, modern yet essentially the same in all times and places.

The Influence of World War I on American Modernist Poetry

Babette Deutsch

Babette Deutsch (1895–1982) was an American poet and literary critic and the author of numerous books, including *This Modern Poetry*. Deutsch writes that the mechanized warfare and massive death of World War I had a profound impact on the sensibilities of American poets. Following the war, the despair of the nation's poets was expressed in the form of satire and themes of death, grief, rootlessness, and the meaninglessness of modern urban life.

During the decade which followed World War I the poets had time to explore the ache a man feels in amputated beliefs as well as in amputated hands and legs. . . . These young poets had not only seen death wholesale, but they had seen it a machine affair, an international industry. . . . Even those who had not been at the front could not escape. They were like men who had lived through the Plague, and who must suffer the added horror of survival under the reign of a plutocracy as dismally vulgar as it was predacious. The chief weapon left them was irony. Only by becoming grotesque could poetry mirror so grotesque a world. . . .

Such poets as Archibald MacLeish, Alan Porter, Horace Gregory, among others, bear witness, however variously, however indirectly, to the fact that they were open to the same literary influences, influences to which the War and its developments made them peculiarly sensitive. They found themselves in a region peopled largely by T.S. Eliot's Hollow Men—straw-brained paralytics going around a prickly pear, discovering that the world ends 'Not with a bang but a whimper'. The nostalgic lines of Allen Tate, with their Elizabethan rhetoric, their Eliotesque symbols, pre-

Excerpted from Babette Deutsch, *This Modern Poetry* (London: Faber & Faber, 1936). Reprinted by permission of the publisher.

senting the contrast between the confusion of our hasty urban culture and an established agrarian order, sing a song of mockery. From a similar elevation, John Peale Bishop surveys the land of his fathers and laughs sardonically at what he sees. Archibald MacLeish, more obviously indebted to Ezra Pound than to Eliot, has a firm hold on the evocative image, the thing seen, tasted, handled. But he, too, likes to have a shot at that gross beast, the vulgus, and to feather his shaft with satire. When he writes, in *Corporate Entity:*

> The Oklahoma Ligno and Lithograph Co
> Weeps at a nude by Michael Angelo,

when he makes *Critical Observations On The Great American Novel,* or, in *Verses For a Centennial* and in *Aeterna Poetæ Memoria,* refers to his more unpleasant fellow-citizens, he proves himself of this distressed company.

HORROR OF DEATH IN THE POETRY OF ARCHIBALD MACLEISH

Yet if a distorted civilization is one of MacLeish's frequent themes, he dwells more persistently on another *motif* recurrent in poetry but emphasized in post-War verse. His work is filled with the horror of death which haunted the Elizabethans, the sense of thieving time which pierced Andrew Marvell and which MacLeish's well-known apostrophe to that seventeenth-century poet expresses with aching intensity. It is characteristic that he sets as an epigraph to *The Pot Of Earth* a passage from *Hamlet:*

> 'For if the sun breeds maggots in a dead dog, being a god-
> kissing carrion,—Have you a daughter?'

> 'I have, my lord.'

> 'Let her not walk i' the sun.'

The poem is built upon an ancient fertility ritual connected with the figure of Adonis, which, like all such rituals, is enacted under the shadow of mortality. It is natural that a poem with such a theme should contain some echoes of *The Waste Land:*

> Seven days I have been waiting for the rain now, . . .

> There was nothing to do, there was nothing to do but wait,
> But wait, but wait, but wait, and the wind whispering
> Something I couldn't understand beneath the door . . .

This is a variation on *What the Thunder Said:*[1]

---

1. *What the Thunder Said* and *A Game of Chess* are the titles of sections of T.S. Eliot's poem *The Waste Land.*

> If there were water we should stop and drink
> Amongst the rock one cannot stop or think

and the rest of that tortured passage, as also on the hysteria
of the lady in *A Game of Chess:*

> 'What is that noise?'
>   The wind under the door.
> 'What is that noise now? What is the wind doing?'
>   Nothing again nothing.

His introduction of moments from contemporary life recall
similar passages from Eliot's poem, and the tragic sense of
waste which dominates it.

The Hamlet of A. MacLeish is another cry of agony, shot
through with Shakespearean echoes, concluding on the
lines which bear the load of dreadful night:

> Thou wouldst not think
> How ill all's here about my heart!

In half a dozen short lyrics he reiterates a grief which is as
old as man, as fresh as the raw clods of an open grave. What
gives this poetry power is MacLeish's gift for the significant
detail, his feeling for cadence, charging the lines with a
halted, *andante*[2] music. What gives it sharpness is his unhappy awareness of these times. Thus, *The End of the World*
offers a picture of the cock-eyed circus that is this world: the
armless ambidextrian is lighting a match between his toes,
the lion biting the complaisant lady's neck, the monkeys are
coughing and swinging in waltz-time, when suddenly the
top blows off,

> And there, there, there overhead, there, there, hung over
> Those thousands of white faces, those dazed eyes,
>   . . . the black pall
> Of nothing, nothing, nothing—nothing at all.

. . . At its best MacLeish's verse is sharp as the New York
sky-line, crisp as the smell of new-cut shavings, troubling as
the beat of a pulse. The success of *Conquistador* is largely
the success of his imagery, his ability to create atmosphere,
to give the special curve and colour of the thing seen, the peculiar tang of the thing on the tongue or in the nostrils, that
which sets one hour apart from others and comes back, long
afterwards, like something palpable, to the mind. . . .

2. slow-tempoed

THE NEED OF A HOMELAND, A MYTH, AND A VOCABULARY

Conquistador is a superb record of a lost world. . . . MacLeish
has suggested that the experience of the Spanish conquerors
has been paralleled in our own time by 'the generation of
men who have moved into and explored and conquered and
debauched the unknown world of modern technics', but
while the idea of this parallel may have helped him to make
the poem a living thing, it has not transpired in the work itself, which therefore remains a smaller and less significant
performance than it might otherwise be. There is abundant
evidence in the body of his work that he feels the lack of the
central unifying force that the older poets found in Church
or State. He cannot be considered a regionalist, but his evo-
cations of his native background in *American Letter*, no less
than his praise of his country in his too much maligned *Frescoes For Mr. Rockefeller's City*, offer testimony to his need for
establishing himself in a place ample enough to afford him
a spiritual as well as a physical home. He is incapable of the
exuberance of that dying veteran, Ernest Walsh, writing in
exile, how as he walked down the aisle toward the altar

> . . . the gargoyles spat and bit off their hands
> And the birds screeched the angels have gone gone
> And the postcard merchants asked have you any
> In America like this meaning
> The Duomo and the half-shown postcard depends
> Whether you are male or female I shake
> My head and say America is uptown
> And downtown overhead and underground
> But we can't get it on a postcard yet

On the contrary, MacLeish recognizes sadly that his country,
his people, is 'neither a land nor a race'. As early as in *The
Hamlet of A. MacLeish* he asked:

> How shall we learn what it is that our hearts believe in?

Nor is he alone in his asking. The need of a homeland, the
lack of a myth, obsesses the poets of the post-War period.

In *Valediction To My Contemporaries*, Horace Gregory cries:

> How shall we find
> the bodies of those unslain, exiled from war
> but now returned, furloughs of exile signed
> from all green ports on earth?

Gregory's apostrophes to such Americans as Ralph Waldo
Emerson, Whitman, Randolph Bourne (all men who had
reaped the grim harvest of war), his tireless exploration of

the native land in which such spirits as his are in perpetual exile, are a more bitter variant of MacLeish's sad asseveration. Only in mockery could the poets now phrase the question which Robert Frost had put in all seriousness a few years earlier:

> How are we to write
> The Russian novel in America
> As long as life goes so unterribly?

With the signing of the Versailles Treaty, meaning had gone out of the world, and since, for the poet, the world and the word are one, meaning had gone out of language. He had to find a new symbol, a new vocabulary. Hence the difficulty of much modern work: the poet communicates not only his personal response to private experience, by his own unique means: he has first to construct the ideal bases of that experience, and his poetry must realize them also. The repressed anguish of Eliot:

> Consequently I rejoice, having to construct
>   something
> Upon which to rejoice
> And pray to God to have mercy upon us

finds an antistrophe in John Peale Bishop's

> The ceremony must be found
>
> Traditional, with all its symbols
> ancient as the metaphors in dreams;
> strange, with never before heard music; continuous
> until the torches deaden at the bedroom door.

In a similar mood the same poet writes:

> Christ is dead. And in a grave
> Dark as a sightless skull He lies
> And of His bones are charnels made.

More dryly, Tate observes:

> Narcissus is vocabulary. Hermes decorates
> A cornice on the Third National Bank. Vocabulary
> Becomes confusion, decoration a blight.

URBAN IMAGERY

. . . The replacement of rural by urban imagery, the obtrusion of science and machine technology, isolated instances of which could be found earlier in the work of verse-makers as various as Maxwell Bodenheim, Louis Untermeyer, and Joseph Auslander, is characteristic of the poetry of this period. Sometimes these elements occur only to be sneered at, as in E.E. Cummings's:

> While you and i have lips and voices which
> are for kissing and to sing with
> who cares if some oneyed son of a bitch
> invents an instrument to measure Spring with?

Sometimes they are conceded special treatment, as in MacLeish's *Einstein,* and Tate's less ambitious poem on the subway, or in MacKnight Black's repeated eulogies of the Corliss engine and his passionate invocations to the sky-scraper, as in *Structural Iron Workers:*

> What love do these men give their women
> That is like the love they spend
> On this iron harlot
> With the sky between her breasts?
>
> What kisses
> Like the red sting of rivets
> Have they left on any lips?
> You will not find
> The full fruit of their loins
> In any daughters, any sons—
> But lift your gaze and stare long
> Toward the sky's edge.

Often these elements of modern life are part of the accepted environment, as in this metaphor of Tate's:

> . . . a vision flashes
> Like the headlong gust from a motor-car.

THE TEMPO OF MODERN LIFE

The rhythms of modern poetry also reflect the *tempo* of modern life, and the noises peculiar to our civilization begin to make themselves heard in our verse. For centuries poets had sought to imitate the voices of birds and of rivers. . . . The contemporary hears fewer larks, nightingales, and placid streams, and more factory-sirens, motor-horns, grinding gears, coughing engines. So one finds Eliot, follow-ing up the 'Twit twit, tereu' of Elizabethan bird-song with the lines:

> At the violet hour, when the eyes and back
> Turn upward from the desk, when the human engine waits
> Like a taxi throbbing waiting . . .

The mention of the 'human engine' of course assists the im-pression, but the blunt movement of the participles in 'Like a taxi throbbing waiting' is as near the pulse of a halted taxi as Milton's liquid syllables are like the flow of gentle waters.

Similarly, in A.S.J. Tessimond's poem, suggested by a Russian film and suggestive of some Soviet poetry, *La Marche des Machines,* the rhythm has the stiff angular character of mechanical motion:

> This piston's infinite recurrence is
> night morning night and morning night and
> death and birth and death and birth and this
> crank climbs (blind Sisyphus) and see
>
> steel teeth greet
> bow deliberate
> delicately lace
> in lethal kiss
> > God's teeth bite whitely tight
>
> slowly the gigantic oh slowly the steel spine
> > dislocates
>
> wheels grazing (accurately missing) waltz
>
> two cranes do a hundred-ton tango against the sky

Thus, all too obviously, in Louis Aragon's *Red Front,* which E.E. Cummings, in spite of his anti-Soviet animus, made the courteous gesture of translating into English verse, one hears the pistons plunge and the whistle scream:

> The red train starts and nothing shall stop it
> UR
> SS
> UR
> SS
> UR
> SS

Harsh Actualities

What particularly distinguishes the work of these men is, however, not that their verse carries the shriek of machinery and the purr of domesticated engines, but that each of them, conveying these noises, could quote the well-known lines:

> But at my back from time to time I hear
> The sound of horns and motors, which shall bring
> Sweeney to Mrs. Porter in the spring.

What disturbs the poets, in fine, is not the horns and motors, but the fact that they are bringing Sweeney to Mrs. Porter—that the season of renewal, of the birth of Christ the Tiger, is to be marked by the union of two creatures vulgar enough to be emblems of the failure of our civilization: poor pieces of a unique mythology. Even Hart Crane, who derived from

Arthur Rimbaud and Emily Dickinson rather than from John Donne and Jules Laforgue, repeatedly staged in his verse the conflict, which eventually brought him to his death, between his transcendental dream and the harsh actualities beating on his nerves. He could mix the sensuous incitements obtained through synæsthesia[3] with a severe abstract quality, and he tangled syntax in his haste to convey at once the rapidity of his sensations and his mystical interpretation of them. But he also found a plainer metaphor than any of his fellows when disgust gagged him:

> The phonographs of hades in the brain
> Are tunnels that re-wind themselves, and love
> A burnt match skating in a urinal—

3. the technique of using imagery that mingles different sense impressions

CHAPTER 3

American Writers of the 1920s and 1930s

American
Modernism

The Lost Generation: Writers in a Time of Transition

Malcolm Cowley

In the following essay, Malcolm Cowley describes the lost generation—the generation of young American writers following World War I, which included F. Scott Fitzgerald, Ernest Hemingway, John Dos Passos, and others. According to Cowley, these writers shared similar experiences—such as the war, American public education, and travel—that led them to view themselves and their world in ways profoundly different from writers of the previous generation. This generation was lost, Cowley states, because it lacked a sense of continuity with the past and because its society was in a period of transition. Cowley was a poet, author, literary critic, and the editor of numerous books on American literature.

This book[1] is the story to 1930 of what used to be called the lost generation of American writers. It was Gertrude Stein who first applied the phrase to them. "You are all a lost generation," she said to Ernest Hemingway, and Hemingway used the remark as an inscription for his first novel. It was a good novel and became a craze—young men tried to get as imperturbably drunk as the hero, young women of good families took a succession of lovers in the same heartbroken fashion as the heroine, they all talked like Hemingway characters and the name was fixed. I don't think there was any self-pity in it. Scott Fitzgerald sometimes pitied himself, and with reason. Hart Crane used to say that he was "caught like a rat in a trap"; but neither Crane nor Fitzgerald talked about being part of a lost generation. Most of those who used

1. *Exile's Return: A Literary Odyssey of the 1920s*

Excerpted from Malcolm Cowley, *Exile's Return: A Literary Odyssey of the 1920s* (New York: Viking Press, 1934).

the phrase about themselves were a little younger and knew they were boasting. They were like Rudyard Kipling's gentlemen rankers out on a spree and they wanted to have it understood that they truly belonged "To the legion of the lost ones, to the cohort of the damned." Later they learned to speak the phrase apologetically, as if in quotation marks, and still later it was applied to other age groups, each of which was described in turn as being the real lost generation; none genuine without the trademark. In the beginning, however, when the phrase was applied to young writers born in the years around 1900, it was as useful as any half-accurate tag could be.

It was useful to older persons because they had been looking for words to express their uneasy feeling that postwar youth—"flaming youth"—had an outlook on life that was different from their own. Now they didn't have to be uneasy; they could read about the latest affront to social standards or to literary conventions and merely say, "That's the lost generation." But the phrase was also useful to the youngsters. They had grown up and gone to college during a period of rapid change when time in itself seemed more important than the influence of class or locality. Now at last they had a slogan that proclaimed their feeling of separation from older writers and of kinship with one another. In the slogan the noun was more important than the adjective. They might or might not be lost, the future would decide that point; but they had already had the common adventures and formed the common attitude that made it possible to describe them as a generation.

THE DECLINE OF REGIONAL INFLUENCES

In that respect, as in the attitude itself, they were different from the writers who preceded them. Sectional and local influences were relatively more important during the years before 1900. Two New England writers born fifteen or twenty years apart––Ralph Waldo Emerson and Henry David Thoreau, for example—might bear more resemblance to each other than either bore to a Virginian or a New Yorker of his own age; compare Emerson and Edgar Allan Poe, or Thoreau and Walt Whitman. Literature was not yet centered in New York; indeed, it had no center on this side of the ocean. There was a Knickerbocker School, there was a Concord School, there was a Charleston School; later there would be a Hoosier School, a Chicago

School. Men of every age belonged to the first three and might have belonged to the others, had these not been founded at a time when writers were drifting to the metropolis.

Publishing, like finance and the theater, was becoming centralized after 1900. Regional traditions were dying out; all regions were being transformed into a great unified market for motorcars and Ivory soap and ready-to-wear clothes. The process continued during the childhood of the new generation of writers. Whether they grew up in New England, the Midwest, the Southwest or on the Pacific Coast, their environment was almost the same; it was a little different in the Old South, which had kept some of its local manners but was losing them. The childhood of these writers was less affected by geography than it was by the financial situation of their parents, yet even that was fairly uniform. A few of the writers came from wealthy families, a very few from the slums. Most of them were the children of doctors, small lawyers, prosperous farmers or struggling businessmen—of families whose incomes in those days of cheaper living were between two thousand and perhaps eight thousand dollars a year. Since their playmates were also middle-class they had the illusion of belonging to a great classless society.

COMMON ADVENTURES

All but a handful were pupils in the public schools, where they studied the same textbooks, sang the same songs and revolted rather tamely against the same restrictions. At the colleges they attended, usually some distance from their homes, they were divested of their local peculiarities, taught to speak a standardized American English and introduced to the world of international learning. Soon they would be leaving for the army in France, where they would be subjected together to a sudden diversity of emotions: boredom, fear, excitement, pride, aloofness and curiosity. During the drab peacemaking at Versailles they would suffer from the same collapse of emotions. They would go back into civilian life almost as if they were soldiers on a long furlough.

Some of them would go to Greenwich Village to begin the long adventure of the 1920s. Only long afterward could the period be described, in Scott Fitzgerald's phrase, as "the greatest, gaudiest spree in history." At first it promised to be something quite different, a period of social and moral reaction. The Prohibition Amendment had gone into effect in

January 1920, strikes were being broken all over the country, and meanwhile Greenwich Village was full of plain-clothes dicks[2] from the Vice Squad and the Bomb Squad. I remember that many young women were arrested and charged with prostitution because the dicks had seen them smoking cigarettes in the street, and I remember that innocent tea-rooms were raided because they were thought to harbor dangerous Reds.[3] Then Warren G. Harding was elected, the Red scare was forgotten and, after a sharp recession in 1921, the country started out to make money; it was the new era of installment buying and universal salesmanship. The young writers couldn't buy luxuries even on the installment plan. They didn't want to advertise or sell them or write stories in which salesmen were the romantic heroes. Feeling like aliens in the commercial world, they sailed for Europe as soon as they had money enough to pay for their steamer tickets.

Nor would this be the end of their adventures in common. Until they were thirty most of them would follow a geographical pattern of life, one that could be suggested briefly by the names of two cities and a state: New York, Paris, Connecticut. After leaving Greenwich Village they would live in Montparnasse (or its suburbs in Normandy and on the Riviera), and some of them would stay there year after year in what promised to be a permanent exile. Others would go back to New York, then settle in a Connecticut farmhouse with their books, a portable typewriter and the best intentions. Whether they were at home or abroad in 1929, most of them would have found a place in the literary world and would be earning a fairly steady income. The depression would be another common experience, almost as shattering as the war.

I am speaking of the young men and women who graduated from college, or might have graduated, between 1915, say, and 1922. They were never united into a single group or school. Instead they included several loosely defined and vaguely hostile groups, in addition to many individuals who differed with every group among their contemporaries; the fact is that all of them differed constantly with all the others. They all felt, however, a sharper sense of difference in regard to writers older than themselves who hadn't shared their adventures. It was as if the others had never undergone

2. detectives   3. communists

the same initiatory rites and had never been admitted to the same broad confraternity. In a strict sense the new writers formed what is known as a literary generation.

Their sense of being different has been expressed time and again in the books they wrote. Take, for example, the second paragraph of a story by Scott Fitzgerald, "The Scandal Detectives," in which he is describing an episode from his boyhood:

> Some generations are close to those that succeed them; between others the gulf is infinite and unbridgeable. Mrs. Buckner—a woman of character, a member of Society in a large Middle Western city—carrying a pitcher of fruit lemonade through her own spacious back yard, was progressing across a hundred years. Her own thoughts would have been comprehensible to her great-grandmother; what was happening in a room above the stable would have been entirely unintelligible to them both. In what had once served as the coachman's sleeping apartment, her son and a friend were not behaving in a normal manner, but were, so to speak, experimenting in a void. They were making the first tentative combinations of the ideas and materials they found ready at their hands—ideas destined to become, in future years, first articulate, then startling and finally commonplace. At the moment she called up to them they were sitting with disarming quiet upon the still unhatched eggs of the mid-twentieth century.

Boys like Ripley Buckner and his friend—who was Scott Fitzgerald under another name—were born shortly before 1900. Since they were in their teens when the twentieth century was also in its teens, it is no wonder that they fell into the habit of identifying themselves with the century. They retained the habit until they—and the century—were well along in the thirties. As representatives of a new age they had a sense of being somehow unique; one catches an echo of it in the affectionate fashion in which Fitzgerald often used the phrase "my contemporaries." It seems to me now that the feeling was insufficiently grounded in fact and that Mrs. Buckner, for example, was closer to her son and his friend than the youngsters realized. Edith Wharton was of Mrs. Buckner's age and she could understand Fitzgerald perhaps better than he understood Mrs. Wharton. Going farther back, many young writers of the 1890s had also been in revolt and had tried to introduce European standards of art and conduct into American literature; they too were a lost generation (and more tragically lost than their successors). The postwar writers, in their feeling that their experiences were unique, revealed their ignorance of the American past. On the other hand, the feeling was real in itself, however ill grounded, and it made them regard all other members of their own age group, whether artists or athletes or business-men, as belonging to a sort of secret order, with songs and passwords, leagued in rebellion against the stuffy people who were misruling the world.

They were not a lost generation in the sense of being un-fortunate or thwarted, like the young writers of the 1890s. The truth was that they had an easy time of it, even as com-pared with the writers who immediately preceded them. Theodore Dreiser, Sherwood Anderson, E.A. Robinson, Edgar Lee Masters and Carl Sandburg were all in their for-ties before they were able to devote most of their time to writing; Sinclair Lewis was thirty-five before he made his first success with *Main Street*. It was different with the new group of writers. Largely as a result of what the older group had accomplished, their public was ready for them and they weren't forced to waste years working in a custom house, like Robinson, or writing advertising copy, like Anderson. At the age of twenty-four Fitzgerald was earning eighteen thou-sand dollars a year with his stories and novels. Hemingway, Thornton Wilder, Dos Passos and Louis Bromfield were in-ternationally known novelists before they were thirty. They had a chance which the older men lacked to develop their craftsmanship in book after book; from the very first they were professionals.

WHY THEY WERE LOST

Yet in spite of their opportunities and their achievements the generation deserved for a long time the adjective that Gertrude Stein had applied to it. The reasons aren't hard to find. It was lost, first of all, because it was uprooted, schooled away and almost wrenched away from its attach-ment to any region or tradition. It was lost because its train-ing had prepared it for another world than existed after the war (and because the war prepared it only for travel and ex-citement). It was lost because it tried to live in exile. It was lost because it accepted no older guides to conduct and be-cause it had formed a false picture of society and the writer's place in it. The generation belonged to a period of transition from values already fixed to values that had to be created. Its members began by writing for magazines with names like *transition, Broom* (to make a clean sweep of it), *1924, This Quarter* (existing in the pure present), *S 4 N, Secession.* They were seceding from the old and yet could adhere to nothing new; they groped their way toward another scheme of life, as yet undefined; in the midst of their doubts and uneasy gestures of defiance they felt homesick for the certainties of childhood. It was not by accident that their early books were almost all nostalgic, full of the wish to recapture some remembered thing. In Paris or Pamplona, writing, drinking, watching bullfights or making love, they continued to desire a Kentucky hill cabin, a farmhouse in Iowa or Wisconsin, the Michigan woods, the blue Juniata, a country they had "lost, ah, lost," as Thomas Wolfe kept saying; a home to which they couldn't go back.

The American Expatriates Fled a Repressive Society

Donald Pizer

During the modernist era, especially following World War I, many American writers lived in Paris for extended periods of time. These writers are referred to as the expatriates. Donald Pizer uses the writing of three such authors—Gertrude Stein, Ernest Hemingway, and Henry James—to illustrate why these writers chose to leave America and call Paris their home. According to Pizer, the expatriates fled to Paris to escape American society's demand for sexual repression and social conformity. Pizer is Pierce Butler Professor of English at Tulane University in New Orleans, Louisiana, where he has taught since 1957. Among his books are *Dos Passos' "U.S.A.": A Critical Study* and *Twentieth-Century American Literary Naturalism: An Interpretation.*

Reduced to its most fundamental level, the expatriate or self-exile state of mind is compounded out of the interrelated conditions of the rejection of a homeland and the desire for and acceptance of an alternative place. The world one has been bred in is perceived to suffer from intolerable inadequacies and limitations; another world seems to be free of these failings and to offer a more fruitful way of life. Although it can be contended that this state of mind has existed since the beginning of civilization, the specific characteristics of expatriation—the particular stifling conditions of one's time and place, the particular appeal of a different set of conditions—have varied in nature and degree from historical moment to historical moment. I would therefore like to suggest some of the distinguishing characteristics of the widespread tendency during the early twentieth century for

American writers to reject American life in favor of life in Paris. And since my interest in this study is not in a sociological or quantitatively historical analysis of American expatriation between the wars—of how many Americans arrived in Paris each year and of where they stayed and what they did—but in the beliefs and values of American expatriate writers as expressed in their own writing about the expatriate experience, in the mythic statement of expatriation, in short, I will introduce the subject by means of several works of fiction that, in relation to one another, suggest the basic character of the interplay between repulsion and attraction for this generation.

Gertrude Stein's "The Good Anna," from *Three Lives* (1909), Ernest Hemingway's "Soldier's Home," from *In Our Time* (1925), and Henry James's account of Lambert Strether's visit to Gloriani's garden, from *The Ambassadors* (1903), are all in their various ways expatriate works even though they do not deal directly with the expatriate experience. All were written after their authors had become expatriates, and all therefore, whether in the depiction of the limitations of American life or of the appeal of Paris, reflect the almost inevitable impulse in the treatment of these subjects to offer an apologia for the condition of self-exile.

AMERICAN MORALISM IN STEIN

Gertrude Stein sets "The Good Anna" in the German-American world of turn-of-the-century Baltimore—the Bridgepoint of the story. Anna, who spends her life as a housekeeper for middle-class employers, is "good" in the sense that she is thrifty, hardworking, religious, and moralistic. These qualities make life difficult for her—"You see that Anna led an arduous and troubled life"—because her employers and acquaintances lack the qualities and Anna sees it as her duty to put things "to rights." Most of her employers are like Miss Mathilda, for whom Anna works for many years, in enjoying a good time and being careless about money, whereas Anna, whose "face was worn, her cheeks . . . thin, her mouth drawn and firm," labors and worries.

Anna is especially severe in her attitude toward sexual transgressions, as Stein initially renders comically by introducing it in relation to Anna's concern over the "wickedness" of her dogs, which were "under strict orders never to be bad one with the other [since] periods of evil thinking came very regularly." A more significant revelation of Anna's nature lies in her response to Miss Mathilda's distinctive form of wickedness: "And then Miss Mathilda loved to go out on joyous, country tramps when, stretching free and far with cheerful comrades, over rolling hills and cornfields, glorious in the setting sun, and dogwood white and shining underneath the moon and clear stars over head, and brilliant air and tingling blood, it was hard to have to think of Anna's anger at the late return." The passage expresses the force of Anna's moralism by contrasting an open and rich natural life with the psychological and emotional restrictions placed on enjoying that life by the presence of a censor. The "good" life, as defined by Anna's beliefs and actions, excludes not only obvious derelictions, such as the sexual, but any act of the spirit which is "wasteful" in the sense of being morally unsanctioned or economically unproductive. And since all in the community—even those who resent Anna's admonitions and rebel against them—accept the premise that she is indeed the "good Anna" and that her values constitute a proper and necessary norm for conduct and belief, Anna is, despite her "arduous" and "troubled" life, a figure of power and control in the world where she functions. Hers is the voice of righteousness, and though that voice may breed opposition, those who rebel are, like her dogs, willful and sinful in their rebellion.

Stein in "The Good Anna" thus portrays an America dominated by an ethos in which the principal commitments are to work, money, and self-discipline (especially in sexual matters), with these constituting both godliness and community worthiness. Many of course fail to live up to the expectations of the ethos, but the expectations—the belief that such commitments constitute the "good" life—pass unchallenged. Miss Mathilda, after many years with Anna, finally goes abroad to live, where she can buy "a bit of porcelain, a new etching and sometimes even an oil painting" without fear of being chastised for excess. But Anna remains in America, still the "good" Anna.

THE IMPACT OF WORLD WAR I IN HEMINGWAY

Hemingway's "Soldier's Home" recapitulates Stein's dissection of the power of a normative moralism in American life but also relates its rejection to the war. Krebs, before his two years in the marines, is a standard product of middle-class

America. From a small Oklahoma town where his father is in real estate, he has gone to a Methodist college in Kansas. A college photograph reveals him "among his fraternity brothers, all of them wearing exactly the same height and style collar."

The war, however, introduces him to the fundamental human realities of death and sex. He fights in several major battles, and after the war he acquires a "not beautiful" German girl friend. Returning home, he has difficulty fitting his life back into the prescribed grooves of belief and behavior. One problem—and this is a theme that Hemingway and John Dos Passos were to exploit more fully in *A Farewell to Arms* and *Three Soldiers*—is that he is disgusted by the convention of "exaggeration" and "untruth" that war needs had imposed on accounts of combat and that he is forced to fall in with in the telling of his own war experiences. He now begins to extrapolate from his understanding of the convention of the lie in wartime to a recognition of its prevalence in his everyday life. As Ezra Pound had put it a few years earlier in his "Hugh Selwyn Mauberly," those who fought

> walked eye-deep in hell
> believing in old-men's lies, then unbelieving
> came home, home to a lie,
> home to many deceits, home to old lies.

Another problem is that Krebs now realizes, from the perspective of his greater range of experience, that he cannot accept his community's belief that life consists of work, money, and religion. These two barriers to reintegration into his world coalesce in his decision to opt out of both community values and community-sanctioned behavior. He expresses his withdrawal most clearly in his attitude toward the girls of the town, girls he finds desirable but not desirable enough to break out of his isolation. "He did not want to get into the intrigue and the politics. He did not want to have to do any courting. He did not want to tell any more lies. It wasn't worth it."

Withdrawal, however, is not an acceptable strategy within Krebs's world, and his parents seek to prod him into reentry. Other young men his age are working and getting married and "are on their way to being really a credit to the community," his mother tells him. When Krebs balks, his mother brings out the heavy artillery of familial love and religious faith. "Don't you love your mother, dear boy?" and "Would you kneel and pray with me, Harold?" are questions she puts to him under the assumption that both she and he accept the premise that a child's love for his mother and his religious belief are intimately related to his role as an American. Krebs responds positively to both questions because he feels sorry for his mother. But he thinks to himself that "he would go to Kansas City" to escape the "consequences" and "complications" that conventional belief is imposing on him at home. Earlier, in relation to his interest in the girls of the town, he had recalled his girl friend in Germany. It had been "simple" there, he remembers. "He did not want to leave Germany. He did not want to come home." Indeed, the stories in *In Our Time* that follow "Soldier's Home" and pursue the experiences of an American protagonist who has served in the war are, with the exception of the final story, "Big Two-Hearted River," set in Europe. The implication is that Krebs will continue the process of self-exile he begins by leaving for Kansas City and will return to Europe, where human relationships are "simpler" in that they lack the "consequences" imposed upon them by an American middle-class value system.

THE ALLURE OF PARIS: LIBERATION FROM REPRESSIVENESS

The attractiveness of Europe for a Miss Mathilda or a Krebs as a way out of the coercive moralism of American life—as a place where the spirit might roam freely and where one could be true to one's feelings without regard to being a credit to the community—had already been emphatically localized in Paris by Henry James in *The Ambassadors*. The middle-aged writer Lambert Strether has led a dull and vaguely unsatisfying life in Woollett, Massachusetts, a town not depicted but the tone of which comes across—largely through the references to Strether's patroness Mrs. Newsome, and the comportment of the Woollett Pococks in Paris—as the moral and emotional equivalent of Miss Mathilda's Baltimore and Krebs's Oklahoma backwater. Strether finds himself in Paris on appointment by Mrs. Newsome to rescue her son from the dangers of Parisian idleness and the possibility of a mésalliance and to return him to work and a proper marriage in Woollett.

Not long after his arrival, Strether is taken to a reception given by the artist Gloriani in the garden of one of the "old noble houses" in the Faubourg Saint-Germain. The intellectual and spiritual density and vibrancy that Strether almost immediately senses in the scene appear to derive principally from the other guests' "liberty to be as they were." "His fellow guests were multiplying, and these things, their liberty, their intensity, their variety, their conditions at large, were in fusion in the admirable medium of the scene." Gloriani himself—"a fine worn handsome face, a face that was like an open letter in a foreign tongue"—also evinces this unique receptivity and freedom and richness, and Strether has the "consciousness of opening . . . all the windows of his mind, of letting this rather grey interior drink in for once the sun of a clime not marked in his old geography."

Gloriani, in keeping with his name, embodies a resplendent mix of freedom and energy, a mix uniting the best in art, society, and nature—as is implied by the setting of an artist's reception in the garden of a fine old house—and explicitly in tune with the new "geography" of Paris rather than the old of Woollett. It is no wonder that, having "drunk in" this potion and having realized as well that despite its invigorating effect it has come too late for him, Strether admonishes the much younger American, Little Bilham, to "live all you can; it's a mistake not to. . . . This place and these impressions . . . have had their abundant message for me, have just dropped *that* into my mind." They have also, of course, helped establish the mythic reality of Paris as the "place" where Americans can lead the kind of life represented in Strether's "impressions" of Gloriani's garden party—a place where the open windows of the receptive spirit can absorb the sun and thus where the gray moral and spiritual climate of Woollett can be exchanged for an atmosphere of a radiant richness and freedom.

F. Scott Fitzgerald Captured the Spirit of His Generation

Malcolm Bradbury

F. Scott Fitzgerald is considered one of the most significant American authors of the modernist era; his novel *The Great Gatsby* is ranked among the greatest works of fiction. In the following excerpt, Malcolm Bradbury explains that Fitzgerald did not merely chronicle the events of his generation; he immersed himself in the lifestyle of the era and created works of fiction that both celebrated and critiqued modern society. *The Great Gatsby* contains several modernist elements, including the fragmentation of history and the use of symbolic and surreal imagery. Bradbury is a novelist, critic, and professor of American Studies at the University of East Anglia in England.

No writer set out more determinedly to capture in fiction the tone, the hope, the possibility, and the touch of despair of the Twenties than Francis Scott Key Fitzgerald. For a long time he appeared to his critics a mere popularizer and chronicler, so obviously immersed in the themes, fashions, and styles of his times that he never achieved the literary power to consider and criticize. . . . Fitzgerald undoubtedly threw himself exotically into the pleasures and the pitfalls of his own gaudy time; he was, more than most, an essentially social novelist. It was he who made sure that the Twenties was known as 'the Jazz Age', that the new goods and chattels, the new expressions and sexual styles, made their way into fiction. His famous essay 'The Crack-Up' sums up this singular identification. The historical development of America in the 1920s, moving from glittering excitement to danger, was his

From *The Modern American Novel*, Revised Edition, by Malcolm Bradbury. Copyright ©1992 by Malcolm Bradbury. Used by permission of Viking Penguin, a division of Penguin Putnam Inc. (U.S.) and Oxford University Press (Canada).

own psychic curve; the Great Crash[1] was the exact analogue of his own psychic crack up; the political reassessment of the Thirties was the match for his own endeavour to put his spiritual house in order. Such identifications were so potent exactly because Fitzgerald always chose to live them as such, making his literary experimentation part of the period's social and sexual experimentation, making the style of his life an essential component of the style of his art. This made his work itself appear innocent, his writing seem short of formal skill. It has taken time for us to see that there was much more, and that the innocent performer of the Twenties became, in his mature work, one of the finest of modern American novelists. . . .

SIGNALLING TO A GENERATION

When, in 1917, he [Fitzgerald] was working on the novel he then called *The Romantic Egoist* and would be published as *This Side of Paradise,* he wrote grandly to his friend Edmund Wilson, 'I really believe that no one else could have written so searchingly the story of the youth of our generation . . .'. *This Side of Paradise* came out in 1920, exactly as the Twenties started, and became an immediate bestseller, rivalling in the lists a work by another Minnesotan, Sinclair Lewis's *Main Street.* But where Lewis satirized the American vanities of the Twenties, Fitzgerald offered an entirely different, quite unsatirical view of the world of post-war modernity. Heavily influenced by Compton Mackenzie's now little-read *Sinister Street,* it followed the period vogue for young man's novels; its young hero, Amory Blaine, is the exemplary post-war dandy, socially and sexually ambitious, who makes his own life the subject of a social and aesthetic experiment, conducted through the pursuit of religion, love, and money. Amory is indeed a 'romantic egoist', drawn on the one hand by a narcissistic investment in his own youth and beauty, and on the other by all the dreamy and fragile promises society and immersion in experience can offer him. Above all there is Princeton's 'glittering caste-system' and the beautiful and wealthy woman who embodies all he desires but stands just beyond his reach. Style becomes a desperate expenditure of the self, and beauty and money turn into transposed versions of each other. Far more energetic than good,

1. the stock market crash of October 1929

the book none the less lays down, if in unresolved form, many of the themes that would subsequently dominate his fiction: the temptation, danger, and damnation of self-love, an awareness of the alluring fragility of all experience, and a compulsive neo-religious idealism that, invested back into American society, somehow attempts to make it shine with a transcendental glory—the themes he would eventually bring into perfect focus in *The Great Gatsby.*

With characteristic honesty Fitzgerald was later to identify the book as 'one of the funniest books since *Dorian Gray* in its utter speciousness', but it was a work that signalled to a generation its presence as a generation, and its remarkable unexpected success threw Fitzgerald into a role he coveted—the style-setter for the times, the filter and promoter of its public moods and sexual fashions. It also enabled him to marry his remote woman, Zelda Sayre, and together the two of them went on to perform the Twenties as an exotic dance of romance and decadent cynicism, as they chased the excitements, spent the wealth, drank the champagne, travelled, enjoyed the playboy delights, and equally consumed the underlying moral and economic fragility. Zelda (eventually a novelist herself) was the new woman, the flapper displaying the boyish toughness, sexual ambiguity, and moral vagueness of a time of changing sexual roles. Scott was equally the new man, capturing style in all its topicality and writing for 'my own personal public—that is, the countless flappers and college kids who think I am a sort of oracle'. Their expensive transatlantic life forced Fitzgerald to write against the clock, in several senses, and he found problems in distancing himself from his own stories or finding time to develop his talent. The titles of his next books of stories—*Flappers and Philosophers* (1920), *Tales from the Jazz Age* (1922)—show his obsession with capturing the period themes. At the same time he was capable of giving his stories a serious treatment and, as he noted, the stories all 'had a touch of disaster in them. . . .' That touch of disaster is very clear in his next novel, *The Beautiful and Damned* (1922), a story about a degenerating hero and a degenerating marriage, which mixes social lyricism with a tale of decadent decline. . . . Hastily written and heavily autobiographical, the book—though perfectly successful—lacks a confident tone, and there was little about it to suggest that his next work would be one of the greatest American novels, the book T.S. Eliot would identify as 'the first step the American novel has taken since Henry James.'

THE GREAT GATSBY: THE TIMELESS
MYTH VERSUS MODERN REALITY

But by now Fitzgerald was growing increasingly conscious of having squandered his talents, and as he began his next book he determined to show himself the conscious artist he believed he could be. That book consequently displays a new seriousness, sometimes explained by the critics as showing for the first time he could stand back and survey his own experience. Yet if anything Fitzgerald's sense of his immersion in his times had increased; . . . he saw it as the writer's task to be a 'performing self', as it has been called, an active agent taking risks with his life and entering all the places where the times are most fully enacted. Both his personal and fictional styles were modes of involvement; but now, in his better work, he began increasingly to understand the compelling forces behind this psychic overextension. With *The Great Gatsby* (1925), one of the most notable of American twentieth-century novels, this mixture of involvement and understanding reaches an extraordinary balance. The book is a classic of formal control (Fitzgerald had learned it in part from Joseph Conrad); it is also a book that seeks exactly to enter its own time and place while reaching beyond it—just as its central character, Jay Gatsby, aims to do. It is the story of a gross, materialistic, careless society of coarse wealth spread on top of a sterile world; on to it is cast an extraordinary illusion, that of the ex-Jay Gatz, the self-created Gatsby. A man whose poor past and corrupt economic supports are hidden in his own glow, Gatsby likewise decorates his entire world through his love for Daisy Buchanan. Society is decadent in one way, Gatsby in another: he is a dandy of desire, a desire that has been redirected from its human or material object into a fantasy, a dream of retaining a past moment in an endless instant of contemplation. His aim, in effect, is to transfigure money into love—a symbolist dream, an assault on reality, the system, the clock of time itself. The clock still ticks, and Fitzgerald hears it; Gatsby is a corrupt dreamer, Daisy a corrupt object of love, married to a violent, damaging husband, surrounded by 'carelessness' and social indifference, her voice full of money. But he grants the grandeur of the invented self and the gaudy worth of its passions: 'The most grotesque and fantastic conceits haunted [Gatsby] in his bed at night. A universe of ineffable gaudiness spun itself out in his brain while the clock ticked on the wash-stand and the moon soaked with wet light his tangled clothes upon the floor.' Gatsby embodies the symbolic aim of the book itself, a figure floating on the American dream while beneath him a confusing record of economic and social facts unravels.

Gatsby is a coarse Platonist, devoted to the pursuit of a 'vast, vulgar and meretricious beauty', but his dream sustains its force, partly because the book allows him to invest naturalist fact with his personal intention, and recognizes symbolist desires, and partly because it is mediated through a narrator, Nick Carraway, who consciously stills the voice of judgement. Carraway's peculiar tolerance comes because he is himself involved in a fantastic life in which he is something of a parvenu, but also because he is the instrument of Fitzgerald's oblique method of interpreting the tale. *Gatsby* is a novel of modern dream-life; and its means call for something more than naturalism or direct moral assessment. It is itself a semi-symbolist text, set in the surreal world of the modern city, New York and its environs, its startling detail thrown up in instants and images—in the shifting fashions in clothes and music, the décor of hotel rooms, the movements of traffic, the ash heaps and the hearses that catch Carraway's eye on his mobile, hyperactive way through the populous landscape. As narrator, Carraway becomes a voice of what Fitzgerald called 'selective delicacy', filtering impression and sensation in an order appropriate to his growing understanding of Gatsby's nature, distributing about him a landscape of generative images, so that Gatsby, who might be thought of as a corrupt product of this world, is gradually distinguished from it, set against it, finally made a victim of its carelessness. The novel's theme is the suffusion of the material with the ideal, of raw stuff becoming enchanted object. This is so not just because of Gatsby's peculiar powers and qualities, but because it is the basis of the mode of writing itself, as it invests Gatsby's actions, parties, and clothes with a distinctive, symbolic glow.

Two alternative worlds, one of careless wealth and the other of ashen poverty, are set in contrast in the novel—watched over by the absent god, the sightless eyes of Dr Eckleberg. But the real contrast is between the contingency of both these worlds and Gatsby's search for a transfiguring vision, for a world beyond the clock of historical time, for a life meaningless unless invested with meaning. Fitzgerald's aim is surreal, the making bright of certain evanescent things so that they have the quality of dream. But at the novel's end that dream is withdrawn, and another surreality, the nightmare of an unmitigated mass of material objects, takes its place. Gatsby's death is the product of carelessness and chance. Nick imagines it:

> I have an idea that Gatsby didn't himself believe that it [the phone call from Daisy] would come, and perhaps he no longer cared. If that was true he must have felt that he had lost the old warm world, paid a high price for living so long with a single dream. He must have looked up at an unfamiliar sky through frightening leaves and shivered as he found what a grotesque thing a rose is and how raw the sunlight was upon scarcely created grass. A new world, material without being real, where poor ghosts, breathing dreams like air, drifted fortuitously about . . . like the ashen, fantastic figure gliding toward him through the amorphous trees.

On the one hand there is the world of time arrested, the past held suspended, of love and dream; on the other there is a modern world of dislocated, rootless, and grotesque images. From the mixture Fitzgerald distils two essential components of modernist writing. The book made him the extraordinary historian of those two interlocking worlds—the world of modern history invested with a timeless myth, where the clock is tilted back like the clock on Gatsby's mantelpiece as he kisses Daisy, and the world of history disinvested, reduced to fragments without manifest order, a modern waste land. This tension and ambiguity persist into the famous ending, where Fitzgerald both recreates 'the American dream', the dream of an innocent, pastoral America created by man's capacity for wonder, and also sees it as a nostalgic desire for that which time itself defeats. As Gatsby is an artistic surrogate, chasing with his 'creative passion' a symbol that is both transcendent and corrupted, *The Great Gatsby* is a symbolist tragedy—about the struggle of the symbolic imagination to exist in lowered historical time, and about that symbol's inherent ambiguity, its wonder and its meretriciousness.

Gatsby is probably Fitzgerald's best, certainly his most finished, book: a realization of his talents in the Twenties, a sign of his power to enter a world both gaudy and destructive and distil a meaning from it. He had succeeded not just in internalizing the times—the spirit of a 'whole race going hedonistic, deciding on pleasure'—but in realizing them as form. But, as Twenties unease grew, Fitzgerald internalized that too, sensing the economic cost to be charged, the moral interest due. Though it was a formal success, *Gatsby* was not a financial one. Fitzgerald now had to undertake the production of countless popular magazine short stories to maintain his life-style, delaying his next novel, which was in any case going through many drafts. Behind the public façade, the marriage to Zelda was now strained, as each fought for self-preservation and survival. The Crash of 1929 destroyed the symbolic base of their existence, and by 1930 what was latent in the inner politics of that marriage— Zelda's schizophrenia, Scott's alcoholism—was evident. 'No ground under our feet', he noted in his ledger, as the lifestyle they had both promoted began to tear to pieces. He now began to read Oswald Spengler, Henry Adams, Sigmund Freud, and Karl Marx, and sensed the need for a 'Great Change'. He grew aware of the historical displacement of the rich, looked towards the roots of his own wealth, began to grant the reality of the historical process and to probe the sexual disorder of the times.

All this went into the plan for his next novel, *Tender Is the Night,* a troubled and troublesome book of which we have two versions. Fitzgerald described it as follows: 'Show a man who is a natural idealist, a spoiled priest, giving in for various causes to the ideas of the haute Burgeoise [*sic*], and in his rise to the top of the social world losing his idealism, his talent and turning to drink and dissipation. Background is one in which the liesure [*sic*] class is at their truly most brilliant & glamorous.' The background is the expatriate, socialite French Riviera where Americans gather, art and wealth converge, the great gaudy spree goes on past its season, and a post-war generation attempts to reconstruct an existence after the war has shelled the old society to death. . . .

Tender Is the Night differs from *Gatsby* in having two methods of presentation. One is spatial–symbolic, a method appropriate to the priestly artist-figure at the book's centre who is seeking to hold on to romantic integrity and wholeness amid destructive time. The other is historical–evolutionary, the story of that time as system, a developing history with which Fitzgerald was not attentively concerned. Process and symbol struggle to give the novel an oblique chronology, and Fitzgerald was never sure of its true order of construction. In fact he began to amend it even after publication, which is why the contemporary reader now has the original and a reconstructed text to choose between.

The novel's incompleteness has a certain appropriateness; for incompleteness and exposure were now a main concern. In the notable essays of 1936 and 1937, 'The Crack-Up' and 'Early Success', he looked at the disintegration of his earlier style in life and art, playing his thirties against his twenties, the Thirties against the Twenties, distilling his concern with exterior and inward dissolution. By now the alcoholism was serious, Zelda was in a mental hospital, and Fitzgerald turned towards Hollywood for a job as screenwriter. His last novel—*The Last Tycoon* (1941)—set there, is yet more incomplete; the book was left unfinished at his early death in 1940.

Ernest Hemingway Used a Precise Style to Depict the Individual in Crisis

Alfred Kazin

In the 1920s, Ernest Hemingway invented a style of writing that combined the simplicity of conversational speech with a sharp focus on details. In the following passage, Alfred Kazin explores elements of the Hemingway style, which was one of the major literary developments of the modernist era. He writes that this distinctive style allowed Hemingway to vividly evoke the intense emotional lives of characters struggling for survival in the midst of tragedy. Kazin, a literary critic, is the author of *On Native Grounds: An Interpretation of Modern American Prose Literature, Bright Book of Life: American Novelists and Storytellers from Hemingway to Mailer,* and *God and the American Writer.*

Ernest Hemingway discovered very early in his career the reductive principle with which he was to identify everything that promised success in his art. Even in his last books his famous style was the mold into which everything else had to fit. *The Old Man and the Sea, Islands in the Stream, A Moveable Feast, Across the River and into the Trees* were all extraordinarily centered, as usual, around a dominating all-absorbing self whose sensations and reflections gave pattern to the story. Even in the indulgent tenderness of *A Moveable Feast* and the suddenly rhetorical simplicities of *The Old Man and the Sea,* there was that extraordinary concentration of subject, place, mood, that enumeration of the world in Hemingway's special style, that was his trademark, his secret—

From Alfred Kazin, *Bright Book of Life* (Boston: Little, Brown, 1971). Copyright ©1969 by Alfred Kazin. Reprinted with the permission of The Wylie Agency, Inc.

and in a writer so superstitious, anxious, competitive—his rabbit's foot.

Unbeatable definiteness of detail, guaranteed precision of effect.... Nothing extraneous, nothing vague. Line was everything. It was unflagging concentration, with its implicit guarantees, that from his first stories, *In Our Time,* gave the "stamp," the magical thing-ness, the determinable and irreducible compressiveness, to Hemingway's writing. A story was a unit of narrative, held together by a centered persona who seemed to hold his life in his hands, to be gambling it for the highest possible stakes. So you always knew where you were. There was a mental warding off of death. But within this context of danger there was a value to the moments, works and days of the hero's existence, a golden savor, that was somehow (just barely) achieved by the fiercest elimination, by the fierceness of reduction. When it worked, there was a luminous, glowing, sacred center of things that was one's intactness. The Hemingway hero comes to regard himself, to cherish himself, by achieving control over a disorder that is different in kind from himself. Everything is founded on the struggle that gives one back to oneself. William Faulkner paid his tribute to the modern sense of purposelessness by speaking of "one anonymous chance to perform something passionate and brave and austere not just in but into man's enduring chronicle ... in gratitude for the gift of time in it." Hemingway jeered at all noble pronouncements, but gave the heroic version of himself what looked like archaic military dignity. He pitted his persona against situations that remained his definition of them—*In Our Time, Winner Take Nothing, Men Without Women, A Lost Generation, A Separate Peace,* "The Killers," *All Is Nada, Hail Nada.*

These stories and sayings were produced in what T.S. Eliot in "East Coker" (1940) was to call "the years of l'entre deux guerres".[1] It was a period that for Hemingway, as for Eliot and so many of the modernist generation, was not "twenty years largely wasted" but the last great practice of a confidence in the purpose of literature that now seems as privileged as aristocracy. The works that made Hemingway famous had cleared his mind of everything past, false, inflated, in order to set the stage for heroic combat between

1. between two wars

the individual and "in our time." More than anyone else in that great generation that believed in "the religion of the word," Hemingway managed, by one word after another, to make the world as linear as his prose, as stripped as a prize ring, as "clean" as an operating room. You were always aware, reading those beautiful early stories, of someone writing with a desperate grace without which there was nothing, of a world so *made* that it flashed out into positiveness only as a fable in relief, cut like an intaglio, sharp as the Sforza face in the painting by Piero della Francesca, dominating the landscape that he owned, and whose hard-won harmonies expressed *him.*

PRECISE RENDERING OF THE INDIVIDUAL IN CRISIS

Confidence was won, just barely, when the "truth" of one's words showed the "precision" of one's feelings, and so won the battle over the "shapelessness," the "mere anarchy," "the panorama of futility and anarchy that is contemporary history." There was, Hemingway liked to say, "a real thing, a fourth or fifth dimension that can be won. . . ." The secret was writing "truly." There had to be a one-to-one correspondence between the object described and the reaction-feeling it stimulated. Even in his last books, where the world would no longer *hold* for him as it once had, where it had plainly shifted out of his control, so that taken as books, his dogged enumeration of "facts" one by one seemed an imposture, rhetorical rather than the "moment of truth," his perfect passagework could move one by its fierce insistency.

> Then he thought, think of it always. Think of what you are doing. You must do nothing stupid.

> He took all his pain and what was left of his long gone pride and he put it against the fish's agony and the fish came over onto his side and swam gently on his side, his bill almost touching the planking of the skiff and started to pass the boat, long, deep, wide, silver and barred with purpose and interminable in the water. [*The Old Man and the Sea*]

> It was wonderful to walk down the long flights of stairs knowing that I'd had good luck working. I always worked until I had something done and I always stopped when I knew what was going to happen next. That way I could be sure of going on the next day. But sometimes when I was starting a new story and I could not get it going, I would sit in front of the fire and squeel the peel of the little oranges into the edge of the flame and watch the sputter of blue that they made. I

THE MEANING OF HEMINGWAY'S STYLE

Philip Young explains the manner in which Hemingway's style conveyed the meaning of his fiction.

A style has its own content, and the manner of a distinctive prose style has its own meanings. The things that Hemingway's style most conveys are the very things he says outright. His style is as communicative of the content as the content itself, and is a large and inextricable part of the content. The strictly disciplined controls exerted over the hero and his nervous system are precise parallels to the strictly disciplined sentences. The "mindlessness" of the style is a reflection and expression of the need to "stop thinking" when thought means remembering the things that upset. The intense simplicity of the prose is a means of saying that things must be *made* simple, or the hero is lost, and in "a way you'll never be." The economy and narrow focus of the prose controls the little that can be absolutely mastered. The prose is tense because the atmosphere in which the struggle for control takes place is tense, and the tension in the style expresses that fact.

Philip Young, "Ernest Hemingway," from *Seven Modern American Novelists: An Introduction.* Ed. William Van O'Connor. Minneapolis: University of Minnesota Press, 1966.

would stand and look out over the roofs of Paris and think, "Do not worry. You have always written before and you will write now. All you have to do is write one true sentence. Write the truest sentence that you know." [*A Moveable Feast*]

The "precision of feeling" here was unanswerable, but this was so because it was one man's intimate experience of danger, dread, anxiety, hope. It spoke for that experience and nothing else: "precision" had been won at the cost of sacrificing anything beyond the quality in danger, the crisis-point, the importance of what the self says it feels. The vividness, timing, tonality, echoing repetitions—Dr. Johnson said that waiting to be hanged concentrates a man's faculties wonderfully—point back to the ordeal. The hero's sense of his own existence, the fierce presentness of his emotions or feelings, were always more convincing in Hemingway's stories than in his novels; the "moment of truth" is always more than the plot. It was only in his greatest "pieces," as one must call them, that his self-obsessed stories were as dramatically convincing as they were emotionally powerful. One believed in the swamp and the haunted soul behind

Nick Adams's fishing in "Big Two-Hearted River" as one could not believe that other people are desperately fighting for their lives in Hemingway's flip introduction of himself into *their* war. "The Germans came over the wall. We shot them one after another, just like that." But when he wrote out of history, out of the confidence that war was a school of style, his sureness expressed itself in rhythms that showed history in the service of art—"Troops went by the house and down the road and the dust they raised powdered the leaves of the trees. The trunks of the trees too were dusty and the leaves fell early that year and we saw the troops marching along the road and the dust rising and leaves, stirred by the breeze, falling and the soldiers marching and afterward the road bare and white except for the leaves." Caporetto, the great episode of the Italian officers being taken out of the line of retreat and shot by military police, stands out in *A Farewell to Arms* because it is a Goya painting of the horrors of war.[2] The expected response is built into the material. The emotions involved are purely tragic, never disturbing, confusing, uncertain. . . .

STYLE RATHER THAN STRUCTURE

Painting and fishing as work toward a specified object interested Hemingway more than the novel as a many-sided form. For his own novels he never thought of plot as a structure with an interest of its own. He made do with the all-important instances of the self doggedly achieving its passage through life, the lyric emphasis of consciousness on itself. The sovereignty of the storyteller, of which Charles Dickens and Honoré de Balzac were equally conscious, became for Hemingway the *matter* of fiction. When he announced that all modern American writing comes out of *Huckleberry Finn,* he was obviously thinking of spoken style. He praised Henry James formally, as one plenipotentiary to another, but not as a deviser in fiction. He had many things to say about Scott Fitzgerald's "weak" character, but the role of coincidence as an agent of disaster in *The Great Gatsby* never interested him any more than did the social contraption that John Dos Passos rigged up in *U.S.A.* to mirror History to itself, or the interlocking sagas of family history and

2. Francisco Goya, a Spanish painter, is known for his dark, grotesquely violent compositions.

Southern history in William Faulkner. Hemingway was by no means the first or the last American writer of fiction to be so much his own presiding situation. But what made the immediate matter in hand excitingly tense, dramatic, always a combat (even when the opponent is rigged and the horrors of war just another battle scene) is Hemingway's fervent belief that if a tragic cause is established, the response is guaranteed—art comes out of style, style out of combat.

The fighter in "Fifty Grand" thinks, "It looked like half a mile down to the ring. It was all dark. . . . Just the lights over the ring." The circumscribed narrow world, the tightening of nature to design as in painting, the handling of weapons, the prize ring, the arena, the making and unmaking of camp, the use of any moment to show only the ultimate responses to life, the line of words in Indian file that is exciting because it conveys the ordeal of consciousness to itself. One item succeeding another with the tread of time itself, Hemingway looking at Nick Adams as Nick Adams looks at his can of beans, the head looking always just one way, directed to nothing but the occasion. The extraordinary replacement of dramatic complexity by a successiveness of words that is the immediate physical experience, the curtailing of everything to the handling of things, the getting on top of difficulties. All these identify obsessive patterning of the smallest experience *with* the deliberate effort it takes to keep alive. The individual person in all his idiosyncrasy, that famous single character as character who had reflected the middle-class tradition of the novel, has been contracted in Hemingway's work to a certain obsessive watchfulness and mindfulness—to a burden of consciousness so haunting and limiting that it makes any complex dramatic structure unnecessary to Hemingway. Even his novels soon came down to one character haunted by danger, reviving each time he could recover his balance by handling each detail in his path with the gravest self-importance.

Hemingway gave a particular and somehow fatal emphasis to the self as the necessary end product of literature. But a belief in the self as the essential *form* of literature was typical of that group of friends—Hemingway, Fitzgerald, Dos Passos, E.E. Cummings, Edmund Wilson—for whom the right words in the right order were the immediate act that cut away the falseness and inconsequence of the world— "the lies, the lies!" as one battle-weary character cried in

Dos Passos's *Three Soldiers*. And left oneself intact. The near was the self. The far-off was the world. Only what was near could be trusted. Because it alone could be used? . . .

WAR AS A SCHOOL OF WRITING

For Hemingway, as for all the best writers of his generation, the great thing about war had been that it was an object lesson for writers and "unmistakable." To be "unmistakable" was Stephen Crane's only rule for "good writing." From the perspective after 1945, Hemingway the Red Cross driver and dilettante of violence was to seem as much a student of other people's wars as Stephen Crane (born 1871) had been of the Civil War.

The first World War was not only a great "experience" for Fitzgerald, Dos Passos, Cummings, Wilson—it was also a school of writing in that most famous of schools for writing, France. Faulkner, who in any event never belonged to this group and had his war experience cracking up an old crate in the Royal Flying Corps in Canada, obviously did not model *Soldiers' Pay* on clean French prose. And 1917–1918 was always to seem less significant to Faulkner than 1861–1865. But looking back now on Hemingway and his nearest friends and rivals, a "lost" generation that found its greatest possible chance in literature by getting to the "Great War" as ambulance drivers, we can see that the famous directness, concreteness, precision so fundamental to these writers arose from the assurance that war was just another tragedy in man's experience. And tragedy was enough to carry a writer in those days, for in tragedy the self was not destroyed from within. With tragedy you knew where you were, always in mortal combat. Death was the only enemy. Constantly facing the greater power of nature and the universe, a man could rise to heroism just as he rose to a clear knowledge of the odds against him in a well-defined godless universe. In tragedy, there was still that instinctive unconscious connection with nature which Hemingway always celebrated lyrically; there was a necessary connection between his sense of the "unmistakable" and the writer's own strength. The "unmistakable" kept man and history in order by keeping them apart. The desired clarity of the lost generation can now be seen as the last example of the pure tragic sense in our literature. The combatants—man and his unfriendly destiny—were like actors well-practiced in the tolerable roles of Achilles and Hector lined up against each other through all eternity. . . .

HEMINGWAY UPSTAGED

After Hemingway, the "unmistakable" as the point of style, his special clarity and grace, was to become a faint memory in the violently flashing images with which Nathanael West rendered the atomized emotions of *Miss Lonelyhearts* and the surrealistically overpainted Hollywood of *The Day of the Locust.* . . . Hemingway's faith in the "unmistakable," the linear, was to become an heirloom that could not be passed on. It would be remembered—it would earn Hemingway the immortality reserved for one who had known how to treasure the moment, how to make style a preservative of one's own sacred experiences. But even before 1939, this particular style of elegant clarity, of confident American downrightness, had been upstaged by Franz Kafka in those books that were to have a greater influence in English than they would ever have in German, by Jean-Paul Sartre in *Nausea,* by James Joyce in the ultimate post-novel that is *Finnegans Wake.* Perhaps the greatest challenge to Hemingway was to come from Faulkner, whose unselfconscious originality of technique, his absorption in the one many-sided story he had to tell, showed narrative not as a triumph *over* experience, but as the struggle of language to find support for the mind in its everlasting struggle with the past.

Hemingway said that he was proud of not writing like "the author of the Octonawhoopoo stories".[3] But Hemingway died of Faulkner as much as he died of Hemingway.[4] In Hemingway's last years it was Faulkner, coming up after having been ignored so long, who was to be a constant shock and bewilderment to Hemingway in the new age of ambiguity. Faulkner was another name for a world—for history—that could not be reduced to a style.

---

3. i.e., Faulkner, whose stories and novels are set in Yoknapatawpha County, Mississippi 4. Hemingway committed suicide in 1961.

The Stream-of-Consciousness Technique in American Modernist Fiction

Frederick J. Hoffman

One of the major stylistic developments of the modernist era was the stream-of-consciousness technique. Influenced by the theories of Sigmund Freud, authors employing this technique attempted to express the unconscious and unspoken thoughts of characters in a way that revealed the processes of the mind. *Ulysses,* a novel by the Irish author James Joyce, is the most renowned example of stream of consciousness in fiction and is considered by many to be one of the two most significant modernist texts, along with T.S. Eliot's poem *The Waste Land.* However, as Frederick J. Hoffman notes, stream of consciousness was successfully used in American fiction, most notably in William Faulkner's novel *The Sound and the Fury.* Hoffman, a literary critic, is the author of *The Twenties: American Writing in the Postwar Decade* and *The Modern Novel in America, 1900–1950.*

Sigmund Freud, in his discussions of the ego, its place in the conscious and the unconscious, and the gravity of its struggle for shape and form in a world of complex and hidden motive, provided a complete set of speculations about the modern soul.[1] . . .

The most important single *formal* result of Freudian influence was . . . the "stream of consciousness" technique. James

1. Freud theorized that the human psyche had three components: the id, consisting of unconscious drives; the ego, which regulates the impulses; and the superego, the moral sense.

From *The Twenties: American Writing in the Postwar Decade,* by Frederick J. Hoffman. Copyright ©1949, 1953, ©1954, 1955 by Frederick J. Hoffman; renewed 1977, 1981, 1982, 1983 by Caroline Hoffman Vasquez. Used by permission of Viking Penguin, a division of Penguin Putnam Inc.

Joyce's *Ulysses* (1922) was the major document. His *Finnegans Wake* also appeared in the 1920s, as "Work in Progress," in *transition* and in the *transatlantic review*. Both works stimulated experiments in fictional prose, some successful, others (like those of A. Lincoln Gillespie in *transition*) wild and nonsensical. Joyce demonstrated in *Ulysses* the possibilities of the new method; he did not claim Freud as his master, though there are evidences in his two major books that he was more than aware of what the "dream work"[2] might contribute to both form and matter.

USING PSYCHOANALYTIC MATTER FOR LITERARY PURPOSE

Most conspicuously indebted to Joyce among American novelists was Conrad Aiken. "I decided very early," Aiken said in reply to a questionnaire (*New Verse*, 1934), "that Freud, and his co-workers and rivals and followers, were making the most important contribution of the century to the understanding of man and his consciousness; accordingly I made it my business to learn as much from them as I could." *Great Circle* (1933), *King Coffin* (1935), and *Blue Voyage* (1927) all testify to Aiken's interest in Joyce and his concern over the Freudian explanation of the human consciousness.

Blue Voyage is in many ways modeled on *Ulysses:* it has its Stephen Dedalus in Demarest, its Leopold Bloom in Silberstein, a merchant of "chewing sweets." The style and design follow clearly the descent of Demarest into the lowest regions of his unconscious and his final rise to the level of rational self-appraisal. As does Joyce in *Ulysses*, Aiken clearly indicates time and place, and allows for an indication of narrative progress in terms of both. Demarest is on a ship, sailing for England. His mind is absorbed by thoughts of his fiancée, Cynthia, whom he expects to see when he arrives. After he has discovered that Cynthia is on the same boat and after she has greeted him coldly, the narrative becomes for a while a monologue, an unconscious reverie. The rest of the novel is a record of Demarest's fight to return to full consciousness of his situation, a progress that is interrupted at one point by an extravagant fantasy, in which he quarrels with his "censor"[3] (in this case, an analyst friend) about the worth of his life and art, and a hallucinatory vision of his

2. Freud believed that dreams were symbolic representations of unconscious fantasies, fears, and conflicts.   3. the voice of the superego

DEFINING STREAM-OF-CONSCIOUSNESS FICTION

Robert Humphrey writes that stream-of-consciousness fiction explores the "prespeech" levels of consciousness in order to reveal the psychic being of characters.

The stream-of-consciousness novel is identified most quickly by its subject matter. This, rather than its techniques, its purposes, or its themes, distinguishes it. Hence, the novels that are said to use the stream-of-consciousness *technique* to a considerable degree prove, upon analysis, to be novels which have as their essential subject matter the consciousness of one or more characters; that is, the depicted consciousness serves as a screen on which the material in these novels is presented.

"Consciousness" should not be confused with words which denote more restricted mental activities, such as "intelligence" or "memory." . . . Consciousness indicates the entire area of mental attention, from preconsciousness on through the levels of the mind up to and including the highest one of rational, communicable awareness. This last area is the one with which almost all psychological fiction is concerned. Stream-of-consciousness fiction differs from all other psychological fiction precisely in that it is concerned with those levels that are more inchoate than rational verbalization—those levels on the margin of attention. . . .

There are two levels of consciousness which can be rather simply distinguished: the "speech level" and the "prespeech level." There is a point at which they overlap, but otherwise the distinction is quite clear. The prespeech level . . . involves no communicative basis as does the speech level (whether spoken or written). This is its salient distinguishing characteristic. In short, the prespeech levels of consciousness are not censored, rationally controlled, or logically ordered. By "consciousness," then, I shall mean the whole area of mental processes, including especially the prespeech levels. . . .

Hence, "consciousness" must not be confused with "intelligence" or "memory" or any other such limiting term. . . . Let us think of consciousness as being in the form of an iceberg— the whole iceberg and not just the relatively small surface portion. Stream-of-consciousness fiction is, to follow this comparison, greatly concerned with what lies below the surface.

With such a concept of consciousness, we may define stream-of-consciousness fiction as a type of fiction in which the basic emphasis is placed on exploration of the prespeech levels of consciousness for the purpose, primarily, of revealing the psychic being of the characters.

Robert Humphrey, *Stream of Consciousness in the Modern Novel.* Berkeley: University of California Press, 1968.

shipmates discussing his life calmly and impudently but with penetrating accuracy. The style and subject matter both participate in the Freudian analysis of the dream world. But it is important to note that Aiken *uses* the psychoanalytic matter to his advantage, conscious that it must be ordered to some literary purpose, the examination of a neurotic state.

WILLIAM FAULKNER'S *THE SOUND AND THE FURY*

The most skillful use of the subconscious is to be found in William Faulkner's *The Sound and the Fury* (1929). Less "literary" in tone than *Ulysses,* it is a more successful adaptation of states of consciousness to narrative purpose. This is partly because Faulkner directs his narrative very clearly in terms of a limited number of perspectives and facts. The central fact is the defection of Candace Compson. The novel is developed according to the four principal judgments of the act, in terms of her sin against moral, family, economic, and traditional proprieties. Faulkner presents the sin and its consequences through the minds of Caddy's three brothers, and finally in terms of the *public* world—the world of Jefferson itself, of the shrunken Compson estate, and of the moral and religious judgment of Dilsey, the Negro servant.

The perspective of the idiot brother Benjy is the most extreme of the four, but only because Faulkner must here articulate and give intelligible form to a mind that neither verbalizes nor discriminates past from present. Benjy's mind works through simple association and the identity of events that bear similarities, however widely separated in time. Since he does not know time, he cannot understand or tolerate change; his insights into Caddy's nature have therefore all been settled at a time before Caddy sinned. His is the moral order of an age of innocence; and that order is rigidly and eloquently upheld in his every response. He reacts by bellowing or whimpering to any suggestion—sight, smell, or movement—that the time of innocence has been changed in the slightest particular. He does not judge persons and acts in terms of a moral order arrived at by reason; he senses disorder, smells out evil, is sensitive to every threat to the family structure.

Like Benjy, Quentin is a monitor of Caddy's moral life. But Quentin's private world—to which Caddy is as essential as she is to Benjy's—is the product of obsessive formulation, ratiocination, conceptualizing. The world of the past is brought back by sensuous images of Caddy as a little girl; but Quentin's memory of the past is not the simple familial order Benjy has seen. He fixes it in terms of concepts of honor and virginity. For him, virginity is a condition of stasis, in which "nothing has happened," and if nothing has happened he can retain his moral design. Caddy's sin has destroyed this design; she has "made things happen" in losing her virginity, in marrying, in giving birth to an illegitimate child. Quentin tries to recover the design—first by an attempt on the life of her first lover, then by trying to fix the blame for the act on himself (incest, by confining the sin, will at least make guilt and atonement possible within the design), finally by committing suicide. He tries to defeat time through death and thus to fix permanently his conceptions of family and personal honor. This is another kind of consciousness, and Faulkner gives it a style and vocabulary quite different from Benjy's. Benjy exists below the level of articulation; Quentin's mind is given excessively to abstracting and codifying, until he drives himself to the ultimate act of abstraction, death by suicide.

Jason's consciousness is totally different from that of either of his brothers. For Benjy, Caddy's sin is a violation of a world of sensation, for Quentin, a loss of honor; for Jason, it is a breach of contract, a legal matter for which legal restitution must be made. The section devoted to his view is liberally supplied with references to money, checks, agreements, investments, profit and loss. Jason is the comically rational character who lives in a common-sense world of calculable facts and figures. He is defeated on a legal technicality; in attempting to recover his "birthright," he appropriates money intended for Caddy's illegitimate daughter, who takes both it and Jason's other savings and escapes with a man from a traveling carnival. His rational world is in the end defeated by the irrational world, which he has never allowed for in his plans.

The prose of these three appraisals follows strictly the requirements of the narrative; there is no display of stylistics for their own sake, no overstepping the bounds of each consciousness. Faulkner neither exploits the unconscious mind for sensational effects nor imposes extraneous matters upon it. The reader is made ready, through the three private reconstructions of the novel's central event, for the final perspective upon the Compsons. It is the external world, the world of the present, as contrasted with Benjy's and Quentin's fixed pasts. Temporally this world is Easter Sunday, 1928, some thirty years after the significant moment of the past; spatially it is reduced to the now small and aging house, actually to Dilsey's kitchen, which is the only place where any genuine living takes place. The reader discovers, finally, that the affairs of the Compson family are not to be judged by any one of the three previous perspectives, but to be evaluated in the somber notes of an old Negro servant, who emerges from her cabin on a wet morning, her skeleton "draped loosely in unpadded skin that tightened again upon a paunch almost dropsical, as though muscle and tissue had been courage or fortitude which the days or the years had consumed."

The Sound and the Fury is a remarkably mature and restrained experiment with the possibilities of "stream-of-consciousness" techniques. Other experimental writing in the decade did not have such successful results. Experiment in so new a thing as the exploration of human consciousness *on its own terms* was handicapped by love of experiment for its own sake: the excitement of innovation was quite often the only incentive. Joyce testified to the brilliant range of improvisation possible in fictional prose, and Faulkner to the sound usefulness of exploring human states and presenting them with insight and depth.

CHAPTER 4

Regional Movements: Renaissance in Harlem and the South

American
Modernism

The Harlem Renaissance: A Florescence of Creativity

Amritjit Singh

In the 1920s, parallel to the soaring careers of Anglo-American modernist writers such as T.S. Eliot, Ernest Hemingway, and F. Scott Fitzgerald, African-American poets and authors were engaged in their own creative flowering in Harlem and other cities nationwide. Known as the Harlem Renaissance, this movement resulted from a combination of social and economic changes that led to the emergence of black racial pride and solidarity in the northern cities. The new racial consciousness found its expression in the poetry and fiction of Claude McKay, Langston Hughes, Zora Neal Hurston, and other young black writers. In this essay, Amritjit Singh, the author and editor of several books on American literature and the Harlem Renaissance, describes the genesis of the movement, the debate over the terminology used to describe it, and the forces that prevented it from developing into a larger black school of American literature. According to Singh, the renaissance fell victim to the white public's preference for stereotypical depictions of blacks as emotionally and sexually uninhibited.

The 1920s in American history were marked by a sociocultural awakening among Afro-Americans. More blacks participated in the arts than ever before, and their number increased steadily throughout the decade. This florescence of creative activity extended to many areas—music, poetry, drama, fiction. In literature, the few Negro novels published between 1905 and 1923 were presented mainly by small firms unable to give their authors a national hearing. However, in the succeeding decade, over two dozen novels by

Excerpted from Amritjit Singh, *The Novels of the Harlem Renaissance* (University Park: Pennsylvania State University Press, 1976), pages 1–25. Copyright ©1976 The Pennsylvania State University. Reproduced by permission of the publisher.

blacks appeared, and most of them were issued by major American publishers.

The needs of this new black self-expression were served by magazines and journals, black as well as white. The twenties gave rise to all-black literary quarterlies and "little magazines," some of rather short duration, such as *Fire, Harlem, Stylus, Quill,* and *Black Opals.* The National Association for the Advancement of Colored People (NAACP) and the National Urban League both published powerful journals, *The Crisis* and *Opportunity* respectively, which encouraged young black writers. *The Messenger,* published by A. Philip Randolph and Chandler Owen, also made stimulating literary contributions from time to time. In addition, the leading journals in America published articles, short stories, poems, and reviews from black writers.

By the middle of the decade, many people had become conscious of this literary upsurge and tried to direct and influence its orientation. Alain Locke, describing himself later as a "midwife" to the younger generation of black writers of the twenties, propounded the concept of a Negro renaissance and tried to develop a movement of black American arts. In March 1925, he edited a special Harlem issue of *Survey Graphic,* which he expanded later that year into an anthology entitled *The New Negro.* This anthology contained the recent work of young black writers and called for continued attempts at racial self-expression within a culturally pluralistic American context. Many black writers answered Locke's call by offering accounts of all strata of black life, from Philadelphia's blue-vein "society" Negroes to Harlem's common folk, including streetwalkers and criminals.

Locke's anthology also initiated a debate on black writing that caused endless controversy in the twenties and continues vigorously today. The term "New Negro," though not original with Locke, caught on in black circles even more than his concept of cultural pluralism. New Negro societies sprang up in several large cities and it became fashionable to declare oneself a member of the New Negro coterie. The fresh interest in the Negro evinced by white writers such as Carl Van Vechten led journals other than *Survey Graphic* to devote entire issues to the Negro. In October 1926, *Palms* featured a "Negro Number" edited by Countee Cullen. Both *The Crisis* and *Opportunity* awarded annual prizes in sponsored literary contests. In 1926, the publishers Albert and Charles

Boni offered a $1,000 cash prize in addition to royalties for the best novel about black life written by a Negro. In June of that year, *Publishers' Weekly* noted the increasing contributions to the literary scene by the "colored race."

TERMINOLOGY

Some scholars and critics have questioned the use of the term "renaissance" to describe the creative activity of blacks in the twenties. They think the term is misapplied because they see no evidence of an earlier Afro-American tradition. The use of the term renaissance is justified by the intense interest of Afro-American writers in coming to terms with the peculiar racial situation in the United States and in exploring their emotional and historical links with Africa and the American South. This interest is prefigured in the work of the nineteenth-century black writers Frederick Douglass, David Walker, William Wells Brown, Martin R. Delany, and Frances E.W. Harper; it culminates in the poetry, fiction, and essays of Paul Laurence Dunbar, James Weldon Johnson, Charles W. Chesnutt, Sutton E. Griggs, and W.E.B. DuBois in the 1890s. The range of black writing in the twenties, best indicated by *The New Negro,* is also reflected in the fine work done by *The Crisis* and *Opportunity* throughout the period with the active participation of intellectuals such as W.E.B. DuBois, Charles S. Johnson, Sterling Brown, and James Weldon Johnson.

These arguments notwithstanding, critics have failed, so far, to evolve a uniform terminology in discussing the black writers of the twenties. It is generally agreed that the phenomenon referred to as the Negro, Black, or Harlem Renaissance appeared on the American scene during the closing years of World War I, was publicly recognized by men such as Alain Locke and Charles S. Johnson in 1924 or 1925, and had begun declining about the time of the stock market crash in 1929. But the critics John Hope Franklin and Sterling Brown prefer to see the Renaissance as an ongoing movement of black arts since the end of World War I. Robert Bone employs the term "Negro Renaissance" for the nationwide upsurge in black writing during the twenties, describing the young black writers centered in Harlem as the Harlem School. Bone contrasts the Harlem School with the so-called Old Guard, but the Renaissance writers' shared impulses and contradictions render these categories critically confusing rather than helpful. Sterling Brown sums up his refusal to call the New Negro phenomenon of the twenties the "Harlem Renaissance" or even a "renaissance":

> I have hesitated to use the term Negro Renaissance for several reasons: one is that the five or six years generally allotted are short for the life-span of any "renaissance." The New Negro is not to me a group of writers centered in Harlem during the second half of the twenties. Most of the writers were not Harlemites; much of the best writing was not about Harlem, which was the show-window, the cashier's till but no more Negro America than New York is America. The New Negro has temporal roots in the past and spatial roots elsewhere in America, and the term has validity, it seems to me, only when considered to be a continuing tradition.

This literary florescence reverberated throughout the country; it was not confined to Harlem. And although short-lived, it was in some sense a renaissance.

For many reasons . . . Harlem has continued to be associated with the New Negro movement. Many socioeconomic and cultural factors made Harlem unique among the all-black communities that developed in Northern cities as a result of the massive urban migration around the time of World War I. The term Harlem Renaissance reflects an awareness of the complexity of the sociocultural forces at work in the New Negro movement and gives Harlem credit for its contributions. . . . The term "Harlem Renaissance" is firmly established in the minds of the reading public as a descriptive label for the emergence of arts among black Americans all over America in the twenties. . . .

WORLD WAR I AND THE GREAT URBAN MIGRATION

World War I became a major factor in the Afro-American's new awareness of himself and his relationship to American democratic ideals. War-born opportunities brought blacks to Northern cities in great numbers, accelerating the population shift generally known as the Great Urban Migration. During the war, black troops marched and fought alongside white Americans to make the world "safe for democracy." The Negro's experiences abroad revealed the discrepancies between the promise of freedom and his own status in American life; and he was led to hope that democracy would also be won at home. After the Armistice in 1918, the blacks became embittered and defiant to find the whites more than ever determined to keep the Negro in his place. As John

Hope Franklin points out, it was not the timorous, docile Negro of the past who said, "The next time white folks pick on colored folks, something is going to drop—dead white folks." The threat posed to legalized white supremacy in the South by returning soldiers and the hostility aroused in the North by a rapidly expanding black population resulted in nationwide expressions of racial animosity. During the "bloody summer" of 1919, race riots erupted in more than twenty-five cities across the nation. Blacks fought back bitterly and audaciously. It was in reaction to these riots that Claude McKay wrote his now famous poem, "If We Must Die," published in *The Liberator.* And in an editorial entitled "Returning Soldiers" in *The Crisis,* DuBois declared:

> Under similar circumstances we would fight again. But by the God of Heaven, we are cowards and jackasses if, now that the war is over, we do not marshal every ounce of our brain and brawn to fight a sterner, longer, more unbending battle against the forces of hell in our own land.

Meanwhile, the urban migration continued. Stimulated by the promise of industrial jobs in the North in the wake of the cessation of European migration, hundreds of thousands of Southern blacks were pouring into Northern cities. By one estimate, over 500,000 lower-class blacks migrated north between 1910 and 1920, and during the twenties another 800,000 blacks abandoned the South, many of them Negro ministers and professionals who followed their clients. In addition, there were migrants from the Midwest, the West, and the West Indies. . . .

The black sharecroppers and farm laborers saw in their move to the cities "a new vision of opportunity, of social and economic freedom," [according to Alain Locke]. In the Northern cities, they hoped to escape the poverty of Southern agriculture and the violence of racial bigotry. The urban migration also meant being crowded into segregated neighborhoods where the blacks could feel their powers as they never had before. They developed a new self-respect and racial consciousness. Segregation stimulated the growth of a black middle class whose main function was to provide services for the black community that did not interest the white businessman. Such services included barber shops, funeral parlors, restaurants, shoe repair shops, beauty shops, and grocery stores, but some Negroes also successfully ran employment and real estate agencies.

The shift to Northern urban centers had its unpalatable side too. First, white hostility threatened the very existence of black neighborhoods. The overcrowding in black communities led to disease and delinquency. Racketeers and profiteers exploited the new migrants, who were for the most part ignorant of the city's ways. Euphoria Blake in Wallace Thurman's [novel] *Infants of the Spring* tells how she moved from the South full of ideas about race uplift, but ended up exploiting her fellow migrants by being an intermediary between jobseekers and employers, between landlords and potential tenants. In addition, intraracial and interregional conflicts arose when blacks of different backgrounds were thrown together into areas only ten to twenty blocks long in most cities.

HARLEM: A RACE-CONSCIOUS, SOPHISTICATED BLACK COMMUNITY

In many ways, Harlem was just another of the new black neighborhoods in Northern cities; it shared their advantages as well as problems. But Harlem differed in that it developed from a white, upper-middle-class suburb, and not from the continued decline of an already poor white area, as was usually the case. In 1925, in an article written for Locke's anthology, *The New Negro,* James Weldon Johnson comments:

> Harlem is not merely a Negro colony or community, it is a city within a city, the greatest Negro city in the world. It is not a slum or a fringe, it is located in the heart of Manhattan and occupies one of the most beautiful and healthful sections of the city. It is not a "quarter" of dilapidated tenements, but is made up of new-law apartments and handsome dwellings, with well-paved and well-lighted streets. It has its own churches, social and civic centers, shops, theaters and other places of amusement. And it contains more Negroes to the square mile than any other spot on earth.

No wonder Harlem became [in the words of Gilbert Osofsky] "a symbol of elegance and distinction, not derogation." Since the promise of a better future seemed more tangible in Harlem, it attracted more migrants, intensifying the process of urbanization in a cosmopolitan setting. The community grew from 14,000 blacks in 1914 to 175,000 by 1925 and more than 200,000 by the beginning of the Depression. Negroes came from all parts of the United States, West Indies, and even Africa, and their interaction led to the growth of a highly race-conscious, sophisticated black community—

something unprecedented in American history. Black writers, painters, and actors from all over the country experienced the magnetic pull of Harlem as the new cultural capital of black America. "In Harlem," wrote Alain Locke in the special Harlem issue of *Survey Graphic,* which he edited in March 1925, "Negro life is seizing upon its first chances for group expression and self-determination." The black's new aspirations and continued frustrations instilled among the common folk a fiery brand of racial chauvinism; it also led to an assertion of black pride by a broad-based middle-class Negro leadership. Because of the diversity of its population, Harlem also became an ideal testing ground for clashing racial and political points of view. What Roi Ottley said about Harlem in 1943 had perhaps even greater validity for the twenties: "It is the fountainhead of mass movements. From it flows the progressive vitality of Black life. . . . To grasp the inner meanings of life in Black America, one must put his finger on the pulse of Harlem."

The new militancy of the Harlem Negro reflected itself in many ways during the period. In 1910, a group of white radicals and black leaders had met in New York to form the NAACP, which pledged itself to work for the abolition of all forced segregation, equal education for black and white children, the complete enfranchisement of the Negro, and the enforcement of the Fourteenth and Fifteenth Amendments. Its organ, *The Crisis: A Record of Darker Races,* edited by W.E.B. DuBois, became an important outlet for black grievances as well as hopes. The first issue of *The Crisis,* published in November 1910, sold 1,000 copies rapidly and by 1918 the circulation figures reached 100,000 per month. The following year, the National Urban League was organized in New York, and "it undertook to open new opportunities for Negroes in industry and to assist newly arrived Negroes in their problems of adjustment in the urban centers." *Opportunity, A Journal of Negro Life* began publication in January 1923 as the expanded organ of the League under the enterprising editorship of Charles S. Johnson. On 28 June 1917, some 10,000 Harlem citizens carrying placards marched down Fifth Avenue in a Silent Parade led by the NAACP to protest the massacre of blacks in East St. Louis. A. Philip Randolph organized the all-black Brotherhood of Sleeping Car Porters and Maids. Although the Brotherhood was not fully recognized as a bargaining agency until 1937, it won the endorsement of the American Federation of Labor, the NAACP, and the National Urban League during the twenties and played a valuable role in the wage agreements of 1926 and 1929 with the Pullman Company. The NAACP launched a nationwide campaign to promote federal antilynching legislation. In 1919, the House of Representatives passed an antilynching bill, but the Southern senators managed to prevent a vote on the measure in the Senate. In Harlem, as elsewhere in Northern cities, numerous small leftist groups were active among the black masses, even though their impact was very limited. . . .

EXTENDING RACE CONSCIOUSNESS INTO THE ARTS

The Harlem Renaissance was a logical extension in the areas of art, music, and literature of the New Negro's racial, cultural, and political thinking. Arna Bontemps traced the origins of the Renaissance to the year 1917, when Claude McKay published a poem entitled "Harlem Dancer" in an obscure magazine. "In that same year, [according to Bontemps,] James Weldon Johnson collected poems he had been writing in a small volume called *Fifty Years and Other Poems,* but none of these verses had the sock of Claude McKay's poetry or of Johnson's own later poems. A serious dramatic presentation with a black cast appeared for the first time on Broadway in that same year." Soon after, many black artists and musicians, including Roland Hayes, Duke Ellington, Louis Armstrong, Bessie Smith, Jelly Roll Morton, W.C. Handy, and Aaron Douglas, came to public attention. . . .

In literature, the first stage of the Harlem Renaissance culminated in the events that led to the publication of *The New Negro* in December 1925. The first of these events was a dinner at the Civic Club on 21 March 1924, for a group called the "Writers' Guild." Charles Johnson describes the dinner in a letter to Ethel Ray (later secretary to Johnson in his *Opportunity* office):

> You could have been of enormous assistance to me this past week when I was arranging for the "debut" of the younger Negro writers. It was a most unusual affair—a dinner meeting at the Civic Club at which all of the younger Negro writers—Cullen, Walter White, Walrond, Jessie Fauset, Gwendolyn Bennett, Alain Locke, M. Gregory, met and chatted with the passing generation—Dubois, Jas. Weldon Johnson, Georgia Douglas Johnson, etc. and with the literary personages of the city: Carl Van Doren, editor of the *Century,* Fred-

erick Allen of *Harper's*, Walter Bartlett of *Scribner's*, Devere Allen of the *World Tomorrow*, Freda Kirchwey of the *Nation*, Paul Kellogg of the *Survey*, Horace Liveright of Boni, Liveright Publishers, etc.—about 100 guests and tremendously impressive speaking. I'll have an account of it in the magazine. It would have given you a first hand introduction to the "last worders" in literature. But principally it served to stimulate a market for the new stuff which these young writers are turning out. The first definite reaction came in the form of an offer of one magazine to devote an entire issue to the similar subjects as treated by representatives of the group. A big plug was bitten off. Now it's a question of living up to the reputation. Yes, I should have added, a stream of manuscripts has started into my office from other aspirants.

Most of the prominent writers of the Renaissance were present at this dinner. (However, Langston Hughes, Claude McKay, and Jean Toomer were out of the country at the time.) Paul Kellogg, the editor of *Survey Graphic*, was also present; he invited Alain Locke to be the guest editor of a special issue devoted to Harlem. Locke accepted the invitation and the March 1925 issue of the *Survey* was entitled "Harlem, the Mecca of the New Negro"; it became "the single most notable achievement of the journal in these years," [according to Clarke A. Chambers]. Two printings totaling 42,000 copies were sold, a record unsurpassed by the *Survey* until World War II. Even before the issue came out, Albert and Charles Boni expressed interest in publishing it later in book form and *The New Negro* was printed in a deluxe edition in December 1925. . . .

WHY DID THE RENAISSANCE FAIL?

It is difficult today to account for all the factors that prevented the growth of a black American school of literature. Harlem Renaissance writing is marked by racialism, but the writers reflect the spirit of the times in their refusal to join causes or movements. "Individuality is what we should strive for. Let each seek his own salvation," says Raymond Taylor, the alter ego of Wallace Thurman in *Infants of the Spring*. As a creative writer, Zora Neale Hurston was interested not in social problems, but in the problems of individuals, black or white. Alain Locke's idea of a black literary movement had political implications, but he did not base it on a rigid social or political ideology. Locke's views were opposed by W.E.B. DuBois, Benjamin Brawley, and Allison Davis, who contended that black writers had a responsibility to defend and uplift the race by portraying educated, middle-class Negroes. Claude McKay, acutely conscious of his position as a black man in Western civilization, asserted his artistic independence while alternating between Marxist and nationalistic ideologies. Wallace Thurman, lost in the world of contemporary bohemia, would not compromise with the high artistic standards he set for himself and others. There were, however, many black writers of the period who—independently or under Locke's influence—resolved their dilemmas of conflicting racial and artistic loyalties in ways resembling Locke's approach.[1] Among these writers are Langston Hughes, Jean Toomer, Rudolph Fisher, Eric Walrond, Sterling Brown, Arna Bontemps, and Zora Neale Hurston.

It is necessary to look outside Harlem and black America for the major explanation of the Harlem Renaissance writers' failure to develop into a cohesive group or movement. In discussing white interest in the Negro, Huggins argues that "the black-white relationship has been symbiotic, [and that] blacks have been essential to white identity (and whites to blacks)." In American history, this black-white symbiosis has resulted in the black being called on to uphold a new stereotype. In the twenties, both in Europe and America, interest in the Negro came to be focused around the cult of the primitive. It had become fashionable in the Jazz Age to defy prohibition and to find joy and abandon in exotic music and dance. In such an atmosphere [in the words of Robert A. Bone] "the Negro had obvious uses: he represented the unspoiled child of nature, the noble savage—carefree, spontaneous and sexually uninhibited." A popular misinterpretation of Freudian theory contributed to the promotion of primitivism. Freud was seen as exalting instinct over intellect in a revolt against the Puritan spirit. In his *Civilization and its Discontents,* Freud had contended that civilization is based upon renunciation of "powerful instinctual urgencies," and the privation of instinctual gratification demanded by the cultural ideal was a major source of neurosis. No wonder, then, that popularized Freudianism became [as stated by Oscar Cargill] "the rationalization of sex primitivism," and gave the "cult of the primitive . . . an extraordinary foothold on this continent.". . .

White American writers had already portrayed the black

1. Locke called for racial self-expression without didacticism or propaganda.

as a person possessing an instinctive simplicity and abandon that contrasted to the fretful and mechanized existence of the white man. In "Melanctha" (1909), Gertrude Stein suggested that instinctive love is best and most satisfying. In 1914, Vachel Lindsay wrote *The Congo: A Study of the Negro Race.* The titles for the three sections of Lindsay's poem reveal his attitude to his subject—"Their Basic Savagery," "Their Irrepressible High Spirits," and "The Hope of their Religion." Lindsay was followed by several white writers, including Eugene O'Neill, E.E. Cummings, and Sherwood Anderson, who saw the Negro's primitivism as a bulwark against increasing standardization. The South was experiencing a Southern Renaissance, which, like the Harlem Renaissance, was notable for its attempted objectivity and detachment. The region's intellectual interest in the Negro was centered at the University of North Carolina, which was considered to be the most progressive school in the South during the postwar years. The Southern writers and scholars who wrote about the Negro during the period include Julia Peterkin, T.S. Stribling, DuBose Heyward, Paul and Elizabeth Lay Green, Frank Graham, Howard Odum, Edward Sheldon, and Frederich Koch. The works of these writers differed from the better-known primitivistic treatments of the Negro, but they contributed to the growing stereotype by concentrating on black common folk, their dialect, and on picturesque aspects of black life.

THE INFLUENCE OF CARL VAN VECHTEN

Carl Van Vechten's *Nigger Heaven* (1926) was the most influential novel, by a white writer, in establishing the image of the Negro as primitive. The book ran into several editions and sold over 100,000 copies; it initiated an unprecedented nationwide interest in the Negro and clearly demonstrated the commercial value of books written about the Negro. And although primitivism had different and wider uses for some black writers—especially Claude McKay—many of the Renaissance writers ignored the challenge of Locke's pluralistic vision under the bandwagon effect of Carl Van Vechten's *Nigger Heaven.* . . .

Although a detailed analysis of *Nigger Heaven* may not be pertinent here, an evaluation of the influence of Van Vechten and his book on the milieu and literary careers of the Harlem Renaissance writers is. *Nigger Heaven* is the story of

Mary Love, a prim and pretty Harlem librarian, who falls in love with Byron Karson, a struggling young writer. Byron, a recent graduate of the University of Pennsylvania, has been told that he has promise, which he interprets to mean: "pretty good for a colored man." Mary Love cannot take sex and love lightly. Randolph Pettijohn, the numbers king, desires her and offers her marriage. "Ah ain't got no education lak you, but Ah got money, plenty of et, an' Ah got love," he tells her. Byron meanwhile fails to find a job compatible with his level of education and refuses to accept a menial job. The exotic and primitive aspects of Harlem life surround Byron's orgiastic affair with Lasca Sartoris, "a gorgeous brown Messalina of Seventh Avenue." Lasca, however, deserts Byron for Pettijohn. Byron avenges himself by impulsively firing two bullets into the prostrate body of Pettijohn, who has already been killed by Scarlet Creeper. At the end, Byron surrenders helplessly to the police.

The unsettling effect of *Nigger Heaven* is best seen in the controversy its publication caused among early reviewers. Many white reviewers questioned its literary value. The *New Republic* thought the book was more successful as a traveler's guide to Harlem than as a novel, and the unimpressed *Independent* called it dull and disappointing in its attempt "to prove that cultivated Negroes talk French and understand the scores of Opera." However, V.F. Calverton praised *Nigger Heaven* for its straightforward presentation of Negro life, and the *New York Times* critic, in a wholly favorable review, concluded that it was a study of the "plight of Colored intellectuals."

For the black reviewers Eric Walrond and Langston Hughes, the book was truthful and objective; Hughes described it as "the first real passionately throbbing novel of contemporary Negro life." But the balance weighed heavily in favor of the book's black detractors. Offended by the title, many simply refused to read the book, and those who read it found the contents distasteful. Allison Davis accused Van Vechten of having "warped Negro life into a fantastic barbarism," while J.A. Rogers suggested that "Van Vechten Heaven" would be a better title for the book, since Harlem seemed to provide "release of soul" for Van Vechten and others, who were satiated by the meager pleasures offered by the "Nordic" world. According to DuBois, the *Police Gazette* was likely to furnish material of a better quality than *Nigger*

Heaven, which was "neither truthful nor artistic. . . . It is a caricature. It is worse than untruth because it is a mass of half-truths"; it is "ludicrously out of focus and undeniably misleading" in trying to express all racial traits in the cabaret life of Harlem, when the overwhelming majority of blacks had never been to cabarets. "The average colored man in Harlem," DuBois added, "is an everyday laborer, attending church, lodge and movie and is as conservative and as conventional as ordinary working folk elsewhere."

CLAUDE MCKAY'S "IF WE MUST DIE"

Claude McKay's poem "If We Must Die" was written in response to the Harlem race riots of 1919, in which blacks fought back against racially motivated attacks.

IF WE MUST DIE

If we must die, let it not be like hogs
Hunted and penned in an inglorious spot,
While round us bark the mad and hungry dogs,
Making their mock at our accursèd lot.
If we must die, O let us nobly die,
So that our precious blood may not be shed
In vain; then even the monsters we defy
Shall be constrained to honor us though dead!
O kinsmen! we must meet the common foe!
Though far outnumbered let us show us brave,
And for their thousand blows deal one deathblow!
What though before us lies the open grave?
Like men we'll face the murderous, cowardly pack,
Pressed to the wall, dying, but fighting back!

From *The Portable Harlem Renaissance Reader.* Ed. David Levering Lewis. New York: Viking, 1994.

The specter of *Nigger Heaven* lurks behind almost all reviews written after 1926. Benjamin Brawley, Allison Davis, and W.E.B. DuBois asserted that some younger black writers and many white writers were misguided by *Nigger Heaven,* and they argued that the emphasis on the exotic and the primitive, the sensual and the bawdy in the depiction of the Negro was detrimental to the black's political future in the United States.

The fad of primitivism cannot be blamed entirely on Van Vechten or on the group of whites who wrote about the Negro in the twenties, but it is reasonable to conclude that the publication of *Nigger Heaven* made many black writers keenly aware of the commercial possibilities of the primitivistic formula, and made it more difficult for the Harlem Renaissance to develop into a black literary movement. The unusual success of *Nigger Heaven* and later of McKay's *Home to Harlem* clearly indicated an eagerness for works exalting the exotic, the sensual, and the primitive. This interest had "no minor effect on certain members of the Harlem *literati* whose work was just what the Jazz Age ordered," [according to Faith Berry]. Thus, black writers who were willing to describe the exotic scene "had no trouble finding sponsors, publishers and immediate popularity." In his autobiography, *The Big Sea,* Langston Hughes recalled the pessimistic judgment of Wallace Thurman, who thought that the Negro vogue had made the Harlem Renaissance writers "too conscious of ourselves, had flattered and spoiled us and had provided too many easy opportunities for some of us to drink gin and more gin."

It is anybody's guess today as to what might have happened if *Nigger Heaven* had not appeared with a bang at a time when the Harlem Renaissance was just struggling to become a conscious movement. However, the book seems to have had a crippling effect on the self-expression of many black writers by either making it easier to gain success riding the bandwagon of primitivism, or by making it difficult to publish novels that did not fit the profile of the commercial success formula adopted by most publishers for black writers.

The Fugitives, the Agrarians, and the Southern Renaissance

Alexander Karanikas

Along with Chicago, New York, and other centers of literary activity, the American south experienced a renaissance in literature during the modernist era. Central to this Southern resurgence was a group of poets, writers, and critics centered at Vanderbilt University in Nashville, Tennessee. These scholars, who initially referred to themselves as Fugitives, and later as Agrarians, rejected many aspects of southern tradition while simultaneously expressing a strong regional allegiance and a determination to protect their way of life from the threat of industrialization. In this selection, Alexander Karanikas describes the Agrarian movement and its contribution to the southern renaissance. Karanikas, a literary critic, is author of *Tillers of a Myth: Southern Agrarians as Social and Literary Critics*, from which this essay is excerpted.

The group of southern writers, poets, and critics remembered as Agrarians chose to make their presence known through the publication of a symposium, *I'll Take My Stand*, twelve essays prefaced by a Statement of Principles, which appeared late in 1930. Symposia have always been popular with devotees of embattled doctrines who wish to explain their goals and influence public opinion. An impressive array of writers is usually gathered to add authority to the position taken. *I'll Take My Stand* was no exception. The volume had impressive authorship, it wished to influence public opinion, and its doctrines were embattled from the start. The Agrarian movement that it helped to launch contributed heavily to the Southern renaissance in literature which has astonished and enriched our century.

Excerpted from Alexander Karanikas, *Tillers of a Myth: Southern Agrarians as Social and Literary Critics* (Madison & London: University of Wisconsin Press, 1966). Copyright, 1996, by Alexander Karanikas. Reprinted by permission of the author.

The publication of the symposium immediately added a new expression to the nation's vocabulary: Southern Agrarianism. The basic assumptions embraced by those two words touched off a controversy which has continued for over three decades. Since 1930 *I'll Take My Stand* has been a convenient guide for identifying one's attitude toward the South. Liberals invariably regard it as a naïve attempt to recapture the past or, worse, to stem the tides of progress. Conservatives usually praise its defense of tradition and the Southern "way of life." Furthermore, it is to *I'll Take My Stand* that scholars first refer when they discuss Agrarianism as a trend in American literature, even though the Agrarians subsequently wrote much more that qualifies as vital doctrine. Ranging widely in its comment, the book has engaged the interest of theologians, sociologists, economists, political scientists, historians, and literary critics. Regional studies of the South cannot avoid mentioning it; anthologies wishing to document the American heritage and the American "mind" have printed excerpts from it.

The writers who jointly challenged the values of industrial society in the symposium were John Crowe Ransom, Donald Davidson, Frank Lawrence Owsley, John Gould Fletcher, Lyle H. Lanier, Allen Tate, Herman Clarence Nixon, Andrew Nelson Lytle, Robert Penn Warren, John Donald Wade, Henry Blue Kline, and Stark Young. Most of the twelve had taught or studied at Vanderbilt University in Nashville, Tennessee. Several had been students there of John Crowe Ransom, an English professor. Ransom, Tate, Davidson, and Warren had already won a modest national reputation as poets through their publication of a literary magazine, *The Fugitive*, in the mid-twenties. According to Tate, the idea of "doing something about the South" had originated about 1926 and soon afterward the writers involved began to organize their energies toward isolation and regional defiance. In their Statement of Principles in *I'll Take My Stand* they encouraged all Southerners to oppose industrial inroads upon their inherited culture; the intrusion of false progress and prosperity emanating from the old enemy, the North, threatened to completely destroy the South's traditional society. . . .

Southern Heritage and the Fugitive Experience

The Agrarians have been so often mentioned as a movement or school that it may be fruitful at the outset to discuss the major factors resulting in their cohesion. Perhaps the most obvious was their Southern birth and residence. The regional heritage into which they were born, and about which they became acutely aware, naturally influenced their emotional and mental development. The recurrence of "Southern" themes, characters, and settings in their creative work clearly indicates that they never forgot the land on which they had walked barefoot in their youth.

Another crucial factor was their collective experience in writing and editing *The Fugitive*. The Nashville and Vanderbilt University environment alone cannot account for this stage of their association. Other young poets practiced their art on that campus, but they did not qualify as Fugitives; Ransom taught many other English majors, but they did not become Tates and Warrens. Perhaps the most that can be said is that at a particular time in the early twenties a group of potential writers happened to meet, become friends, and eventually exchange poems. Led by Ransom and encouraged by interested citizens of Nashville, these talented poets managed to put out nineteen issues of their journal from 1922 to 1925. *The Fugitive* ranks as one of the finest of the little magazines that enriched the literary twenties. Its success in launching several important careers is already well known. Some authorities also credit it with having initiated the entire Southern literary renaissance. . . . Perhaps even more than the magazine itself, the Fugitive anthology [published in 1928] drew national attention to the Nashville writers. In his review of it, Edmund Wilson speculated that the South now seemed ripe for a literary renaissance comparable to the one in Ireland. "By reason of its very leisure," he wrote, "its detachment from the industrial world and its strong local tradition, the South at present enjoys unique advantages for the cultivation of literature; and it is not impossible to image its playing . . . a role similar in some respects to that which eighteenth-century Ireland has played in respect to modern London."

The Fugitive experience did more than launch the individual careers of its participants; it also taught them the valuable habit of collaboration. They met frequently to discuss poetry, criticism, and philosophy and to help each other revise. The choice of the name "Fugitive," as they explained it, meant they were fleeing from the stultifying Brahminism of the Southern cultural tradition—from its maudlin roman-

ticism, its parochialism, its superficiality, its sentimental-
ism. They wanted to write a hard intellectual poetry, not
particularly local or regional, that escaped the appalling
mediocrity of what had been passing as Southern verse. At
this time of separation from one aspect of their heritage, they
would have approved Howard Mumford Jones's ridicule of
Southern romanticism.

> A thousand stories have created the legend that is the South.
> Way down upon the Suwanee river the sun shines bright on
> my old Kentucky home where, bound for Louisiana, Little
> Eva has a banjo on her knee, and Old Black Joe, Uncle Remus
> and Miss Sally's little boy listen to the mocking-bird and
> watch a sweet chariot swing low one frosty morning! The gal-
> lant Pelham and his comrades bend forever over the hands of
> adorable girls in crinoline; under the duelling oaks Colonel
> Carter of Cartersville and Marse Chan blaze away at each
> other with pistols by the light of the silvery moon on Mobile
> Bay. It matters little now, Lorena, the past is in the eternal
> past, for I saw thee once, once only, it was on a July midnight
> and the full-orbed moon looked down where a despot's heel
> is on thy shore, Maryland, my Maryland.

SPIRITUAL SECESSION

The Fugitives' rejection of the overly romantic in favor of the
classical and intellectual, however, comprised only a narrow
basis for disaffiliation from the Southern tradition. Indeed, for
a number of reasons, the Fugitives soon developed a very mil-
itant loyalty to their region's culture. This process went hand
in hand with a wider ideological unity as they found themselves in rebellion against the majority, or non-Southern portion, of American culture. Another important aspect of their
cohesion, therefore, is their identity as a Southern manifesta-
tion of post–World War I disillusionment. Although the Fugitive-Agrarians never renounced their American citizenship
or entertained serious thoughts of expatriation, *I'll Take My
Stand* did signify a spiritual secession from the nation as a
whole. Some critics deemed it a social and cultural revolution; others called it simply another example of personal
alienation. No doubt it had elements of both.

The twenties were rife with instances of such alienation.
Hardly any writer of the time accepted at its face value the
arrogant commercialism which touted itself as the new civilization. Writers fled from the monstrous money power in
every geographical and spiritual direction. Never before had
art been in such peril of becoming merely a commodity in a

community of Babbitts.[1] Many writers, therefore, sought ways in which to rebel and still create without any loss of integrity. Among other observers, Solomon Fishman has written about how this splintering of the American cultural tradition affected the artist. Fishman includes the Southern Agrarians among those he talks about in *The Disinherited of Art*. Of them and other disaffiliates he says:

> The key to this cycle of American literature is the term "alienation." It includes a whole constellation of attitudes associated with the literary twenties: isolation, individualism, bohemianism, dissidence, rejection, rebellion, disillusion, pessimism, defeat, decadence, disintegration, escape, exile. Alienation, in brief, implies a centrifugal impulse, the detachment of the particle from the mass.

Some of these attitudes apply to the Agrarians; others do not. In regard to "escape" and "exile," the Nashville writers refused to join the exciting exodus to Paris, resisting the bohemian lures and intellectual pleasures so movingly recounted by Malcolm Cowley in *Exile's Return* (1934). Not that Ransom and Tate loved art any less than did the genuine expatriates. They might have made Nashville into a remote mountain outpost of dadaism, for instance, but they did not for a number of explainable reasons. They and some of their associates had been to Europe to soldier, to study, or to write; but the Europe of Ransom and Tate was not the animated bohemia of Malcolm Cowley. Nowhere in Agrarian literature can we find praise for such a rootless, cosmopolitan, and "modern" life. Even had the Agrarians been able to dwell for long in the Paris cafés, it is doubtful that their latent traditionalism would have permitted any deep dissociation from home, their "region of memory." Indeed, as happened with certain other expatriates like Thomas Wolfe, self-exile abroad might have had the effect of attaching them even more strongly to their native land.

However, "rejection" and "disillusion" were certainly two attributes of the Agrarian rebellion. They rejected industrialism, the prevailing "American way"; certain critics have accused the Agrarians of also rejecting everything which contributed to the dissolution of the medieval world. They were disillusioned with democracy because of the rise of an industrial society and the defeat of the South in the Civil

---

1. a reference to George Babbitt, the crassly materialistic and conformist main character of Sinclair Lewis's novel *Babbitt*

War. They referred to democracy in the North as a "plutocracy" which travestied the ideals of the founding fathers. They said that the North had defeated the South only because it had more industries producing more and better arms. Thus, industrialism, along with science and technology, had long been an enemy of the traditional South.

FINDING T.S. ELIOT

In addition to the general postwar disillusionment, another source of Agrarian cohesion was the discovery of T.S. Eliot's teachings about the value to literature of a social tradition. *The Sacred Wood* had appeared in 1920. In it Eliot included his epochal essay, "Tradition and the Individual Talent." Two years later he wrote *The Waste Land.* Of the Fugitives it was Tate who "found" Eliot and soon began, as he affirmed, "an impertinent campaign in Eliot's behalf in the South." We may assume the campaign engaged, first of all, his Fugitive friends. Perhaps Ransom's subsequent violent condemnation of *The Waste Land* had some remote connection with Tate's increasing addiction to Eliot's literary theories, to his drifting away from neoclassicism. Be that as it may, Eliot's well-known argument runs as follows. Since the modern world is spiritually splintered—without a control in faith, often with no faith at all—the writer of sensibility needs a *tradition* to validate his views, to nourish his art, to formalize his life, and to find and recognize his God. It must be a concrete and usable tradition, unlike that of the Neo-Humanists which was too abstract; it must be anchored in a place and a time. For Eliot the time of Dante seemed best to fulfill these requirements. In an organic, enduring, traditional society the great artist, having no need to invent his subject matter, can concentrate his creative energies on brilliant, formal, aesthetic realization.

Learning from Eliot the literary value of a tradition, the Agrarians—so the argument goes—searched their own backgrounds and found in the Old South the necessary tradition. The Old South had an aristocracy, a kind of serfdom, a ritualized religion, a code; in short, it was a stable, organic, and spiritually unified society like the Middle Ages. It was also merely a legend, one might be quick to say; but as an inspiration for literature, need a legend be scientifically verifiable?

So much, at the moment, for the argument that Eliot's theories were a possible cause of Agrarian coalescence. That

ALLEN TATE'S ENGAGEMENT WITH THE PAST
Richard Gray cites Allen Tate's poem "Ode to the Confederate Dead" to illustrate the poet's technique of involving the reader in the creation of a southern myth.

[Tate uses] myth as an extension of fact rather than a denial of it. . . . That is to say, his purpose in describing the plantation South in the way he does is not to present a complete distortion of the historical past, but to articulate what *might* have happened if its best energies had been realized. . . . It is a sophisticated strategy, but an unconcealed one, so that readers are never in doubt of what is happening.

Not only is it unconcealed: in Tate's best work, this engagement of the present with the past is even emphasized, and this primarily by means of the device of the narrator. In the "Ode to the Confederate Dead," for example, the conflict between the "active faith" of previous generations and the fragmentation of the present one is presented in terms of a series of memories. The narrator, a man who characterizes the contemporary failure, stands by the monuments raised to those killed fighting for the South during the Civil War; and as he describes their lives, or rather what he imagines their lives to have been, the description is transformed into a celebration. The persons described are metamorphosed into an heroic alternative to the plight of the person describing. That is the drama of the poem, accounting for the extraordinary poignancy of lines like the following.

> Turn your eyes to the immoderate past,
> Turn to the inscrutable infantry rising
> Demons out of the earth—they will not last.
> Stonewall, Stonewall, and the sunken fields of hemp,
> Shiloh, Antietam, Malvern Hill, Bull Run.
> Lost in that orient of the thick-and-fast
> You will curse the setting sun.
>
> Cursing only the leaves crying
> Like an old man in a storm
> You hear the shout, the crazy hemlocks point
> With troubled fingers to the silence which
> Smothers you, a mummy, in time.

The point, as I see it, is that here and elsewhere in the poem Tate actually dramatizes the mythologizing process. . . . The reader shares with an identifiable narrator the experience of creating an idea, a complex of possibilities, out of a historical fact.

Richard Gray, *The Literature of Memory: Modern Writers of the American South.* Baltimore: Johns Hopkins University Press, 1977.

other causes were also at work almost goes without saying. Any literary history of the 1920's has to reflect the multiple alienations among its writers and that most of these alienations converged upon an anti-industrial, anti-machine, anti-capitalist bias. The Southern Agrarians, no doubt influenced by the general spirit of dissent, emerged as one of the trends most critical of civilization in the United States. It was the particularity of the Agrarians, their special kind of revolt, their basic assumptions, and the unusual conditions they made for accepting nationalism which set them apart.

Because they were more or less the products of their times, the Agrarians reacted similarly to three major influences: the varied sources of regional discord, the challenge posed by the "New South," and their own role in the Southern literary renaissance. Certain events in each of these categories further strengthened their personal ties, clarified and deepened their common ideology, and hardened their will to attack the revealed enemy. As for regional discord and the challenge of the New South, the Scopes trial[2] and the labor violence at Gastonia, [North Carolina, in 1929] were only two major events symbolizing the danger to the Southern tradition; even more insidious were the thousand-and-one signs that the money-hungry New Southerners were increasing their power everywhere.

PROGRESS AND REACTION

Strong forces were at work undermining the Southern tradition and many of them formed part of the aftermath of World War I: new wealth for the middle classes (much of it from military camps), new war-born industries, a confident commercial spirit, wider opportunities for the returned veterans both Negro and white, a stronger nationalism dimming further the memory of the Civil War, a vast uneasiness among the Negro people, and the beginnings of a critical literature. Other forces included the spread of modernism in the Southern churches, the growth of liberal curricula in education, a wider acceptance of science, and a more enlightened and aggressive press.

Every move forward, however, produced a countermove on the part of those who feared change. Professor Edwin

2. a 1925 trial in Dayton, Tennessee, in which science teacher John T. Scopes was accused of violating Tennessee's law against teaching Darwin's theory of evolution in public schools; also known as the "monkey trial"

Mims, head of the English department at Vanderbilt, under whom Ransom and other Agrarians taught or studied, saw this process in 1926 when he wrote in *The Advancing South:*

> The reactionary forces, stung to renewed action by evidences of the growth of the progressive spirit, are more outspoken, more belligerent, more apparently victorious, but their citadels are gradually being undermined by the rising tide of liberalism. The South, once so potent in the life of the nation, is passing through not only a remarkable industrial development, but an even more important and significant intellectual renascence.

By the end of the twenties the Agrarians had taken their stand with those "reactionary forces" that Mims spoke about. The epithet "Young Confederates" might have received added point from their going to the refrain of the Confederate marching song "Dixie" for their title, *I'll Take My Stand.* On the other hand, advocates of the New South like Mims welcomed progress, liberalism, and industrialism. Indeed, in more ways than one, *I'll Take My Stand* was written as an answer to *The Advancing South.*

The simple dichotomy between progress and reaction which Mims used, however, had deeper and more complex implications which must be briefly examined here. Contrary to what the Agrarians were to believe, the backward Southern hinterland did not always reject every influence coming from the North; and not all of these influences, by any standard, could qualify as liberal or progressive. For example, ugly race riots in Chicago and elsewhere in the North influenced the revival of the Ku Klux Klan, with its new headquarters in Atlanta. Various hysterias of national origin found regional sustenance in the South. The great steel strike in 1919, led by socialists like William Z. Foster, proved to many that Bolshevism[3] was possible in America; in the view of A. Mitchell Palmer, the Attorney-General, it had to be crushed both above and below the Mason-Dixon line, by the use of midnight raids, jailings, and deportations. The traditional xenophobia that had often deprived Southern industry of the skills of immigrants now increased in magnitude, as the whole nation prepared laws to limit further immigration. The widely used epithet "radical alien" had a Southern definition, often meaning a "damned Yankee" or anyone interfering with the caste system under which the

3. Communist revolution

Negro lived. Full-page horror stories in Northern tabloids depicting scenes of a coming "red terror" or "yellow peril" had their Southern counterparts in neurotic fears expressed about the Negro, the Jew, and the Catholic. There were "liberal" books written that accuse the fundamentalists of conspiring to set up a theocracy, a union of church and state in which science and reason would have to surrender to the Bible as the revealed word of God. Conversely, many a fundamentalist preacher blared forth the warning that godless scientists and teachers were trying to impose atheism on the youth, to "destroy" Jesus Christ, under the pretense of advancing progress and truth.

THE SOUTHERN LITERARY RENAISSANCE

In the midst of these many tensions—some critics say because of them—the South in the twenties experienced an upsurge in literary creation. Louise Cowan loses no time in assigning the credit; her Introduction [to *The Fugitive Group* (1959)] begins, "The Nashville poets who published the little magazine *The Fugitive* during the early half of the 1920's have the distinction of being the inaugurators of the Southern literary renaissance." The . . . compilation of *Southern Renascence* (1953), together with so much else since the twenties, testifies to the rich fulfillment of what was then more a welcomed promise than a fact. For several decades no Southerner has needed to feel embarrassed by the literary output of his region. However, in the days when H.L. Mencken derided the South as the "Sahara of the Bozart" and when the Ku Klux Klan and the "monkey trial" were powerful regional symbols, it was a novel idea indeed to expect great literature from the land of lynch mobs and boll weevils. Some writers doubted that what was happening should be dignified with the title "renaissance." Others completely overlooked the latent literary impulse and sought to rationalize its apparent dearth. Thus, the novelist Corra Harris, writing with unmistakable charm, explained: "We are less intellectual than Northern people because we have more natural sense and do not feel, as they do, an artificial craving for culture to make up for a native deficiency." Miss Harris, it should be understood, was not trying to be funny.

During the mid-twenties and after, the reference by Edwin Mims to a "renascence" found many echoes both North and South. In commentaries of the late twenties, various reasons were given for the literary awakening. First was the active sense of tragedy and evil possessed by Southerners as being the only Americans ever to have suffered military defeat—indeed, to have known the violent despoilment of their homes. From its knowledge of death and grief the South had a deeper and more profound source for its art than did other regions. In William Faulkner, the South had a prime example of a writer who plumbed the most fearful reaches of this source. Secondly, the Southerner felt the sense of having lost a "precious object" because of the gradual demise of the Southern tradition and the "backward glance" of the bereaved Southern writer after World War I. According to at least one important Agrarian, Allen Tate, it was this look toward the past which more than anything else inspired the literary renaissance. It certainly inspired Tate's great "Ode to the Confederate Dead" and his novel *The Fathers*. A third causative factor for the upsurge in regional writing was thought to be the passive nature of Southern society, its rural backwardness, its lack of nervous hurry-and-go. Edmund Wilson commented in 1928, "It is perhaps the only section of the country where the educated classes possess at once enough cultivation, existences sufficiently unhurried and an intimate enough share in the life of their communities to produce intellectual work of real richness and depth." A fourth cause was alleged to be the influence of the industrial and social revolution loosely labeled the "New South," with its worship of mass education, science, modernism, commerce, and progress. To the liberal, this revolution was bound to be the reason for anything good, including literature, that was produced in his region.

Even those observers who welcomed the signs of progress —in terms of what today is called the gross national product—sensed something different in the South, a residue of emotions unlike any to be found elsewhere. E.C. Lindeman touched upon this facet of the South when he wrote: "And there is something about the people—something deep and frightening at times, something which has grown out of suffering, something indigenous which might, if it were creatively released, provide the most potent stimulus for cultural advance since New England civilization disintegrated." Still another source sensitive to incipient trends, the *Saturday Review of Literature,* commented that if that malaise of "the restless mind which results in literature is stirring any

where in the United States it should be in the new South.
The South is a box of fireworks awaiting a spark." This condition resulted mainly from the "racial and regional characteristics" diametrically opposed to the "leveling influence of
prosperous mechanization."

In 1927 Herschel Brickell wrote, "The dreary desert [the
South] has become an oasis, at the moment the center of literary interest in this country." He found it no "exaggeration
to speak of a renaissance of literature in the South." He
praised Faulkner as "delightfully cosmopolitan" and cred-
ited him with knowing as much about writing "the prose to
which we give the convenient tag 'modern' as any habitué of
the corner made by the crossing of the Boulevards Montparnasse and Raspoil in Paris. . . ." Among the newer poets
Brickell singled out Tate, Ransom, and Fletcher as three who
showed that "the Renaissance does not lack its singers."

Howard Mumford Jones, an important witness of the
South's cultural scene, found not only a social awakening
but also bewilderment. Writing in 1929 about the Southern
legend, Jones said that nobody in the North knew what was
going on in the cultural life of the South and, for that matter,
not many Southerners knew either. "The intellectual quick-
ening which has accompanied its industrial development
has resulted in a series of bewildering shifts of values. It is a
Georgia newspaper, the Columbus *Enquirer Sun,* which first
effectively shattered the silence of the Ku Klux Klan." He
snapped back at those who attacked the South while over-
looking serious problems in their own back yard. "It might
be interesting," he wrote, "to weigh the stupidities of the
Dayton trial in a little Tennessee town against the cruelties
of the Sacco-Vanzetti case[4] in cultivated Massachusetts, just
as it would be possible to balance the power of travelling
evangelists to sway illiterate whites against the morbid hold
of tabloid newspapers over the emotions of half-baked clerks
and silly stenographers." Lest the enthusiasts overpraise the
new Southern literature, Jones soon asked the question: Is
there a Southern renaissance? No, was his answer, at least
not yet. He praised the book reviews of Donald Davidson and
others, but he disliked Ransom's and Tate's nostalgia for the
civilization of the slave system. Jones maintained, finally,

---

4. the 1920–21 murder trial of Italian immigrants Nicola Sacco and Bartolomeo
Vanzetti; critics believed the defendants, who were subsequently executed in 1927, received an unfair trial due to their anarchist views.

that there would be no great literature, "merely regional studies and topical books," until the South again stood for a significant idea.

Today, literary historians no longer doubt the reality of the renaissance or the vital role played in it by the Fugitive-Agrarians. Their part in the awakening helps to identify them as a distinct school; what they did is usually discussed as a collective effort. All the group's cohesive factors were reflected in the writing of *I'll Take My Stand.* Its importance as a generative and unifying force cannot be exaggerated; its articles of belief created a common intellectual ground for the participants. The "Twelve Southerners" were busy with research and writing projects of their own; yet they joined to initiate the new social and cultural movement and assumed responsibility for its success or failure.

CHAPTER 5

Evaluating American Modernists and Their Contribution

American Modernism

American Modernists Revolted Against Genteel Tradition

Malcolm Cowley

Malcolm Cowley was a poet, author, literary critic, and the editor of numerous books on American literature. The following selection was excerpted from his foreword to his book *After the Genteel Tradition: American Writers Since 1910*, which was originally published in 1936. Cowley contends that the American writers of the 1920s (who have subsequently been labeled modernists) deliberately rebelled against a genteel tradition. This tradition was characterized by a puritanical morality, excessive optimism, and a reverence for English literary forms. American modernists rejected these traditions in favor of sensuality, realism, and an emphasis on distinctively American literary styles and subject matter.

December 10, 1930, was a significant date. At a meeting in Stockholm attended by the King of Sweden and the Swedish Academy, the Nobel Prize was formally presented to the author of "Main Street" and "Babbitt." He was the first American to be measured and weighed and certified as an international giant of letters. . . .

Two days later, when Sinclair Lewis made his acceptance speech before the Swedish Academy, . . . "The American Fear of Literature" was his subject. His address was front-page news in the American papers, and it remains a historical document of considerable meaning.

It seems that Dr. Henry Van Dyke had taken umbrage. Speaking as a member of the American Academy of Arts and Letters, he declaimed that the award of the Nobel Prize to a man who had scoffed so much at American institutions was an insult to our country. Lewis, after reporting the incident,

Excerpted from Malcolm Cowley, Foreword, *After the Genteel Tradition*, edited by Malcolm Cowley (Gloucester, MA: Peter Smith, 1936).

suggested to his Swedish audience that Dr. Van Dyke might
call out the Marines and have them landed in Stockholm to
protect American literary rights. But he also had more serious comments to offer. Dr. Van Dyke, he said, was an almost
official representative of the "genteel tradition" that for half
a century had been the persistent enemy and slow poisoner
of good writing in America:

> Most of us—not readers alone but even writers—are still
> afraid of any literature which is not a glorification of every-
> thing American, a glorification of our faults as well as our
> virtues. . . . We still most revere the writers for the popular
> magazines who in a hearty and edifying chorus chant that
> the America of a hundred and twenty million population is
> still as simple, as pastoral, as it was when it had but forty mil-
> lion . . . that, in fine, America has gone through the revolu-
> tionary change from rustic colony to world empire without
> having in the least altered the bucolic and Puritanic simplic-
> ity of Uncle Sam.

In the new American empire it was possible for a writer
to make plenty of money: he could have his butler and his
motor and his villa at Palm Beach, where he could mingle
almost on terms of equality with the barons of banking. But
still, if he took his profession seriously,

> . . . he is oppressed by something worse than poverty—by the
> feeling that what he creates does not matter, that he is ex-
> pected by his readers to be only a decorator or a clown, or
> that he is good-naturedly accepted as a scoffer whose bark is
> probably worse than his bite and who certainly does not
> count in a land that produces eighty-story buildings, motors
> by the million and wheat by the billions of bushels. And he
> has no institution, no group, to which he can turn for inspi-
> ration, whose criticism he can accept and whose praise will
> be precious to him.

Lewis began to call the roll of the groups or institutions
that ought to be friendly to creative writing. The American
Academy? It contains so very few of the first-rate writers that
"it does not represent literary America of today—it represents only Henry Wadsworth Longfellow." The American
universities? Some four of them have shown some real interest in contemporary creative literature. But most of the
others have exemplified "the divorce in America of intellectual life from all authentic standards of importance and reality. . . . To a true-blue professor of American literature in
an American university, literature is not something that a
plain human being, living today, painfully sits down to pro-

duce. No, it is something dead; it is something magically produced by superhuman beings who must, if they are to be regarded as artists at all, have died at least one hundred years before the diabolical invention of the typewriter." And what about our literary criticism? "Most of it," Lewis said, "has been a chill and insignificant activity pursued by jealous spinsters, ex-baseball reporters and acid professors." There have been no valid standards because there has been nobody capable of setting them up. Worse still, there have been the false and life-denying standards of critics like William Dean Howells and Henry Van Dyke, who were "effusively seeking to guide America into becoming a pale edition of an English cathedral town."

Fortunately the younger generation has untied itself from their stepmotherly apron strings. A whole new literature has come of age, a literature that tries to express the sweep and strength and beauty-in-ugliness of the American empire as it is today. There are a dozen American writers worthy of receiving the Nobel Prize. But no matter which of them had been chosen, there would have been the same outcry from the academicians and from the Humanists drily embattled in their college libraries.

In the most significant part of his speech, Lewis enumerated the great men and great achievements of the 1920's. He imagined what the older and more genteel critics would have said to each possible choice of the Swedish Academy:

Suppose you had taken Theodore Dreiser.

Now to me, as to many other American writers, Dreiser more than any other man, marching alone, usually unappreciated, often hated, has cleared the trail from Victorian and Howellsian timidity and gentility in American fiction to honesty and boldness and passion of life. Without his pioneering, I doubt if any of us could, unless we liked to be sent to jail, express life and beauty and terror. . . .

Yet had you given the prize to Mr. Dreiser, you would have heard groans from America; you would have heard . . . that his style is cumbersome, that his choice of words is insensitive, that his books are interminable. And certainly respectable scholars would complain that in Mr. Dreiser's world, men and women are often sinful and tragic and despairing, instead of being forever sunny and full of song and virtue, as befits authentic Americans.

And had you chosen Mr. Eugene O'Neill, who has done nothing much in American drama save to transform it utterly, in ten or twelve years, from a false world of neat and competent trickery to a world of splendor and fear and greatness, you would have been reminded that he has done something far worse than scoffing—he has seen life as not to be neatly arranged in the study of a scholar but as a terrifying, magnificent and often quite horrible thing akin to the tornado, the earthquake, the devastating fire.

And had you given Mr. James Branch Cabell the prize, you would have been told that he is too fantastically malicious. So would you have been told that Miss Willa Cather, for all the homely virtue of her novels concerning the peasants of Nebraska, has in her novel, "A Lost Lady," been so untrue to America's patent and perpetual and possibly tedious virtuousness as to picture an abandoned woman who remains, nevertheless, uncannily charming even to the virtuous, in a story without any moral; that Mr. Henry Mencken is the worst of all scoffers; that Mr. Sherwood Anderson viciously errs in considering sex as important a force in life as fishing; that Mr. Upton Sinclair, being a Socialist, sins against the perfectness of American capitalistic mass production; that Mr. Joseph Hergesheimer is un-American in regarding graciousness of manner and beauty of surface as of some importance in the endurance of daily life; and that Mr. Ernest Hemingway is not only too young but, far worse, uses language which should be unknown to gentlemen; that he acknowledges drunkenness as one of man's eternal ways to happiness. . . .

Dreiser and O'Neill, James Branch Cabell, Willa Cather, H. L. Mencken, Sherwood Anderson, Upton Sinclair, Joseph Hergesheimer and Ernest Hemingway: this list of distinguished writers needs a few emendations. The speaker himself should most certainly be added to it. So too should Van Wyck Brooks, the first critic to express many of the ideas that Lewis was presenting to the Swedish Academy. So too should "the really original and vital poets, Edna St. Vincent Millay and Carl Sandburg, Robinson Jeffers and Vachel Lindsay and Edgar Lee Masters," mentioned in another passage of the same address. On the other hand, Ernest Hemingway might have been omitted here, since he belongs by age and spirit to another generation. But with a very few changes of this order, the list would be definitive. Sinclair Lewis, in his speech at Stockholm, had named the prominent figures of the era in American literature that was just then drawing to a close.

But he did more than merely catalogue the "great men and women in American literary life today." He also specified the reasons for their greatness (and in quoting what the academic critics would say against them he was praising them still more, by indirection). Thus, Dreiser had "cleared the way from Victorian and Howellsian timidity and gentility." O'Neill had seen life "as not to be neatly arranged in the study of a scholar." Willa Cather had been "so untrue to America's patent and perpetual and possibly tedious virtuousness as to picture an abandoned woman . . . in a story without any moral" (though the moral was there, if Lewis had tried to find it). Mencken had offended the godly by scoffing at evangelism; Sherwood Anderson had offended them by not scoffing at sex; and even Hemingway had fitted into the same pattern of negation and defiance by using "language which should be unknown to gentlemen." It seemed to Sinclair Lewis that all these writers were united into one crusading army by their revolt against the genteel tradition.

But just what was the nature of this tradition against which so many writers were rebelling?

In its general outlines it resembled Victorianism in England, but it was less relieved and softened by hypocrisy. The real Victorians had the privilege of leading their private lives behind locked doors—some of them locked so securely that they have never yet been opened—but the Americans of the eighties and nineties lived as it were behind plate-glass windows. There is a story repeated by Burton Rascoe in his introduction to "The Smart Set Anthology" that sets the tone of the whole period. It seems that Robert Louis Stevenson, passing through New York, paid a visit to Richard Watson Gilder, the editor and high panjandrum of the *Century Magazine.* Mr. Gilder happened to have heard some not very terrible rumors about Mr. Stevenson's private affairs. In England these rumors would have been disregarded, on the ground that they had never been printed in the *Times* or made the subject of a debate in Parliament. But to Mr. Gilder they indicated that his guest was not quite respectable, and so he refused to invite Mr. Stevenson into his editorial sanctum. . . . When Edward VII, then Prince of Wales, was entertained by American ladies at Lake Lucerne, near Saratoga, he surprised and horrified them by the freedom of his manners. They had expected "something more seemly" from Victoria's son.

The truth is that Victorianism, transplanted to America, had become intermingled with native characteristics, and notably with New England Puritanism. This in turn had become the tendency to divide practical life from the life of the mind, just as Sunday was divided from the days of the week. In "America's Coming-of-Age," Van Wyck Brooks discusses the subject with great acuteness. Practical life, he says, had become a hard, dirty scramble in which the only justifiable aim was to get ahead, be successful, make money—but meanwhile the life of the mind was supposed to be kept as spotless and fragrant with lavender as a white Sunday dress. The two sides of Puritanism might be united in a single man—for example, in Andrew Carnegie, who made a fortune by manufacturing armor plate and then spent it in promoting peace by impractical methods, and in building libraries where the men in his rolling mills, who worked twelve hours a day and seven days a week, would never have time to acquire culture.

But the Victorian spirit in America was also intermingled with the defiant optimism that grew out of pioneering and land speculation. There were always better farms to the westward. Prices would always go up, and the mortgage would be paid at the last moment, even while the sheriff was pounding at the door. . . . With this background of belief, many American books had the same innocently hopeful atmosphere as American real-estate developments; they were like cement sidewalks laid down in the wilderness with the absolute certainty that, some day, there would be a skyscraper on this corner lot now covered with sagebrush. To fail or even to be discouraged in the midst of so many opportunities was not only a sign of weakness; it was a sin like adultery, and it could scarcely be mentioned in novels written for decent people.

These two features of the genteel tradition are no more important than others that have been less widely analyzed or attacked. For example, the tradition was connected with and encouraged by the new American bourgeoisie that had grown up after the Civil War. Many of the genteel writers were themselves poor devils starving in garrets, but the general tone was set by men like Howells and Gilder and Henry Van Dyke who were used to eating at the tables of millionaires. And the general tone was refined and bloodless. "Culture" was regarded as a foreign accomplishment to be learned and exhibited like golf or table manners—almost as a commodity to be bought like a new John Keats manuscript for Mr. Morgan's library. In any case, it had nothing to do with the back streets where people quarreled and made love and died without benefit of Samuel Coleridge or Walter Pater.

Still another feature of the genteel tradition was that it centered on the Atlantic seaboard, with its magazines and publishing houses in Boston or New York and its shrines of culture at Harvard and Princeton. But these were minor centers and minor shrines. In reality the genteel writers looked toward London and Oxford and shared their intellectual enthusiasms at a distance of several years. There had ceased to be any continuous literary life in the United States; and writers here were oppressed by a feeling of provincialism, of being away from the heart of things and following other people's fashions.

In revolting against gentility, the writers praised by Sinclair Lewis had revolted against every feature of the genteel tradition. Instead of being Puritan, they were not only anti-Puritan but in some cases candidly sensual, given to praising sexual freedom and to justifying drunkenness "as one of man's eternal ways to happiness." Instead of being optimistic, they painted a world in which "men and women are often sinful and tragic and despairing." Instead of belonging to the North Atlantic seaboard, most of them had their roots in the Midwest or the South. Instead of being inspired by English models, they either tried to create a strictly American tradition, in the American language, with saints and folk heroes like Abe Lincoln and Johnny Appleseed, or else they followed theories like socialism and Freudianism that had never played much part in English thought, having originated on the continent of Europe. But most of all, the new literary movement was a revolt of the middle classes against conventions that did not fit their own lives and prevented them from using their first-hand observations.

On this last point, Sinclair Lewis was unusually eloquent:

> I had realized in reading [Honoré de] Balzac and [Charles] Dickens that it was possible to describe French and English common people as one actually saw them. But it had never occurred to me that one might without indecency write of the people of Sauk Centre, Minnesota, as one felt about them. Our fictional tradition, you see, was that all of us in Midwestern villages were altogether noble and happy; that not one of us would exchange the neighborly bliss of living on Main Street for the heathen gaudiness of New York or Paris or Stockholm. But in Mr. [Hamlin] Garland's "Main Traveled Roads" I discovered that there was one man who believed that Midwestern peasants were sometimes bewildered and hungry and vile—and heroic. And, given this vision, I was released; I could write of life as living life.

American Modernists Were Defenders of Genteel Tradition

Marcus Klein

Marcus Klein rejects the common view that American modernists rebelled against genteel cultural and literary traditions. He states that the American modernists were members of a social aristocracy who resented their loss of privileged status in the wake of urbanization and mass immigration during the early decades of the twentieth century. According to Klein, the writings of F. Scott Fitzgerald, T.S. Eliot, Ezra Pound, and others reveal that the modernists were disturbed by what they perceived as the mongrelization of American society due to the influx of foreign immigrants—especially southern and eastern Europeans, Slavs, and Jews. Klein is a professor emeritus at the State University of New York at Buffalo. He has edited and written several books on American literature, including *Foreigners: The Making of American Literature, 1900–1940*, from which this excerpt was taken.

New writers in a moment of what was indeed crucial historical change, circa 1912, had put themselves to the invention of new expression: a new language (which, in the words of T.S. Eliot, struggled "to express new objects, new groups of objects, new feelings, new aspects") and new techniques, new freedoms, new conventions, the pressure in poetry of original observation, "direct treatment of the 'thing,'"[1] original discovery, and experiment above all. The strategy in turn had demanded an attitude toward history. And what was invented by Ezra Pound and Eliot and some others was an ingenious paradox: lacking a plausible Golden Age or a rele-

1. Ezra Pound, "A Retrospect," 1918

vant Augustan Age, there could be a *new tradition,* which would serve as a tactical base for an attack upon the present. The present was conceived to be the desuetude[2] of romanticism. . . . Pound, by way of direct assault on the "emotional slither" of most poetry written since 1450, discovered the true classics in Anglo-Saxon, Provençal, early Italian, and then subsequently Chinese and Japanese literatures. Eliot assumed leadership of the revival of the metaphysical poets when he reviewed Herbert Grierson's anthology in 1921, and took the occasion to eliminate from the canon most poets from John Milton through Alfred Tennyson. And by how much the new tradition was a tactic, conceived for its present usefulness in liberating poetry from the immediate past, was to be indicated by the fact that Eliot not so long afterward, in the period after 1933, read back into the canon many of those poets whom he primarily had succeeded in banishing.

But this discovered tradition, no matter where discovered and no matter how arbitrary or fleeting its contents, had never been only a congeries[3] of serviceable inventions. For one thing, it had enjoined a tremendous amount of scholarship or, more exactly, a taste for the supposed authority of traditional literary-historical scholarship—from which followed the virtual definition of literature as the enterprise of an intellectual aristocracy. Like modern science, as was quite part of the general intention, literature was to require special academic training, and of course not everyone went to the university. To a remarkable extent, the modernism made by Americans had a Harvard education.

More important, the new tradition, conceived to allow a new progress for poetry, in fact denied progress as, for all of its recovery of historical fragments, it denied history. History became static omnipresence. In "Tradition and the Individual Talent," that singularly influential essay, Eliot had put the matter most directly. The "historical sense," he said, was "nearly indispensable to any one who would continue to be a poet beyond his twenty-fifth year," but then he had gone on to define the key term in such a way that history was neither sequential nor consequential, but a kind of completeness in itself, unmoving and immovable:

the historical sense involves a perception, not only of the

2. discontinuance   3. collection

past-ness of the past, but of its presence; the historical sense compels a man to write not merely with his own generation in his bones, but with a feeling that the whole of the literature of Europe from Homer and within it the whole of the literature of his own country has a simultaneous existence and composes a simultaneous order. This historical sense, which is a sense of the timeless as well as of the temporal and of the timeless and of the temporal together, is what makes a writer traditional. And it is at the same time what makes a writer most acutely conscious of his place in time, of his own contemporaneity.

And it followed that the writer who was to be traditional and contemporaneous at the same time had also to be reactionary, in the pure sense that he would approach the present and define himself in the present by asserting the presentness of the past, which was to say, precisely, the tradition of the past. . . .

A DISPOSSESSED SOCIAL ARISTOCRACY

American makers of the modern movement were with remarkable uniformity of a certain class, one which might well think of itself as a dispossessed social aristocracy. Besides Eliot, Pound, and Ernest Hemingway, the makers included Gertrude Stein, Wallace Stevens, E.E. Cummings, Marianne Moore, F. Scott Fitzgerald, Hilda Doolittle, John Dos Passos (in his earlier career), John Gould Fletcher, perhaps William Faulkner, and some dozens of others in supporting roles— Margaret Anderson, Sylvia Beach, Gorham Munson, and so on. They were the inventors. They were all of a distinct generation, all with the exception of Stein and Stevens born in the 1880s and 1890s. (Gertrude Stein was born in 1874, Stevens in 1879.) More to the point, by actual fact of birth they tended—as in the cases of Eliot, Pound, Cummings, Stevens, Moore, Faulkner, Fitzgerald, and Stein and Dos Passos—to come from old American stock. (Gertrude Stein was Jewish, but from an old American family nonetheless; her *Making of Americans* was in one aspect a monograph on that subject. Dos Passos was a bastard, but raised in such circumstances that he had standing in elevated society; he was a kind of royal bastard.) The American Eliots, as T.S. Eliot well knew, dated back to the year 1670. Ezra Pound, as Pound well knew, went back somewhat further, on the Pound side to the 1630s and on his mother's side back to circa 1623. Moreover, the various makers almost without exception came from families which either were wealthy or had been wealthy. These inventors constituted, whether by actual fact of birth or not, a beleaguered gentry, forced quite abruptly, by real history, to assert a glamorous antiquity. It was another function of the "tradition," then, that it provided a homeland for upper-class aliens.

The post hoc myth, adduced principally by Malcolm Cowley in *Exiles' Return*, was that a generation's exile, metaphorical and literal, was consequent upon disillusion: the American makers of modern literature were refugees from an America that suddenly had lost its old idealisms and that had in the period after the First World War gone wildly, grubbily commercial. But that case for the matter was at best an ideal approximation. For one thing, the commercialism which putatively had disillusioned these idealists had been as much a fact of the 1880s, say, as of the 1910s and 1920s. If anything, the sheer business thrust of American civilization had been the more blatant in the years of the robber barons, prior to the turn of the century. For another thing, it was precisely in the time of the coming-of-age of these idealists that the muckrakers were revealing the symbiotic corruption of the leading businessmen and the leading politicians in Eliot's St. Louis, Ezra Pound's Philadelphia, Hemingway's Chicago, and the Minneapolis next door to F. Scott Fitzgerald's St. Paul. And those fine old American values (to which, most particularly, Fitzgerald had alluded) would have been difficult to corroborate in the contemporary knowledge of these particular persons.

But these persons were exiles truly, nonetheless. The country had changed, and in such a way as to rob them of what they very well might have assumed to be their cultural security, their cultural standing, their cultural rights.

URBANIZATION AND IMMIGRATION

Civilization in America was not even where it had been before, and therefore was not what it had been before. The Jeffersonian ideal of a country of small farmers, which Ezra Pound in particular was to invoke, had long ago been betrayed by history. Now as this generation came of age, its successor, the America of the comfortable, quite homogeneous small town, after the turn of the century just beginning to be idealized, was also in process of being betrayed. The fact, if not yet quite the realization, was exactly contemporary with this generation. In the single decade of the 1880s, the urban population of the United States increased by more than 50 percent. In the next decade it increased by another (exponential) approximately 36 percent, and then, after the turn of the century, in the decade 1900-1910, by an additional approximately 40 percent, and then by still another 30 percent in each of the following two decades. By 1922, when, in *The Waste Land,* Eliot published his discovery that the mythical waste land was the modern city (using London as his specific example, to be sure, but having America in mind), well over half of that country from which he was exiled lived in the modern city. . . .

Not that the particular Americans who made the modern movement were small towners—a good number of them were, in fact, already suburbanites—but they were by and large so situated in their individual growings-up that they might be greatly threatened by the particular form of American urbanization. It was another cause of their exile that their country had been invaded, occupied, and culturally ravaged, by barbarians.

In terms of its personnel, the primary fact of American urbanization was the so-called Second, or New, or Great Immigration, beginning in the 1880s and reaching its peak in the years 1905-10. Except for the unfortunate incursions of the Irish on the East Coast and the Chinese on the West Coast and the Scandinavians in the middle, immigration for a half century heretofore had been largely a cultural beneficence. Now the country was being overrun by immigrants in numbers far surpassing anything that had been known and, more to the point, of nationalities (if these landless peasants, these ghetto refugees could be said to have nationality) scarcely available to imagination. These Sicilians and Greeks and Slavs and Polish-Russian Jews who filled the cities spoke in tongues which in themselves were an affront, except perhaps that an amount of sophistication might perceive them to be comic. Having no law, these immigrants had no society. Having no cultivation, they had no culture. Being southern and eastern Europeans, they were not northern and western Europeans. And they made the de facto culture of American cities. They arrived in such numbers that it became difficult, and indeed an urgent, question to determine what an American was, and then they insisted upon clustering and spawning. In 1930, when the episode of the

New Immigration had stabilized, some 14 million persons living in the United States had been born elsewhere, very largely in southern and eastern Europe, and another 25-million-plus persons were first-generation native born. Another 12 million persons, it might be added, were black, so that between 40 and 50 percent of the entire population of the United States consisted of persons who had at best an ambivalent relationship to any such essentialized, mainstream American tradition as anybody might propose. (Southern blacks began arriving in the northern cities in large numbers when northern industry began to subsidize the war in Europe; the so-called Great Migration began in 1916, when a million southern blacks went North. In the decade of the 1920s the black population of the northern cities was compounded by an additional 64 percent.) Civilization in the United States was located in the cities, and the cities were ghetto conglomerates. By 1930 the "great cities," those with a total population of a million or more, were made up of persons *two-thirds* of whom were either foreign born or first-generation native born.

After such assault, what gentry assumptions any old Americans might have had could have had no more than dubious pertinence in America.

EXPLOITING THE LOSS OF PRIVILEGE

On the other hand, the loss of America conferred peculiar opportunity. The young sons of the old stock, growing up in the time of the assault, might find themselves to be not only dispossessed but also a glamorously defeated nobility, having old values (not otherwise specific) to be honored and a lineage (not necessarily detailed) to be invoked. Suggestions for the literary exploitation of such loss were already plentiful at the turn of the century, in modes ranging from popular chivalric romances to high decadence. And then shortly afterward there was the Henry Adams of the *Education,* who more pertinently than anyone else—more so certainly than Jules Laforgue or Tristan Corbière[4]—defined the *cultural authority* of American modernism. Adams of course had rare authority indeed. He could make unique claim to a prominent American heritage which the America of the new age had betrayed. The insult was personal and conveyed

4. French symbolist poets who influenced modernist writers

plausible privilege. Adams was eloquently credible when he said of himself in the *Education:*

> His world was dead. Not a Polish Jew fresh from Warsaw or Cracow—not a furtive Yacoob [sic] or Ysaac still reeking of the Ghetto, snarling a weird Yiddish to the officers of the customs—but had a keener instinct, an intenser energy, and a freer hand than he—American of Americans, with Heaven knew how many Puritans and Patriots behind him, and an education that had cost a civil war. He made no complaint and found no fault with his time; he was not worse off than the Indians or the buffalo who had been ejected from their heritage.

But if Adams was particularly privileged, still the young generation of the modern masters engaged in inventing themselves, it happened, just when the *Education* became public—could very well participate, and in accents not very much different. Ezra Pound could suggest, with just a small amount of self-conscious irony, that "one"—that is, Pound himself—"could write the whole social history of the United States from one's family annals." To do so, moreover, would be to illustrate the abrupt contemporary mongrelization of that history. A Philadelphia neighbor of his youth "was not only a gentleman but the fine old type. And his son is a stockbroker, roaring himself hoarse every day in the Wheat Pit . . . and *his* son will look like a Jew, and his grandson . . . will talk Yiddish. And this dissolution is taking place in hundreds of American families who have not thought of it as a decadence." And for Eliot there was a family feeling of what must be called dynasty, now assaulted if not yet quite defeated. His mother had written a biography of her father-in-law, William Greenleaf Eliot. (Had her subject been her own father, then her motive might presumably have been merely filial.) The lost cause became high principle, "tradition" precisely, especially when Eliot could address those fine few who might be presumed to understand. So his series of lectures to the University of Virginia in 1933 was conceived as further reflections on "Tradition and the Individual Talent," and Eliot would say to these southerners:

> You have here, I imagine, at least some recollection of a 'tradition,' such as the influx of foreign populations has almost effaced in some parts of the North, and such as never established itself in the West: though it is hardly to be expected that a tradition here, any more than anywhere else, should be found in healthy and flourishing growth. . . . Yet I think that the chances for the re-establishment of a native culture are perhaps better here than in New England. You are farther

away from New York; you have been less industrialized and less invaded by foreign races.

And again, a true traditionalism would require that

> The population should be homogeneous; where two or more cultures exist in the same place they are likely either to be fiercely self-conscious or both to become adulterate. What is still more important is unity of religious background; and reasons of race and religion combine to make any large number of freethinking Jews undesirable.

A CLASS DEFINED BY RACE AND ETHNICITY

. . . This literary generation was a social class, defined as American social classes tend to be defined, along ethnic and racial lines. Hence the "tradition," which however conceived—whether rooted in Eliot's Anglo-Catholicism or Fitzgerald's mythical Middle West or Hemingway's Michigan woods or Faulkner's magnolia South, or wherever—had the effect of excluding all of the abrupt barbarians.

Hence also a mode of social references in the literary discourse of this generation which occasionally made blatant the relationship between the "tradition" and an ethnic exclusiveness. There was, for convenient instance, the celebrated comic moment in *The Great Gatsby* when Fitzgerald told the names, in a half-dozen paragraphs, of the people who came to Gatsby's parties:

> From farther out on the Island came the Cheadles and O.R.P. Schraeders, and the Stonewall Jackson Abrams of Georgia, and the Fishguards and the Ripley Snells. Snell was there three days before he went to the penitentiary, so drunk out on the gravel drive that Mrs. Ulysses Swett's automobile ran over his right hand. The Dancies came, too, and S.B. Whitebait, who was well over sixty, and Maurice A. Flink, and the Hammerheads, and Beluga the tobacco importer, and Beluga's girls.

And so on. Who were the Cheadles and the Stonewall Jackson Abrams of Georgia and the Fishguards and the Snells? The answer, in all obviousness, was that they were mongrels. They were debasers of the social coin: imagine a man named Abrams who has dared to call himself Stonewall Jackson and who has also dared to come from (American) Georgia. Such names were very funny, and not only to Francis Scott Key Fitzgerald, because the class implication to which Fitzgerald was appealing was after all understood by most of his readers.

Hence, more forthrightly, an early trifle by E.E. Cummings (the rebellious son of a rebellious father who, although rebellious, was still minister of the South Congregational Church of Boston):

IKEY (GOLDBERG)'S WORTH I'M TOLD $ SEVERAL MILLION
FINKELSTEIN (FRITZ) LIVE
AT THE RITZ WEAR
earl & wilson COLLARS

Hence Ezra Pound's principled anti-Semitism, only the later virulence of which was plausibly insane. Hence, more seriously, Eliot's stock characters Sweeney and Bleistein. Eliot was indeed ambivalent about the former, although never about the latter, and about the former never in such a way as to confer fellow-feeling: Sweeney was to be envied his animality, perhaps. But Sweeney and Bleistein were metaphors, plainly, by which a traditionalist measured the decline of the West. And it would have required some peculiar effort or naiveté to regard Eliot's metaphors as being fortuitous or idiosyncratic, as though he might just as well have named his characters by other names. The metaphor functioned because Sweeney was the name for an Irishman and Bleistein was the name for a Jew. More precisely still, what was plainly meant was a shanty Irishman with low appetites and the slimy Jew whose

lustreless protrusive eye
Stares from the protozoic slime
At a perspective of Canaletto.

Of course no specific slur was intended. Some of everybody's best friends were Irish, Jewish, or whatever. (Sir) Jacob Epstein had come to London from New York's Lower East Side, and everybody knew and liked him. T.S. Eliot wrote fan letters to Groucho Marx. Such utterance did not have a literal bearing. It did, however, affirm a convention by which a literal society was to be known. An American gentry might have been dispossessed, but it was therefore—asserting its exclusiveness. It might have been exiled from America, but it still owned and could defend civilization. The property was plainly posted: No Irish Permitted, Jews Not Welcome, Caucasians Only. And given the actualities of the contemporary history of American culture, these postings were to a considerable extent the device by which the property—Civilization, Culture, Kulcher, Tradition—was to be defined.

Modernism Is an Exclusively White, Western Movement

Houston A. Baker Jr.

In the following excerpt, Houston A. Baker Jr. writes that the modernist movement represented an attempt by wealthy white Anglo-Saxon males to protect their privileged status in the face of dramatic social and cultural change. Baker states that as an Afro-American, he finds it difficult to identify with the works of modernist writers—including such American authors as F. Scott Fitzgerald, T.S. Eliot, and Eugene O'Neill. Baker is an English professor and the director of the Center for the Study of Black Literature and Culture at the University of Pennsylvania. He is the author of several books on black American literature.

Promising a wealth of meaning, [the term "modernism"] locks observers into a questing indecision. . . . Teased out of thought by the term's promise, essayists often conclude with frustratingly vague specifications. Harry Levin's essay "What Was Modernism?" for example, after providing lists, catalogues, and thought problems, concludes with the claim that modernism's distinguishing feature is its attempt to create "a conscience for a scientific age." Modernism's definitive act, according to Levin, traces its ancestry to "Rabelais, at the very dawn of modernity."

Such an analysis can only be characterized as a terribly general claim about scientific mastery and the emergence of the modern. It shifts the burden of definition from "modernism" to "science" without defining either enterprise.

Robert Martin Adams, in an essay bearing the same title as Levin's, offers a key to modernism's teasing semantics. Adams writes:

> Of all the empty and meaningless categories, hardly any is inherently as empty and meaningless as "the modern." Like "youth," it is a self-destroying concept; unlike "youth," it has a million and one potential meanings. Nothing is so dated as yesterday's modern, and nothing, however dated in itself, fails to qualify as "modern" so long as it enjoys the exquisite privilege of having been created yesterday.

Adams implies that bare chronology makes modernists of us all. The latest moment's production—by definition—instantiates "the modern." And unless we arbitrarily terminate modernism's allowable tomorrows, the movement is unending. Moreover, the temporal indeterminacy of the term allows us to select (quite randomly) structural features that we will call distinctively "modern" on the basis of their chronological proximity to us. We can then read these features over past millennia. Like Matthew Arnold in his Oxford inaugural lecture entitled "On the Modern Element in Literature," we can discover what is most distinctively modern in works a thousand years old. . . .

A RESPONSE TO RADICAL UNCERTAINTY

Yet for Anglo-American and British traditions of literary and artistic scholarship there is a tenuous agreement that some names and works *must* be included in any putatively comprehensive account of modern writing and art. Further, there seems to be an identifiable pleasure in listing features of art and writing that begin to predominate (by Virginia Woolf's time line) on or about December 1910.

The names and techniques of the "modern" that are generally set forth constitute a descriptive catalog resembling a natural philosopher's curiosity cabinet. In such cabinets disparate and seemingly discontinuous objects share space because that is the very function of the cabinet—to house or give order to varied things in what appears a rational, scientific manner. Pablo Picasso and Ezra Pound, James Joyce and Wassily Kandinsky, Igor Stravinsky and Paul Klee, Constantin Brancusi and H.D. are made to form a series. Collage, primitivism, montage, allusion, "dehumanization," and leitmotivs are forced into the same field. Friedrich Nietzsche and Karl Marx, Sigmund Freud and James Frazer, Carl Jung and Henri-Louis Bergson become dissimilar bedfellows. Such naming rituals have the force of creative works like *Ulysses* and *The Waste Land*. They substitute a myth of unified purpose and intention for definitional certainty. Before succumbing to the myth, however, perhaps we should examine the "change" that according to Woolf's calendar occurred on or about December 1910.

Surely that change is most accurately defined as an acknowledgment of radical uncertainty. Where precisely anyone or anything was located could no longer be charted on old maps of "civilization," nor could even the most microscopic observation tell the exact time and space of day. The very conceptual possibilities of both time and space had been dramatically refigured in the mathematics of Albert Einstein and the physics of Werner Heisenberg. A war of barbaric immensity combined with imperialism, capitalism,

---

MODERNISM IS GRIM READING

Richard Poirier states that one of the distinguishing characteristics of modernist writing is that it is deliberately difficult reading.

The phenomenon of grim reading—that is what I would like to offer as my initial definition of modernism. Modernism happened when reading got to be grim. I locate modernism, that is, in a kind of reading habit or reading necessity. I am concerned with the degree to which modernist texts—and it should be remembered that in the annals of twentieth-century literature these texts are by no means in the majority—mostly prevent our asking questions about any spontaneous act of reading, even when it is accompanied by a high degree of learned competence. Modernism in literature can be measured by the degree of textual intimidation felt in the act of reading. That act can become, especially in the classroom, a frightened and unhappy experience in which we are made to feel not only inferior to the author but, in the face of constant reminders that he is himself dissatisfied with what he has just managed to put before us, totally uncritical. . . . I would say that modernism is to be located not in ideas about cultural institutions or about the structures of life in or outside literary texts. It is to be found, rather, in two related and historically verifiable developments: first, in the promotion, by a particular faction of writers, of the virtues and necessities of difficulty and, second, in the complicity of a faction of readers who assent to the proposition that the act of reading should entail difficulties analogous to those registered in the act of writing.

Richard Poirier, "The Difficulties of Modernism and the Modernism of Difficulty," *Humanities in Society*, vol. 1, 1978.

and totalitarianism to produce a reaction to human possibilities quite different from Walt Whitman's joyous welcoming of the modern. Whitman in the nineteenth century exulted: "Years of the modern! years of the unperform'd!"

For T.S. Eliot, on or about December 1910, the completed and expected performance of mankind scarcely warranted joy. There was, instead, the "Murmur of maternal lamentation" presaging

> Cracks . . . and bursts in the violet air
> Falling towers
> Jerusalem Athens Alexandria
> Vienna London
> Unreal.[1]

Eliot's speaker, however, is comforted by the certainty that there are millennia of fragments (artistic shrapnel) constituting a *civilization* to be mined, a cultured repertoire to act as a shore against ruins. F. Scott Fitzgerald's Tom Buchanan in *The Great Gatsby* might therefore be a more honestly self-conscious representation of the threat that some artists whom we call "modern" felt in the face of a new world of science, war, technology, and imperialism. "Civilization's going to pieces," Tom confides to an assembled dinner party at his lavish Long Island estate while drinking a corky (but rather impressive) claret. "I've gotten to be a terrible pessimist about things," he continues.

PROTECTING THE TOWERS OF WHITE MALE SUPREMACY

Now, I don't mean to suggest that Anglo-American, British, and Irish moderns did not address themselves with seriousness and sincerity to a changed condition of humankind. Certainly they did. But they also mightily restricted the province of what constituted the tumbling of the towers, and they remained eternally self-conscious of their own pessimistic "becomings." Tom's pessimism turns out to be entirely bookish. It is predicated upon Lothrop Stoddard's[2] (which Tom remembers as "Goddard's") racialist murmurings. What really seems under threat are not towers of civilization but rather an assumed supremacy of boorishly racist, indisputably sexist, and unbelievably wealthy Anglo-Saxon males. One means of shoring up one's self under perceived threats of "democratization" and a "rising tide" of color is to resort to elitism—to

---

1. from *The Waste Land*   2. Stoddard expressed white supremacist views in his 1920 book *The Rising Tide of Color Against White World Supremacy.*

adopt a style that refuses to represent any *thing* other than the stylist's refusal to represent (what Susan Sontag refers to as an "aesthetics of silence"). Another strategy is to claim that one's artistic presentations and performances are quintessential renderings of the unrepresentable—human subconsciousness, for example, or primitive structural underpinnings of a putatively civilized mankind, or the simultaneity of a space-time continuum. Yet another strategy—a somewhat tawdry and dangerous one—is advocacy and allegiance to authoritarian movements or institutions that promise law and order.

Regardless of their strategies for confronting it, though, it was *change*—a profound shift in what could be taken as unquestionable assumptions about the meaning of human life—that moved those artists whom we call "moderns." And it was only a rare one among them who did not have some formula—some "ism"—for checking a precipitous toppling of man and his towers. Futurism, imagism, impressionism, vorticism, expressionism, cubism—all offered explicit programs for the arts *and* the salvation of humanity. Each in its turn yielded to other formulations of the role of the writer and the task of the artist in a changed and always, ever more rapidly changing world.

Today, we are "postmodern." Rather than *civilization*'s having gone to pieces, it has extended its sway in the form of a narrow and concentrated group of powerbrokers scarcely more charming, humane, or informed than Tom Buchanan. To connect the magnificent achievements, breakthroughs, and experiments of an entire panoply of modern intellectuals with fictive attitudes of a fictive modern man (Fitzgerald's Tom) may seem less than charitable. For even though Tom evades the law, shirks moral responsibility, and still ends up rich and in possession of the fairest Daisy of them all (though he ends, that is to say, as the capitalist triumphant, if not the triumphant romantic hero of the novel), there are still other modes of approach to the works of the moderns.

MODERNISM IS ALIEN TO AFRO-AMERICANS

Lionel Trilling, for example, provides one of the most charitable scholarly excursions to date. He describes modern literature as "shockingly personal," posing "every question that is forbidden in polite society" and involving readers in intimate interactions that leave them uneasily aware of their personal beings in the world. One scholarly reaction to

Trilling's formulations, I'm afraid, is probably like that of the undergraduates whom he churlishly suggests would be "rejected" by the efforts of William Butler Yeats and Eliot, Pound and Marcel Proust. It is difficult, for example, for an Afro-American student of literature like me—one unconceived in the philosophies of Anglo-American, British, and Irish moderns—to find intimacy either in the moderns' hostility to *civilization* or in their fawning reliance on an array of images and assumptions bequeathed by a *civilization* that, in its prototypical form, is exclusively Western, preeminently bourgeois, and optically white.

Alas, Fitzgerald's priggishly astute Nick [Carraway in *The Great Gatsby*] has only a limited vocabulary when it comes to a domain of experience that I, as an Afro-American, know well: "As we crossed Blackwell's Island a limousine passed us, driven by a white chauffeur, in which sat three modish negroes, two bucks and a girl. I laughed aloud as the yolks of their eyeballs rolled toward us in haughty rivalry." If only Fitzgerald had placed his "pale well-dressed negro" in the limousine or if Joseph Conrad [in his novella *Heart of Darkness*] had allowed his Africans actually to be articulate or if D.H. Lawrence [in his novel *Women in Love*] had not suggested through Birkin's reflection on African culture that

> thousands of years ago, that which was imminent in himself must have taken place in these Africans: the goodness, the holiness, the desire for creation and productive happiness must have lapsed, leaving the single impulse for knowledge in one sort, mindless progressive knowledge through the senses, knowledge arrested and ending in the senses, mystic knowledge in disintegration and dissolution, knowledge such as the beetles have, which live purely within the world of corruption and cold dissolution.

Or if only Eugene O'Neill had bracketed the psycho-surreal final trappings of his Emperor's world [in his play *The Emperor Jones*] and given us the stunning account of colonialism that remains implicit in his quip at the close of his list of dramatis personae[3]: "The action of the play takes place on an island in the West Indies, as yet un-self-determined by white marines." If any of these moves had been accomplished, then perhaps I might feel at least some of the intimacy and reverence that Trilling suggests.

But even as I recall a pleasurable spring in New Haven

---

3. characters

when I enjoyed cracking Joycean codes in order to teach *Ulysses*, I realize that the Irish writer's grand monument is not a work to which I shall return with reverence and charitably discover the type of inquisition that Trilling finds so engaging: "[Modern literature] asks us if we are content with our marriages, with our family lives, with our professional lives, with our friends." I am certain that I shall never place *Ulysses* in a group of texts that I describe, to use Trilling's words, as "spiritual" if not "actually religious." Perhaps the reason I shall not is because the questions Trilling finds— correctly or incorrectly—intimately relevant to his life are descriptive only of a bourgeois, characteristically twentieth-century, white Western mentality. As an Afro-American, a person of African descent in the United States today, I spend a great deal of time reflecting that in the world's largest geographies the question Where will I find water, wood, or food for today? is (and has been for the entirety of this century) the most pressing and urgently posed inquiry.

In "diasporic," "developing," "Third World," "emerging"— or whatever adjective one chooses to signify the non-Western side of Chenweizu's title "The West and the Rest of Us"—nations or territories there is no need to pose, in ironical Audenesque ways, questions such as Are we happy? Are we content? Are we free?[4] Such questions presuppose at least an adequate level of sustenance and a sufficient faith in human behavioral alternatives to enable a self-directed questioning. In other words, without food for thought, all modernist bets are off.

---

4. a reference to W.H. Auden's poem "The Unknown Citizen"

American Modernists Were Intellectually Shallow

Ernest Earnest

In the following essay, Ernest Earnest concludes that the literature of the American modernist era, which he calls the second American renaissance, is ultimately disappointing—especially when compared to the first renaissance of the mid-1800s, which includes the work of Walt Whitman, Ralph Waldo Emerson, and Henry David Thoreau. According to Earnest, American authors of the 1910s and 1920s— such as Ernest Hemingway, T.S. Eliot, F. Scott Fitzgerald, and many others—underestimated the richness of American culture, rejected basic American values, and failed to explore universal themes. Earnest is the author of numerous books on American literature and intellectual life, including *Expatriots and Patriots: American Artists, Scholars, and Writers in Europe* and *The Single Vision: The Alienation of American Intellectuals*.

There are several criteria for evaluating a literary period: its impact on its own time, its legacy to later periods, its creation of enduring works, its achievement in comparison with that of other eras. . . .

Judged by its impact on its own time, the literary work of the second American renaissance[1] can scarcely be overestimated. . . .

The writers of those golden years had finally broken the shackles of the genteel tradition; they had created new kinds of poetry; they had transformed the theater from entertain-

1. the period from 1910 to 1930; the first American renaissance occurred in the middle decades of the nineteenth century, represented by Edgar Allan Poe, Ralph Waldo Emerson, Henry David Thoreau, Nathaniel Hawthorne, Herman Melville, and Walt Whitman.

Excerpted from Ernest Earnest, *The Single Vision: The Alienation of American Intellectuals* (New York: New York University Press, 1970). Copyright ©1970 by New York University. Reprinted with permission.

ment into a serious forum; they had made literary experimentation not only respectable but mandatory; they had developed a body of literary criticism hitherto unequalled in the United States; and above all they had made literature exciting and controversial, had made it as perhaps never before or since a vital part of the American scene. Why then is their total effort so disappointing? Why was their legacy of so little use to their successors?

PROMISES UNFULFILLED

There is some justice in [literary critic] Maxwell Geismar's comment on the period:

> For this entire movement of the American twenties, fresh and promising, varied in talent and bold in achievement, seems to end almost everywhere on a note of negation and exhaustion. Winesburg, Ohio, gave way to New York, and New York to Paris and Capri, and Capri to the Wasteland. This was the last resort, the true home of these innovators and rebels.

[Poet and literary critic] Malcolm Cowley spoke of a "feeling of promises unfulfilled and powers never translated into deeds or works." He cited the inferior later work of Theodore Dreiser, Sinclair Lewis, and Willa Cather; the retirement of Van Wyck Brooks from contemporary literature; Carl Sandburg traveling around with a guitar. He could have added the decline of Ernest Hemingway after *A Farewell to Arms* and cited the T.S. Eliot of *The Cocktail Party* and *The Confidential Clerk.* A significant number of the writers took the escape route of alcohol, among them Lewis, Ring Lardner, Hart Crane, and of course F. Scott Fitzgerald. Hemingway's highly autobiographical *The Snows of Kilimanjaro* is a kind of confession that high living had blighted his talent. The sense of alienation in the writers of the era was in itself a debilitating force.

Cowley suggested that the rich promise was blighted by the War, . . . the failure of the hope raised by Woodrow Wilson's promises, . . . and the complete victory of big business. This explanation is inadequate. The notes of negation and defeat had been sounded before the War; and the vintage years came in the 1920s. . . .

UNFOUNDED CRITICISM OF THE AMERICAN SCENE

Bernard De Voto may be closer to the truth in his theory that the writers were viewing the scene through literature instead of looking at the realities of American life. But one can hardly accuse Dreiser, Lewis, Fitzgerald, and John Dos Passos of a bookish view of life. For better or worse they kept their eyes on the American scene. De Voto is of course right in arguing that they failed to see the whole picture, the dynamic side of a society which had created the most powerful nation on earth, which was feeding half the globe, and which even in the Harding-Coolidge era gave more of its citizens freedom and economic opportunity than was enjoyed anywhere else. Until the gates were partially shut by the exclusion act of 1921, thousands of immigrants annually abandoned the old world for the new.

It might even be argued that the basic idealism of Americans was a major cause for the bitter criticism of their own country. Human beings and human institutions always fell short of the utopian vision which had existed since the Declaration of Independence and which characterized our literature from Thomas Jefferson to Vernon Louis Parrington. Lincoln Steffens discovered that in Europe business and political corruption was so institutionalized as to be an accepted way of life as opposed to the American attack on these evils. It is symbolic that a major difference between a Carol Kennicott and an Emma Bovary is that the American woman tried to improve a dull village; whereas the French woman merely tried to escape one through sexual adventure.

This utopianism is related to the only-in-America fallacy. Just as Shelley, fleeing Regency England, envisioned a Greek isle which preserved a golden age and to which he could flee with Emilia, so American writers pictured happy European peasants and villagers far different from the people of Spoon River and Winesburg.[2] Standardization, which seemed so crass in a Ford car, looked quaint when a European peasant cut grain with a sickle unchanged in design for hundreds of years. In this myopia the American rebels displayed a certain amount of provinciality. Although they had read Henrik Ibsen, George Bernard Shaw, and H.G. Wells, they often failed to recognize that these writers had been at war with the same genteel tradition which American writers found so stultifying at home.

The pervasive theme of escape from a stultifying cultural

2. the fictional settings of Edgar Lee Masters' poetry collection *Spoon River Anthology* and Sherwood Anderson's short story collection *Winesburg, Ohio*

environment to Chicago, New York, or Paris is a reflection of the social mobility possible to Americans. This social and spatial mobility which . . . accounted for the rapid settling of a vast land mass, is obviously related to the utopian dream of finding a better world. In the twentieth century it often took the form of a reverse trek back to the city, the Eastern seaboard, or Europe.

The effect of the rapid social change of the twentieth century, especially the effect of increasing urbanization on mores and values [was significant]. However, despite the impressive body of fiction and criticism reflecting the new values, it is difficult to name a single literary work which deals with this phenomenon of social change. Almost without exception the writers rejected the older village and middle-class values, but no one of them revealed that the nation as a whole was revising these values. The huge success of a *Spoon River, Main Street* [by Sinclair Lewis], or a *What Price Glory* [by Eugene O'Neill] is testimony to a widespread new climate of opinion. H.L. Mencken and his cohorts made much of the anti-evolution statute of Tennessee[3]; they had little or nothing to say of the growth of great universities throughout the nation, fine metropolitan museums and symphony orchestras, or the creation of a Mayo Clinic or a Rockefeller Foundation for research.

The cultural wasteland depicted by Brooks, Mencken, Waldo Frank, Ludwig Lewisohn, Lewis, William Carlos Williams, and others had as early as 1912 begun a revolution in English poetry. With the exception of William Butler Yeats there was probably no British twentieth-century poet as important as Robert Frost, Ezra Pound, Eliot, Wallace Stevens, E.E. Cummings, or even Masters and Vachel Lindsay—certainly none as original—until the appearance of W.H. Auden, Stephen Spender, and Louis Mac Neice in the 1930s. The editor of a leading American publishing house remarked that about 1929 his company began to issue more native than foreign work. Obviously a new tide had been running for some years.

Important sources of this myopia about the American scene were the literary and academic establishments. Both were dominated by the Jamesean view of our culture.[4] Until

---

3. a law that barred teaching the theory of evolution in schools   4. the view that American culture was insubstantial and shallow, as expressed by Henry James

the thirties and forties few college alumni had ever had a course in American literature. One English major who graduated from a prominent college in 1923 remembers that by then he had never read anything by Emerson, Thoreau, Melville, James, or Whitman except *Captain My Captain* [by Whitman]. On his way to the doctorate he never met any of these in the classroom. . . .

THE DESTRUCTION OF VALUES

The limitations of the academic world help to explain but do not justify the myopia of so much of the intellectual community. It is not, as [poet Archibald] MacLeish charged, that they were irresponsible; instead throughout the whole period there is a note of passionate conviction. They wanted nothing less than to make over the United States. But . . . the intellectuals of the second renaissance were too ready to destroy everything hitherto standing. The occupational hazard of the intellectual is to subordinate everything to some single utopian purpose; he is disturbed by the untidy and the nonrational inheritances from the past. This is nowhere more evident than in the willingness of both the leftists and the conservatives to jettison the humane values of the liberal tradition. It is also evident in the attempt to reduce romantic love to a biological function and to equate family relationships to Oedipus complexes.

The same tendency appears in the rejection of middle-class values, especially as reflected in small-town life. Certainly the American small town, like villages everywhere, had mean and narrow characteristics, but it was surely not the joyless place depicted by the intellectuals. The singing around the piano, the dancing to the Victrola, the church "sociables," the ball games, the family picnics and young peoples' doggie roasts, the men's hunting and fishing provided a kind of relaxed enjoyment of life. Men and women worked hard but at a less driving pace than was customary in the city. Sentimentalized as it was, Thornton Wilder's *Our Town* (1938) is at least as true as *Main Street*. Fitzgerald understood something of this when he had Nick Carraway [in *The Great Gatsby*] say:

> That's my Middle West—not the wheat or the prairies or the
> lost Swede towns but the thrilling returning trains of my
> youth, and the street lamps and sleigh bells in the frosty dark,
> and the shadows of holly wreaths thrown by lighted windows

on the snow. I am part of that, a little solemn with the feel of those long winters, a little complacent from growing up in the Carraway house in a city where dwellings are still called through decades by a family's name.

To an extent matched nowhere in the world the middle-class people of the Gopher Prairies and Zeniths sent their boys and girls to college. There was an economic motive of course, as there always is in the preparation for a career. But it is surely no accident that so many of the intellectuals of the second renaissance traveled the road from a village or provincial city to college and then to literature: Pound, Eliot, Lewis, Cather, Fitzgerald, Stevens, Williams, Hart Crane, Allen Tate, William Faulkner—to mention only a few. Obviously there must have been some seedbed of intellectual culture, some respect for the things of the mind and spirit. In fact the literary flowering of the period is the best refutation of the oft repeated charge that America was a cultural wasteland. No renaissance springs up *de novo*[5]; it is always the product of a culture.

It was the failure to recognize the vigor of our native culture which was a major defect of the writers between 1910 and 1930. There was an adolescent quality in the revolt, a rebellion against one's father. In the late 1930s and early 1940s writers like Brooks and MacLeish began, like Mark Twain, to discover how much the old man had learned in a few years. . . .

A PAUCITY OF ENDURING WORKS

Another way of evaluating the literature of a period is to consider the enduring quality of its finest works. In his discussion of the American novel, John W. Aldbridge is certainly too sweeping in saying that "Gatsby is one of the very few books left from the twenties that we are still able to read with any kind of enduring pleasure." Certainly one would have to include *Winesburg, Ohio* (although its date is 1919), [Hemingway's] *The Sun Also Rises* and *A Farewell to Arms* and possibly [Faulkner's] *The Sound and the Fury* and [Thomas Wolfe's] *Look Homeward, Angel*. And in any discussion of the movers and shakers of the period it is easy to forget such good novels as Edith Wharton's *Age of Innocence*, Ellen Glasgow's *Barren Ground* and *The Romantic Comedians*, Joseph Hergesheimer's *Java Head*. However, although

5. over again

these reflect the sensibility of the twenties they are essentially re-creations of the past.

It is ironic that the rebels who were so contemptuous of America's literary past created few novels of the stature of *The Scarlet Letter, Moby Dick, Billy Budd, Huckleberry Finn, Daisy Miller, Portrait of a Lady, The American, The Ambassadors, The Wings of the Dove,* and *The Golden Bowl.* Even a partial list of the novels and stories of Henry James indicates how much more impressive was his achievement than that of many of the later novelists. In fact today Lewis is almost unreadable and Dreiser only somewhat less so.

One reason for this is that James probed more deeply into the psyche: Isabel Archer, Christopher Newman, Lambert Strether, Milly Theale, Maggie Verver are more complex characters than Carrie Meeber, Frank Cowperwood, Clyde Griffiths, Carol Kennicott, or George Babbitt. Sam Dodsworth is a cruder reworking of Christopher Newman. As Philip Young pointed out Hemingway tended to draw a single male character—a projection of himself. The people in Dos Passos' novels tend to merge into a kind of montage.

In poetry it might be a moot question whether Eliot is greater than Walt Whitman, but as Pound said of Whitman, "it was you who broke the new ground." As is well known, Eliot's technique in *The Waste Land* owes much to Pound. One need not agree with Richard Aldington who said of Eliot, "what is original in his poetry is not good, and what is good is not original," but it is doubtful that such an Alexandrian technique is a step forward.

Certainly Whitman and Emily Dickinson can stand comparison with such major twentieth-century figures as Eliot, Frost, and Stevens. And not all critics would agree that Frost is a major poet. However it is possibly true that the first third of this century was richer in poetic achievement than any comparable period in American literature. It may well be that the poetry of the era will be more enduring than the prose. Often the poetry touches deeper levels of feeling, and at its best, like that of Whitman and Dickinson it explores fundamental questions.

CONTRASTING THE CONTENT OF THE TWO RENAISSANCES

So too did the prose of Emerson, Thoreau, Hawthorne, and Melville. It is this very concern with fundamental questions which has made Thoreau a revolutionary force in this century—the teacher of Ghandi and Martin Luther King. Today there are Thoreau societies in France and England and two in Japan. Hawthorne's stories and Melville's *Moby Dick* explore the nature of evil: is it inherent in the creation or is it a human creation? *Billy Budd* dramatizes the ever-recurring problem of law versus justice. The questions with which the nineteenth-century writers dealt are those with which we are concerned and with which our grandchildren will be concerned after us.

By contrast, many of the preoccupations of the prose writers [of the 1920s]—including the novelists—such matters as puritanical views of sex, Prohibition, the exploitation of labor, the New Humanism, Agrarianism, the alleged cultural desert—are all hopelessly dated.

Several exceptions come to mind; Hemingway with his stoic creed for dealing with a meaningless universe; Joseph Krutch with a somewhat similar response; Stevens with his aesthetic acceptance of life and death; O'Neill with his sense of man's tragic fate; and Eliot with his concern with spiritual sterility.

Hemingway's nihilism at times verged on the melodramatic and his "grace under pressure" too often became a tough-guy prose. The creed of the bullfighter and the hunter is inadequate for the complex modern world.

In Krutch's world even the physical and aesthetic satisfactions are absent. He gave a paranoid picture of the discomforts of contemporary life, a paranoia verging on melodrama.

In Stevens' world the musing woman finds that "Death is the mother of beauty," and that

> Divinity must live within herself;
> Passions of rain or moods in falling snow;
> Grievings in loneliness, or unsubdued
> Elations when the forest blooms; gusty
> Emotions on wet roads on autumn nights;
> All pleasures and all pains, remembering
> The bough of summer and the winter branch.
> These are the measures destined for her soul.

Seldom has the aesthetic creed found finer expression. This world where "Deer walk upon our mountains, and the quail/Whistle about us their spontaneous cries," is all very lovely, but it lacks the terror of Melville's shark-filled sea; or the brutality of the world Hemingway had experienced in a war where soldiers casually pot Germans as they come over a garden wall; or the psychic turmoil of Faulkner's characters which leads to their self-destruction. An exclusively tragic view of life can omit the basic human aesthetic and sensuous satisfactions, but one which deals only with these satisfactions is incomplete. Stevens leaves small room for tragedy.

On the other hand, O'Neill at his best as in *Desire Under the Elms* or *Mourning Becomes Electra* was dealing with the great themes of Aeschylus and Sophocles. But like so much of the work of the twenties O'Neill's work as a whole leaves the impression of negation and defeat. In a way the nihilism of *The Iceman Cometh* (1939) and *A Long Day's Journey into Night* (1956) is the logical conclusion to his earlier work. Nevertheless, as Krutch has pointed out, O'Neill did deal with two great questions: "the question of human responsibility for what is called Fate and the question of what general truth the tragic situation illustrates...perhaps the questions which true tragedy always raises."

ELIOT VERSUS WHITMAN

The limitations of Eliot lie not in the questions he asked but in his evidence and his answers. Eliot, like so many of his contemporaries, glamorized the past and gave a one-sided picture of modern life. Granting his premise that modern society is spiritually sterile his plea for a return to medieval theology was an inadequate solution to the dilemmas created by historical scholarship and modern science. The theology to which he returned was based on a cosmology and a social order neither of which was relevant to the modern world. In *Ash Wednesday* and *The Journey of the Magi* this theology is implied rather than stated, but in his prose works, especially *The Idea of a Christian Society* (1940) Eliot called for an authoritarian state church embracing most of society. "A spirit of excessive tolerance is to be deplored." This is strikingly similar to Fascist and Communist ideology.

Here again a comparison with Whitman is revealing. *The Journey of the Magi is* based upon a literal acceptance of the story of the birth and crucifixion of the God-man. Whitman dealt with the crucifixion in contemporary terms. In *A Sight in Camp in the Daybreak Gray and Dim* he told of finding three dead soldiers behind the hospital tent. Possibly he intended to suggest the trinity or the three crucifixions; in any case when he lifted the blanket from one figure he found

a face nor child nor old, very calm, as of
beautiful yellow-white ivory;

Young men I think I know you—I think this face
 is the face of Christ himself,
Dead and divine and brother of us all, and here
 again he lies.

For Eliot the crucifixion took place once long ago; for Whitman it was an ever recurring tragedy. Eliot's vision led him to seek an authoritarian theology; Whitman's raised questions about war and man's inhumanity to man.

A LITERATURE OF EPHEMERAL SURFACES

The foregoing comparisons between nineteenth-century American literature and that between 1910 and 1930 support the view that despite its immense vitality, the second renaissance was intellectually shallow. This shallowness appears in the misreading of the American past, in the considerable misrepresentation of the contemporary scene, in the failure to recognize the basic values of our society, and in the failure to deal adequately with fundamental questions. Too often it was a literature of ephemeral surfaces. Taken as a whole it lacks breadth of social and philosophical vision.

American Modernists Strove to Improve American Society

C. Barry Chabot

Most literary critics emphasize the effects that modernist writers had on the form and style of literature. C. Barry Chabot, the chair of the English department at Miami University in Oxford, Ohio, maintains that American modernist writers attempted to change not only the formal aspects of poetry and fiction, but also the institutions of American society. Chabot insists that Willa Cather, T.S. Eliot, Ezra Pound, and other American modernists tried to use their writing to create social and economic equality and a greater sense of community in American society.

I want to claim that [American modernist writers] share a common project that we can now see resulted in the emergence of American literary modernism as a distinctive and unusually strong body of literature. That project took form around a shared dismay about the character of American social and cultural life in the early years of this century. In *New York Intellect,* Thomas Bender observes that Van Wyck Brooks and his contemporaries more often understood themselves as a generation than as a class, but that they were nonetheless drawn primarily from the middle class. "The Young Intellectuals," he writes, "were the first generation to come of age within a bourgeois culture that had consolidated itself politically, financially, and culturally." These writers came to maturity in the years immediately after the muckrakers and American literary naturalists[1] had expressed alarm about the lives increasingly allotted to the less fortunate classes. Although the Young Intellectuals were typically among the ben-

---

1. Muckrakers exposed social and economic injustices; naturalists depicted the ugly realities of American society.

Excerpted from C. Barry Chabot, *Writers for the Nation: American Literary Modernism* (Tuscaloosa: University of Alabama Press, 1997). Copyright ©1997 The University of Alabama Press. Reprinted with permission from the publisher.

eficiaries of the new social order, they followed the naturalists in drawing up a lengthy and varied list of grievances against the quality of life it made available—it was exploitative, it was too industrial, it was changing too quickly, its culture had become refined to the point of irrelevance; but, whatever the particulars, such complaints eventually and centrally concluded that the nation no longer afforded its citizens with terms for living companionable lives. American literary modernism, in other words, involves the recognition that even the seemingly fortunate are victimized by current economic and social life. As I understand it, American literary modernism was primarily animated by efforts to repair this deficiency, to imagine conditions that would either restore to the national life the possibility that all citizens could enjoy access to functioning and supportive communities, or, failing restoration, at least provide something by way of a substitute. On these terms, the emergence of American literary modernism was not only roughly contemporaneous with the progressivism of a Herbert Croly or Walter Lippmann but was also animated by similar convictions about the nation's needs. It is not an accident, in other words, that the *New Republic, The Masses,* and *Seven Arts* all began publication in New York City within a few years of one another. In a brief memoir about *Seven Arts,* James Oppenheim, its founding editor, explains that he had been "inanely jealous of the gang of fellows who had shot the *New Republic* into existence, a 'journal of opinion,' mind you, when the real thing would be a journal of art," since he believed that "that lost soul among nations, America, could be regenerated by art, and that the artist was always a Jean-Christophe with the power to do the job." American literary modernists were not always able to muster or to sustain such confidence in their ability to accomplish this collective mission, but they were united by their sense of its urgency, as by the seriousness with which they pursued their self-appointed charge.

STRATEGIES FOR CHANGE

American literary modernists also differed as to the specific strategies they favored for meeting their nation's apparent needs. . . . I have found it helpful to conceive of these strategies primarily along two axes: first, whether the imagined alternatives to a lamentable present were to be found in the past or in the future, and second, whether they involved primarily personal or more thoroughly social changes. For instance, Willa Cather represents an alternative that is simultaneously personal and oriented toward the past. After working for many years in industrial Pittsburgh and then New York, Cather came to the conclusion that the era of her childhood in Nebraska, and other frontier communities even more remote in time and place, had uniquely provided conditions for satisfying lives. She had little conviction that such conditions could be restored and was prepared to draw comfort from contemplating memories and reconstructions of such lost social moments. T.S. Eliot and Allen Tate were both, like Cather, notoriously oriented toward the past, but both were more sanguine than she about the possibilities for restoring or preserving what they took to be preferable ways of life. Both also recognized that such acts of preservation required the cultivation of social institutions compatible with those forms of life; accordingly, both for a time resigned themselves to engaging in a period of social agitation. In their different ways, then, Eliot and Tate represent a strategy that is similar to Cather's in being oriented to the past, and different in being broadly social in nature. Another poet, Wallace Stevens, represents a strategy that is both personal, because it is dependent upon the resources of the individual imagination, and oriented toward the future, toward an integration that the poet's imagination must continuously provide. The emergence of Harlem in the years just after World War I lent credence to the belief that a new day was already at hand for African Americans. The rhetoric of the New Negro era oscillates between celebrating the changes that had occurred as already inaugurating that new day and taking them as promissory notes due in the very near future. These expectations were in time frustrated, but for a brief cultural moment it was imaginable that in enclaves like Harlem the benefits of full citizenship were at last becoming available to African Americans. Finally, in the thirties a group of writers emerged that imagined an alternative that, like Stevens's, was oriented toward a possible future, and yet that recognized, as did Eliot and Tate, that their aspirations were dependent upon the transformation of the nation's extant institutions. . . .

Writers from the thirties . . . are more commonly thought to represent a decisive and deliberate break from American literary modernism and a reversion to an earlier, seemingly less sophisticated, literary program. When American literary modernism as a whole is understood primarily as a response to the felt needs of the nation, and when it is recognized that those needs consistently included the provision of a sense of community, then the novelty of the proletarian fiction of the thirties[2] can be understood as deriving primarily from the solution it proposes. The community it envisions for a troubled nation is thoroughly egalitarian, and it is willing to engage directly in the political process in order to bring such a community into existence. Whereas Eliot and the Agrarians[3] recognized the institutional and thus political dimensions of their own rather different visions, they characteristically stopped short of involving themselves directly in the political process. Although it largely lay dormant for some years, this radical and more directly political variant of American literary modernism was present from the first, where it can be found during the teens in the pages of *The Masses* and even in Van Wyck Brooks's *America's Coming-of-Age*. If in the teens there was an emerging consensus about the need to restore some sense of community to the nation, few American writers and intellectuals were then prepared to adopt such seemingly radical solutions, believing that the process of reform already evident in the progressive movement would eventually prove sufficient. When conditions dramatically worsened in the thirties, it became easier for many to imagine that only equally dramatic changes in the social fabric could suffice.

RESTORING LITERATURE AND SOCIAL INSTITUTIONS

What must seem most odd about the conception of American literary modernism proposed here is my claim that it was preoccupied by the need to restore some sense of community to the nation. Modernism is usually thought to be at best indifferent to social life, to be preoccupied by narrowly aesthetic concerns. At its worst, the examples of Ezra Pound and, to a lesser degree, T.S. Eliot are taken to demonstrate that modernism possessed an inherent affinity for fascism. . . . American literary modernists *were* concerned about the state of our literature and *were* dedicated to its renewal. However, they typically understood that state as symptomatic of the state of society as a whole, and recognized that

2. fiction that criticized the capitalist economic system and sympathized with the poor
3. a group of southern writers who sought to preserve southern rural traditions in the face of industrialization

their success in reviving the former required doing as much for the latter. The genteel poems that these writers abhorred had equally genteel readers, and the modernists were as interested in changing the mental habits of the latter as they were in altering the diction and form of the former. If Pound, Eliot, and others assumed that their project involved restoring to literature a degree of the vigor it possessed at other times and places, they also assumed that it needed to be complemented by the wholesale restoration of traditional social institutions. Since they are exemplary moderns, their example makes claims that modernism per se is inherently conservative, even fascistic, initially plausible. I would argue, however, that their conservatism derives from their tendency to assume that only the traditional institutions that in another era had seemingly made available the sense of community were capable of doing so in their own. They would no doubt have agreed with the Blum brothers in Willa Cather's *A Lost Lady,* who believed that "a fortunate and privileged class was an axiomatic fact in the social order." Not all American literary modernists shared this questionable assumption. Van Wyck Brooks, the writers associated with *The Masses,* and many others in the thirties believed that socialism or other altogether new forms of social life could provide people with that crucial sense. The latter were not prepared to accept economic and social privilege as essential features of stable societies; they believed, instead, that it must be possible to distribute social benefits equitably among all members of a community. Certainly the New Negro writers did not accept the social and economic places historically allotted by this nation to African Americans. American literary modernists, in other words, commonly recognized that any sense of community had been eroded among their contemporaries and were united in their efforts to make it again widely available. They differed in their judgments as to the means through which this could most effectively be accomplished, and thus they advocated various remedies. Some of these remedies were clearly compatible with fascism; just as clearly, others were not. Thus American literary modernism as a whole possessed no inherent political bias, conservative or otherwise. What it did possess was a strong conviction that history had at some point (a point these writers would identify differently) deprived them and their contemporaries of a sense of community, as well as a commitment to rectifying that regrettable absence. They proposed a variety of remedies, each with its peculiar political inflection. . . .

It seems to me important to stress that these writers were unable to imagine and implement genuine solutions to the social and cultural difficulties that so concerned them. No one else has either, so in large measure the problems they addressed remain our problems, often now exacerbated with the passage of time. We should honor them now as much for the courage and intellectual seriousness they displayed in assuming such broadly social responsibilities as for the power of the literature they thereby produced. In the end, I would argue that that power derives precisely from the intensity and perceptiveness of their engagement with matters of the greatest cultural urgency.

CHRONOLOGY

1859

British naturalist Charles Darwin's *Origin of Species* published

1900

Sigmund Freud's *Interpretation of Dreams* published

1905

Fauvist Exhibit in Paris

1912

Poetry: A Magazine of Verse founded by Harriet Monroe

1913

Armory Show in New York; Willa Cather's *O, Pioneers!* published; Robert Frost's *A Boy's Will* published in London; Vachel Lindsay's *General William Booth Enters Heaven* published; Igor Stravinsky's *Rites of Spring* debuts

1914

Margaret Anderson launches the *Little Review* in Chicago; the *Egoist* and *Blast* magazines are established in London; Frost's *North of Boston* published in London; Amy Lowell's *Sword Blades and Poppy Seeds*, Gertrude Stein's *Tender Buttons* published

1915

Alfred Kreymborg founds *Others* magazine in New York; the *Ballet Russe* tours America; Edgar Lee Masters's *Spoon River Anthology*, Ezra Pound's *Some Imagist Poems*, Van Wyck Brooks's *America's Coming of Age* published; German-born physicist Albert Einstein publishes his general theory of relativity

1916

H.D.'s *Sea Garden*, Carl Sandburg's *Chicago Poems* published

1917

U.S. enters World War I; T.S. Eliot's *Prufrock and Other Observations* published

1918

Sandburg's *Cornhuskers* published; World War I ends

1919

Race riots erupt in Harlem during the Red Summer; Sherwood Anderson's *Winesburg, Ohio*, John Crowe Ransom's *Poems About God* published

1920

Schofield Thayer establishes the *Dial*, a monthly review; Eliot's *The Sacred Wood* (essays), F. Scott Fitzgerald's *This Side of Paradise*, Ezra Pound's *Hugh Selwyn Mauberley*, Sinclair Lewis's *Main Street*, Edith Wharton's *The Age of Innocence* published

1921

John Dos Passos's *Three Soldiers*, Marriane Moore's *Poems* published; *Broom: An International Magazine of the Arts* comes out in Rome, Berlin, and New York; the *Double Dealer* magazine debuts in New Orleans

1922

e.e. cummings's *The Enormous Room*, Eliot's *The Waste Land*, Fitzgerald's *Tales of the Jazz Age*, Fitzgerald's *The Beautiful and Damned*, James Joyce's *Ulysses*, Claude McKay's *Harlem Shadows*, Eugene O'Neill's *The Emperor Jones*, Lewis's *Babbitt* published; Southern Fugitive movement establishes the *Fugitive* magazine

1923

Eliot becomes editor of the *Criterion*; Wallace Stevens's *Harmonium*, Jean Toomer's *Cane* published

1924

Countee Cullen's *Color*, Ernest Hemingway's *In Our Time*, Thomas Mann's *The Magic Mountain* published; *Opportunity* magazine hosts a dinner to celebrate the recent outpouring of African-American writing in Harlem

1925

Anderson's *Dark Laughter*, Dos Passos's *Manhattan Transfer*, Fitzgerald's *The Great Gatsby*, Pound's *Cantos I–XVI*, Ellen Glasgow's *Barren Ground*, Franz Kafka's *The Trial*, Stein's *The Making of Americans*, William Carlos Williams's

In the American Grain published; in the "monkey trial" in Dayton, Tennessee, high school teacher John T. Scopes is tried for teaching Darwin's theory of evolution

1926

William Faulkner's *Soldier's Pay*, Hemingway's *The Sun Also Rises*, Langston Hughes's *The Weary Blues*, Kafka's *The Castle*, Alaine Locke's anthology *The New Negro*, Carl Van Vechten's *Nigger Heaven* published

1927

Conrad Aiken's *The Blue Voyage* published

1929

Faulkner's *The Sound and the Fury*, Hemingway's *A Farewell to Arms*, Thomas Wolfe's *Look Homeward, Angel* published; Wall Street crashes on October 29, signaling the beginning of the Great Depression

1930

Hart Crane's *The Bridge*, Eliot's *Ash Wednesday* published; the Southern Agrarian movement at Vanderbilt University publishes the symposium *I'll Take My Stand*

1932

Hemingway's *Death in the Afternoon*, John Steinbeck's *The Pastures of Heaven* published

1934

Fitzgerald's *Tender Is the Night*, Langston Hughes's *The Ways of White Folks*, Zora Neale Hurston's *Jonah's Gourd Vine* published

1936

Dos Passos's *U.S.A.*, Faulkner's *Absalom, Absalom!* published

1937

Hemingway's *To Have and Have Not* published

1939

World War II begins; Steinbeck's *The Grapes of Wrath* published

1940

Hemingway's *For Whom the Bell Tolls* published

1941

U.S. enters World War II on December 7

For Further Research

CRITICISM AND LITERARY HISTORY ON
MODERNISM AND THE MODERNIST ERA

Robert Martin Adams, "What Was Modernism?" *Hudson Review*, vol. 31, no. 1, Spring 1978.

Joseph Warren Beach, *American Fiction, 1920–1940.* New York: Macmillan, 1942.

Arna Bontemps, ed., *The Harlem Renaissance Remembered.* New York: Dodd, Mead, 1972.

Malcolm Bradbury and James McFarlane, *Modernism, 1890–1930.* London: Penguin Books, 1976.

Stanley K. Coffman Jr., *Imagism: A Chapter for the History of Modern Poetry.* New York: Octagon Books, 1972.

Paul K. Conkin, *The Southern Agrarians.* Knoxville: University of Tennessee Press, 1988.

Malcolm Cowley, *A Second Flowering: Works and Days of the Lost Generation.* New York: Viking, 1973.

James De Jongh, *Vicious Modernism: Black Harlem and the Literary Imagination.* New York: Cambridge University Press, 1990.

Marc Dolan, *Modern Lives: A Cultural Re-Reading of "The Lost Generation."* West Lafayette, IN: Purdue University Press, 1996.

Elizabeth Drew, with John L. Sweeney, *Directions in Modern Poetry.* 1940. Reprint, New York: Gordian Press, 1967.

Peter Faulkner, *Modernism.* New York: Harper & Row, 1977.

Maxwell Geismar, *The Last of the Provincials: The American Novel, 1915–1925.* 1943. Reprint, Boston: Houghton Mifflin, 1949.

Maxwell Geismar, *Writers in Crisis: The American Novel, 1925–1940.* 1941. Reprint, New York: Hill and Wang, 1961.

Michael J. Hoffman and Patrick D. Murphy, eds., *Critical Essays on American Modernism.* New York: G.K. Hall, 1992.

Irving Howe, ed., *Literary Modernism.* New York: Fawcett, 1967.

Glenn Hughes, *Imagism and the Imagists: A Study in Modern Poetry.* Stanford, CA: Stanford University Press, 1931.

Hugh Kenner, *A Homemade World: The American Modernist Writers.* New York: Knopf, 1974.

Jacob Korg, *Language in Modern Literature: Innovation and Experiment.* New York: Barnes and Noble, 1979.

David Levering Lewis, ed., *The Portable Harlem Renaissance Reader.* New York: Viking, 1994.

Harry Levin, "What Was Modernism?" *Refractions: Essays in Comparative Literature.* New York: Oxford University Press, 1966.

Randy Malamud, *The Language of Modernism.* Ann Arbor: University of Michigan Research Press, 1989.

Michael North, *The Dialect of Modernism: Race, Language, and Twentieth-Century Literature.* New York: Oxford University Press, 1994.

C.E. Bechhofer Roberts, *The Literary Renaissance in America.* London: W. Heinemann, 1923.

Louis D. Rubin Jr., *The Wary Fugitives: Four Poets and the South.* Baton Rouge: Louisiana State University Press, 1978.

Lisa M. Steinman, *Made in America: Science, Technology, and American Modernist Poets.* New Haven, CT: Yale University Press, 1987.

Louis Untermeyer, *American Poetry Since 1900.* New York: Henry Holt, 1923.

William Van O'Connor, ed., *Seven Modern American Novelists: An Introduction.* Minneapolis: University of Minnesota Press, 1959.

Ronald Harold Wainscott, *The Emergence of the Modern in American Theater, 1914–1929.* New Haven, CT: Yale University Press, 1997.

Ellen Williams, *Harriet Monroe and the Poetry Renaissance: The First Ten Years of Poetry, 1912–1922*. Urbana: University of Illinois Press, 1977.

Austin McGiffert Wright, *The American Short Story in the Twenties*. Chicago: University of Chicago Press, 1961.

Thomas Daniel Young, *Waking Their Neighbors Up: The Nashville Agrarians Rediscovered*. Athens: University of Georgia Press, 1982.

CRITICISM AND LITERARY HISTORY THAT INCLUDES THE MODERNIST ERA

John M. Bradbury, *Renaissance in the South: A Critical History of the Literature, 1920–1960*. Chapel Hill: University of North Carolina Press, 1963.

J.A. Bryant Jr., *Twentieth-Century Southern Literature*. Lexington: University Press of Kentucky, 1997.

Stanley Cooperman, *World War I and the American Novel*. Baltimore: Johns Hopkins University Press, 1967.

Miles Donald, *The American Novel in the Twentieth Century*. New York: Harper & Row, 1978.

Bernard Frank Dukore, *American Dramatists, 1918–1945*. New York: Grove Press, 1984.

Eleanor Flexner, *American Playwrights, 1918–1938: The Theatre Retreats from Reality*. New York: Simon and Schuster, 1938.

Richard Gray, *The Literature of Memory: Modern Writers of the American South*. Baltimore: Johns Hopkins University Press, 1977.

Donald Heiney, *Recent American Literature*. Woodbury, NY: Barron's Educational Series, 1958.

Frederick J. Hoffman, *The Modern Novel in America, 1900–1950*. Chicago: Henry Regnery, 1951.

John Hollander, ed., *Modern Poetry: Essays in Criticism*. New York: Oxford University Press, 1968.

Alfred Kazin, *On Native Grounds: An Interpretation of Modern American Prose Literature*. New York: Reynal & Hitchcock, 1942.

Jordan Yale Miller, *American Drama Between the Wars: A Critical History*. Boston: Twayne, 1991.

David Perkins, *A History of Modern Poetry: Modernism and After.* Cambridge, MA: Harvard University Press, 1987.

Richard Ruland and Malcolm Bradbury, *From Puritanism to Postmodernism: A History of American Literature.* New York: Viking, 1991.

Alan Shucard, Fred Moramarco, and William Sullivan, *Modern American Poetry, 1865–1950.* Boston: Twayne, 1989.

HISTORICAL BACKGROUND

Ralph K. Andrist, ed., *The American Heritage History of the 20's and 30's.* New York: American Heritage, 1970.

Stanley Cohen, *Reform, War, and Reaction: 1912–1932.* Columbia: University of South Carolina Press, 1973.

Lynn Dumenil, *The Modern Temper: American Culture and Society in the 1920s.* New York: Hill and Wang, 1995.

John Kenneth Galbraith, *The Great Crash, 1929.* Boston: Houghton Mifflin, 1954.

Robert Goldston, *The Great Depression: The United States in the Thirties.* New York: Bobbs-Merrill, 1968.

Barry D. Karl, *The Uneasy State: The United States from 1915 to 1945.* Chicago: University of Chicago Press, 1983.

Walter Lord, *The Good Years: From 1900 to the First World War.* New York: Harper, 1960.

Richard Brandon Morris and James Woodress, eds., *Boom and Bust: 1920–1939.* New York: McGraw-Hill, 1976.

Michael E. Parrish, *Anxious Decades: America in Prosperity and Depression, 1920–1941.* New York: Norton, 1992.

Geoffrey Perrett, *America in the Twenties: A History.* New York: Simon and Schuster, 1982.

Milton Plesur, ed., *The 1920s: Problems and Paradoxes.* Boston: Allyn and Bacon, 1969.

Arthur M. Schlesinger Jr., *The Crisis of the Old Order, 1919–1933.* Boston: Houghton Mifflin, 1957.

Elizabeth Stevenson, *Babbitts and Bohemians: The American 1920s.* New York: Macmillan, 1957.

INDEX

Across the River and into the Trees
(Hemingway), 112
Adams, Henry, 167–68
Adams, Robert Martin, 171–72
Advancing South, The, 149
Aeterna Poetae Memoria
(MacLeish), 83
African Americans
in Harlem, 132–34
modernism is alien to, 175–77
and primitivism, 136–40
urban migration of, 130–32
see also Harlem Renaissance
Age of Innocence, The (Wharton),
22, 183
Agrarians, 25, 141–42
formation of, 142–43
influences of, 146, 148
Northern forces against, 148–50
political involvement of, 191
rebellion against non-Southern
culture by, 144–46, 148
see also South, the
Aiken, Conrad, 121, 123
Aldbridge, John W., 183
Aldington, Richard, 58, 65
All the King's Men (Warren), 47–48
allusion, 79–80
Ambassadors, The (James),
102–103
America
immigration in, 166–67
Sinclair on literature of, 155–59
societal changes in, 15
urbanization, 165–66
Victorianism in, 159–61
see also American modernism;
South, the
American Letter (MacLeish), 85
American modernism, 162–64
accomplishments of, 178–79
as alien to African Americans,
175–77
characteristics, 13–14

concrete vs. abstract language in,
44–46
contrasted with America's literary
past, 184–86
distrust of words in, 47–50
enduring works of, 183–84
vs. European modernism, 14, 36,
37, 40, 41
fiction of, 22–24
on historical progress, 33
influences of, 14–16
immigration/urbanization,
165–67
visual arts, 16–18
World War I, 22–23, 82–83,
100–102
as intellectually shallow, 187
lack of regional influences in,
92–93
as reaction to radical uncertainty,
172–74
as rebellion against genteel
tradition, 158–61
as rejection of culture, 31–33
rejection of rhetoric in, 46–47
relativism in, 34
restoring literature and social
institutions through, 191–93
as revolt against prevalent style,
28–30
subjectivity in, 30–31
truth vs. sincerity in, 35
unfounded criticism of, 179–83
unfulfilled promises of, 179
variations in, 25–26
writers of,
desire to change society, 188–89
desire to improve society, 189–90
loss of privileges, 167–69
on need for community, 190–91
protecting white male
supremacy, 174–75
racial/ethnic exclusiveness of,
169–70

social aristocracy in, 164–65
strategies for changing society,
    189–90
see also Agrarians; Harlem
    Renaissance; poetry; *names of
    individual writers*
Anderson, Margaret, 164
Anderson, Sherwood, 39–40
on African-American primitivism,
    137
in Chicago, 36–37
Sinclair Lewis on, 158, 159
anti-intellectualism, 41–42
Aragon, Louis, 88
Armory Show (art exhibit), 17–18
Ash Wednesday (Eliot), 186
"At a Station in the Metro" (Pound),
    19
Auslander, Joseph, 86
Autumn Salon (art exhibit), 16

Babbitt (Lewis), 22
Baker, Houston A., Jr., 171
Barren Ground (Glasgow), 22, 183
Baudelaire, Charles-Pierre, 32
Beach, Sylvia, 164
Beautiful and the Damned, The
    (Fitzgerald), 106
*Bedford Glossary of Critical and
    Literary Terms, The* (Murfin and
    Ray), 14
Bender, Thomas, 188
Benn, Gottfried, 30
"Big Two-Hearted River"
    (Hemingway), 115–16
Billy Budd, 184, 185
Bishop, John Peale, 83, 86
Black Opals (journal), 128
Blast (magazine), 20
Blue Voyage (Aiken), 22, 121, 123
Bodenheim, Maxwell, 86
Bogan, Louise, 56
Bone, Robert, 129
Boni, Albert and Charles, 128–29
Bontemps, Arna, 134, 136
Boyd, Ernest, 39
Boy's Will, A (Frost), 62
Bradbury, Malcolm, 22–23, 24, 104
Brawley, Benjamin, 135–36, 139
Brickell, Herschel, 152
Bromfield, Louis, 96
Brooks, Van Wyck, 160, 188
Brotherhood of Sleeping Car
    Porters and Maids, 133–34
Brown, Sterling, 129, 130, 136
Brown, William Wells, 129
Browning, Robert, 58–59

Cabell, James Branch, 36, 158

Calverton, V.F., 138
Canzoni (Pound), 57
Carnegie, Andrew, 160
Cather, Willa
oriented toward the past, 190
Sinclair Lewis on, 158, 159
Cézanne, Paul, 16
Chabot, C. Barry, 188
Chesnutt, Charles W., 129
Chicago, 36–37
Chicago Poems (Sandburg), 39
Chicago Tribune, 37
Civic Club dinner, 134–35
Collinwood, R.G., 48
Conquistador (MacLeish), 84, 85
Corporate Entity (MacLeish), 83
Cowan, Louise, 150
Cowley, Malcolm, 91, 155
disappointment in American
    modernism, 179
expatriate literature of, 145, 165
"The Crack-Up" (Fitzgerald), 104,
    111
Crane, Hart, 22, 39
harsh actualities in poetry of,
    88–89
as part of lost generation, 91
use of rhythm 69
*Crisis: A Record of Darker Races,
    The* (journal), 128, 129, 133
Criterion (magazine), 41
*Critical Observations On The Great
    American Novel* (MacLeish), 83
Cubists, 17
Cullen, Countee, 25, 128
cummings, e.e.
ethnic exclusiveness in, 169–70
social aristocracy of, 164
translation by, 88
use of imagery, 86–87
use of rhythm, 69

Dadaism, 20
Darwin, Charles, 15
Davidson, Donald, 142, 152
Davis, Allison, 135–36, 138, 139
death
and influence of World War I on
    poetry, 83–84
in *The Waste Land*, 78
Delany, Martin R., 129
Desire Under the Elms (O'Neill), 186
Deutsch, Babette, 82
De Voto, Bernard, 179–80
Dickinson, Emily, 69, 184
Disinherited of Art, The (Fishman),
    145
Domesday Book (Masters), 39
Doolittle, Hilda, 19, 20

as exemplary Imagist, 69–71
and Ezra Pound, 58, 59, 65
social aristocracy of, 164
Dos Passos, John, 24, 46, 96
emphasis on self in literature of,
117–18
social aristocracy of, 164
Douglas, Aaron, 134
Douglass, Frederick, 129
Dreiser, Theodore, 36
as naturalist, 18
Sinclair Lewis on, 157, 159
DuBois, W.E.B., 129, 133
on *Nigger Heaven*, 138–39
on portrayal of African
Americans, 135–36
on race riots, 131
Duchamp, Marcel, 16, 17
Dudley, Helen, 56
Dunbar, Paul Laurence, 129

"Early Success" (Fitzgerald), 111
Earnest, Ernest, 178
Eastman, Max, 37
Education (Adams), 168
Einstein, Albert, 15, 16, 173
Eliot, T.S., 13, 19
banishment of poets by, 163
compared with Walt Whitman,
184, 186–87
concrete language used by, 45
disappointment in, 179
ethnic exclusiveness of, 170
European influence on, 14
exploiting loss of social privilege
by, 168–69
on historical sense, 163–64
impact on poetry, 72–73
influence on Agrarians, 146
as modernist and traditionalist,
20–21
oriented toward the past, 190
political involvement of, 191
social aristocracy of, 164
uncertainty in, 174
use of concrete by, 45–46
use of tempo of modern life, 87
World War I influence on, 23
see also Waste Land, The
Ellington, Duke, 134
Ellmann, Richard, 51
Emperor Jones, The (O'Neill), 176
End of the World, The (MacLeish),
84
Enormous Room, The (cummings),
22
European modernism
vs. American modernism, 36, 40, 41
influence on American

modernism, 14
Exiles' Return (Cowley), 145, 165
expatriates, 180–81
Fugitives as, 144, 145
Imagist poets as, 64–65
literary works of, 99
lost generation as, 23, 94
Expressionists, 17
Exultations (Pound), 57

Farewell to Arms, A (Hemingway),
183
fascism, 191, 192
Fathers, The (Tate), 151
Faulkner, William, 151
on death of language, 45
impact on Hemingway's
literature, 119
on purposelessness, 113
use of concrete by, 45–46
use of stream-of-consciousness
by, 123–25
war in literature of, 118
Fauvists, 16, 17, 18
Feidelson, Charles, Jr., 51
Ficke, Arthur Davis, 56
fiction, 22–24
see also American modernism;
individual titles
"Fifty Grand" (Hemingway), 117
Fifty Years and Other Poems
(Johnson), 134
Finnegans Wake (Joyce), 119, 121
Fire (journal), 128
Fisher, Rudolph, 136
Fishman, Solomon, 145
Fitzgerald, F. Scott, 91
changes in, 110–11
contributions of, 24
lifestyle reflected in fiction of,
104–106
on lost generation, 95
social aristocracy of, 164
World War I influence on, 23
see also Great Gatsby, The
Flappers and Philosophers
(Fitzgerald), 106
Fletcher, John Gould, 142, 152, 164
Flint, F.S., 64, 66, 67, 68
Flowering of the Rod, The
(Doolittle), 70
Foster, William Z., 149
Franklin, John Hope, 129, 130–31
free verse
in Imagism, 59–60, 68–69
Frescoes For Mr. Rockefeller's City
(MacLeish), 85
Freud, Sigmund, 15–16
and primitivism, 136

and stream-of-consciousness, 120, 121
Frost, Robert, 19, 62–63, 86, 184
　use of concrete by, 67
　on Woodrow Wilson, 46
Fugitive, The (magazine), 142, 143
Fugitives, 25
　rebellion against non-Southern culture by, 144–46, 148
　Southern heritage of, 143–44
　see also South, the
Futurism, 20

Game of Chess, A (MacLeish), 84
Gauguin, Paul, 16
Gautier, Judith, 59
genteel tradition, 156
　rebellion against, 159–61
Gilder, Richard Watson, 159
Glasgow, Ellen, 36
Golden Bough, The (Frazer), 78–79
Gombrich, E.H., 33
"The Good Anna" (Stein), 99–100
Goodman, Paul, 29
Graham, Frank, 137
Gray, Richard, 15, 17, 21, 64
Great Circle (Aiken), 121
Great Gatsby, The (Fitzgerald), 22, 107–10
　African Americans in, 176
　American small town in, 182–83
　as enduring work, 183
　ethnic exclusiveness in, 169
　lack of rhetoric in, 46
　uncertainty in, 174
Great Immigration, 166
Great Urban Migration, 130–32
Green, Elizabeth Lay, 137
Green, Paul Lay, 137
Greenwich Village, 37, 93–94
Gregory, Horace, 82, 85
Griggs, Sutton E., 129

Hamlet of A. MacLeish, The (MacLeish), 84, 85
Handy, W.C., 134
Harding, Warren G., 94
Harlem (city), 132–34
Harlem (magazine), 128
Harlem Renaissance, 24–25
　beginning of, 127–29, 134–35
　effect of *Nigger Heaven* on, 139–40
　reasons for failure of, 135–37
　and social change, 190
　terminology used to describe, 129–30
Harlem School, 129–30
Harper, Frances E.W., 129
Harris, Corra, 150

Hayes, Roland, 134
Heart of Darkness (Conrad), 176
Heisenberg, Werner, 173
Hemingway, Ernest, 13, 96
　contributions of, 23–24
　disappointment in, 179
　European influence on, 14
　nihilism in, 185
　as part of lost generation, 91
　Sinclair Lewis on, 159
　style of, 112–14, 115
　　through individual in crisis, 114–16
　　vs. structure, 116–18
　upstaged by other authors, 119
　use of concrete by, 45–46
　World War I influence on, 23, 100–102, 118
Hergesheimer, Joseph, 158
Hesse, Herman, 30–31
Heyward, DuBose, 137
history
　broken, in *The Great Gatsby*, 109
　discontinuity in, 30–31, 53
　progress in, 33
　T.S. Eliot on, 163–64
Hoffman, Frederick J., 120
Howe, Irving, 28, 39
Howells, William Dean, 157
Hughes, Langston, 25, 136, 138
"Hugh Selwyn Mauberly" (Pound), 101
Hulme, T.E., 40, 64
　on distrust of words, 48
　influence on Ezra Pound, 59
Humphrey, Robert, 122
Hurston, Zora Neale, 25, 135, 136

Iceman Cometh, The (O'Neill), 186
Idea of a Christian Society, The (Eliot), 186
ideogrammic method, 71
"If We Must Die" (McKay), 131, 139
I'll Take My Stand (essays), 25, 141–42, 149, 153
imagery, 42
　in *The Waste Land*, 77–78
　urban, 86–87
　see also Imagism
Imagism, 19–20
　changes in free verse made by, 59–60
　influences of, 58–59
　lack of abstraction in, 49–50
　origins of, 64–65
　rules of, 65–69
immigration, 166–67
Impressionism, 16
Industrial Revolution, 15

In Our Time (Hemingway), 22
Islands in the Stream (Hemingway), 112

James, Henry
  expatriate literature of, 102–103
  lasting impression of, 184
  as naturalist, 18
Java Head (Hergesheimer), 183
Jeffers, Robinson, 69, 158
Johnson, Charles S., 129, 133, 134–35
Johnson, James Weldon, 129, 132, 134
Jones, Howard Mumford, 144, 152–53
journals
  African American, 128, 133, 135
  of lost generation, 96–97
  poetry, 20, 37
Journey of the Magi, The (Eliot), 186
Joyce, James, 20, 31
  Hemingway upstaged by, 119
  use of stream-of-consciousness, 120–21

Kafka, Franz, 31, 119
Kandinsky, Wassily, 16
Karanikas, Alexander, 141
Kazin, Alfred, 112
Kellogg, Paul, 135
King Coffin (Aiken), 121
Klee, Paul, 32
Klein, Marcus, 162
Kline, Henry Blue, 142
Knowles, John, 48
Koch, Frederich, 137
Kreymborg, Alfred, 19, 37
Krutch, Joseph Wood, 49
Ku Klux Klan, 149

La Marche des Machines (Tessimond), 88
Lanier, Lyle H., 142
Last Tycoon, The (Fitzgerald), 111
Levin, Harry, 171
Lewis, Sinclair, 24, 36
  compared with Fitzgerald, 105
  Nobel Prize acceptance speech by, 155–59
  on revolt against genteel tradition, 161
Liberator, The, 131
Lindeman, E.C., 151
Lindsay, Vachel, 19, 37, 158
  on African Americans, 137
Little Review (magazine), 20, 36, 39
Locke, Alaine, 129, 135

anthology of, 128
and black pride, 133
London, 64–65
Long Day's Journey into Night, A (O'Neill), 186
Look Homeward, Angel (Wolfe), 183
lost generation, the, 23, 91–92
  adventures of, 93–95
  compared with earlier writers, 95–96
  lack of regional influences on, 92–93
  reasons for being lost, 96–97
  war's effect on, 118
  see also American modernism, writers of
Lost Lady, A (Cather), 192
Lowell, Amy
  on Edgar Lee Masters, 38
  and Imagism, 20, 67
  influence of, 37
  on new poetry movement, 18–19
Lowes, John Livingston, 68
Lukacs, Géorg, 33
Lume Spento, A (Pound), 57
Lytle, Henry Nelson, 142

Mackenzie, Compton, 105
MacLeish, Archibald, 82
  influence of World War I on, 83–84
  on need for a homeland, 85
magazines. *See* journals
Main Street (Lewis), 22, 105
Making of Americans, The (Stein), 43
Malinowski, Bronislaw, 48–49
Manhattan Transfer (Dos Passos), 22, 24
Mann, Thomas, 32
"The Man with the Blue Guitar" (Stevens), 21
Marx, Karl, 15
Masses, The (magazine), 37, 189
Masters, Edgar Lee, 19, 158
  in Chicago, 36–37
  Spoon River poems of, 37–39, 60–61
Matisse, Henri, 16
McKay, Claude, 131, 134
  poem on race riots by, 139
  political ideology of, 136
  use of primitivism, 137
Melville, Herman, 185
Mencken, Henry, 158
  Sinclair Lewis on, 159
  unfounded criticism by, 181
Meredith, George, 68
Messenger, The (journal), 128

migration, African American,
  130–32
Millay, Edna St. Vincent, 158
Mims, Edwin, 148–49, 150
Mizener, Arthur, 49
Moby Dick (Melville), 185
Modern American Poetry,
  1865–1950 (Shucard et al.), 15
modernism
  defined, 14–15, 51–52, 171–72
  see also American modernism
Monet, Claude, 16
Monroe, Harriet, 18, 56, 58, 60, 65
Moody, William Vaughan, 56
Moore, Marianne, 68, 69, 164
Moramarco, Fred, 15
Morton, Jelly Roll, 134
Mosquitoes (Faulkner), 50
Mourning Becomes Electra
  (O'Neill), 186
Moveable Feast, A (Hemingway), 112
Munson, Gorham, 164
Murfin, Ross, 14
myth
  in Southern poetry, 147
  in *The Waste Land*, 78–79

National Association for the
  Advancement of Colored People
  (NAACP), 128, 133, 134
National Urban League, 133
Nausea (Sartre), 119
New Negro, The (anthology), 128,
  129, 132, 134, 135
New Negro movement, 130
New Republic, 138, 189
New Spoon River, The (Masters), 39
Nietzsche, Friedrich, 16, 34
Nigger Heaven (Van Vechten),
  137–40
Nixon, Herman Clarence, 142
Nobel Prize, 155
North of Boston (Frost), 63
Nude Descending a Staircase
  (Duchamp), 17

Objectivism, 21, 42–43
"Ode to the Confederate Dead"
  (Tate), 147, 151
Odum, Howard, 137
Ogden, C.K., 48
Old Guard, 129–30
Old Man and the Sea, The
  (Hemingway), 112
O'Neill, Eugene
  on African American primitivism,
    137
  nihilism in, 186
  Sinclair Lewis on, 157–58, 159

Opportunity: A Journal of Negro
  Life, 129, 133
"Oread" (Doolittle), 69–70
Others (magazine), 20
Ottley, Roi, 133
Our Town (Wilder), 182
Owsley, Frank Lawrence, 142
Oxford History of English
  Literature, 52

Pale Horse, Pale Rider (Porter),
  46–47
Palmer, Mitchell, 149
Palms (journal), 128
Paris, 23, 102–103
Paterson (Williams), 41, 71
Perkins, David, 72
Personae (Pound), 57
Peterkin, Julia, 137
Picasso, Pablo, 16, 31
Pisan Cantos (Pound), 57
Pizer, Donald, 98
Poe, Edgar Allan, 69
poetry
  anti-intellectual, 41–42
  conveying harsh actualities, 88–89
  distrust of general statement in,
    48, 49
  of Fugitives, 143
  influence on visual arts, 17
  literary eras, contrasts in, 184
  myth in, 147
  on need for a homeland in, 85–86
  objectivism in, 42–43
  tempo of modern life in, 87–88
  urban imagery in, 86–87
  and World War I, 18–22, 82–83
  see also Imagism; *names of*
    individual poets
Poetry: A Magazine of Verse, 18, 36,
  37, 56, 181
  essay on Imagism in, 65–66
  Ezra Pound's involvement with,
    57, 58
  first years of, 60
  Sandburg's poems in, 61
Poirier, Richard, 173
Porter, Alan, 82
Porter, Katherine Anne, 46–47
post-Impressionism, 16
Pot of Earth, The (MacLeish), 83
Pound, Ezra, 13, 22, 56–58
  changes in free verse made by,
    59–60
  essay on Imagism by, 65–66, 67, 68
  exploiting loss of social privilege,
    168
  as Imagist, 19–20, 49, 64–65
  influences of, 58–59

on rules of Imagism, 68–69
social aristocracy of, 164
World War I in literature of, 101
primitivism, 136–40
Prufrock and Other Observations
(Eliot), 79

Quill (journal), 128

race riots, 131
poem on, 139
Randolph, A. Philip, 133–34
Ransom, John Crowe, 22, 25, 69,
143, 152
opposition to industrialism, 142
rejection of rhetoric, 46
Rascoe, Burton, 159
Ray, Ethel, 134
Ray, Supryia M., 14
Red Front (Aragon), 88
"The Red Wheelbarrow"
(Williams), 42
Reedy, William Marion, 37
Reedy's Mirror (journal), 37, 60
Richards, I.A., 48
Ripostes (Pound), 59
Robinson, Edward Arlington, 19
Roethke, Theodore, 69
Rogers, J.A., 138
Romantic Comedians, The
(Glasgow), 183
Romantic Egoist, The (Fitzgerald),
105
Romanticism
poetry's revolt against, 18
relationship with Imagism, 66
Ruland, Richard, 23, 24

Sacred Wood, The (Eliot), 146
Sandburg, Carl, 19, 61, 158
in Chicago, 36–37
as revolutionary poet, 38–39
on use of superfluous words, 68
Sartre, Jean-Paul, 119
Sayre, Zelda, 106, 110, 111
"The Scandal Detectives"
(Fitzgerald), 95
Schoenberg, Arnold, 31
Separate Peace, A (Knowles), 48
Seven Arts (journal), 189
sexual mores
in Gertrude Stein's work, 99–100
of 1920s, 106
Sheldon, Howard, 137
Shucard, Alan, 15, 16
*Sight in Camp in the Daybreak Gray
and Dim, A* (Whitman), 186–87
Sinclair, Upton, 18
Singh, Amritjit, 127

Sinister Street (Mackenzie), 105
Smith, Bessie, 134
Snows of Kilimanjaro, The
(Hemingway), 179
socialism, 192
"Soldier's Home" (Hemingway),
100–102
Soldiers' Pay (Faulkner), 118
Sound and the Fury, The
(Faulkner), 22
as enduring work, 183
stream-of-consciousness in,
123–25
South, the
literary awakening in, 150–53
modernism in, 148–50
Southern Renaissance, 137
see also Agrarians
Southern Renascence, 150
Spender, Stephen, 31
on the modern, 53–54
Spirit of Romance, The (Pound), 57
Spoon River Anthology (Masters),
37–38, 60–61
Spring and All (Williams), 41
Steffens, Lincoln, 180
Stein, Gertrude
on African Americans, 137
compared with William Carlos
Williams, 43
on lost generation, 91
on moral/sexual restrictions,
99–100
as naturalist, 18
social aristocracy of, 164
Stevens, Wallace, 20
on imagination, 22
oriented toward the future, 190
social aristocracy of, 164
on use of superfluous words, 68
Stevenson, Robert Louis, 159
stream-of-consciousness
influence of Freud on, 121, 123
in James Joyce, 123
in *The Sound and the Fury*,
123–25
in *The Waste Land*, 80
through prespeech levels of
consciousness, 122
Stribling, T.S., 137
Structural Iron Workers (Black), 87
Struggle of the Modern, The
(Spender), 53
Stylus (journal), 128
Sullivan, William, 15
Sun Also Rises, The (Hemingway),
22, 183
Survey Graphic (journal), 128, 133,
135

symbolism, 66
  in *The Great Gatsby*, 108
  in *The Waste Land*, 77–78
Symons, Julian, 36

Tagore, Rabindranath, 60
Tales from the Jazz Age
  (Fitzgerald), 106
Tate, Allen, 22, 151, 152
  on industrialization, 25, 142
  influence on poetry by, 82–83
  oriented toward the past, 190
  on T.S. Eliot, 146
  use of myth, 147
  use of urban imagery, 87
Tate Gallery, 57
Taylor, Raymond, 135
*Tendencies in Modern American
  Poetry* (Lowell), 37
Tender is the Night (Fitzgerald),
  110–11
Tessimond, A.S.J., 88
This Side of Paradise (Fitzgerald),
  105
Thoreau, Henry David, 184–85
Three Soldiers (Dos Passos), 22,
  117–18
Thurman, Wallace, 135–36
Toomer, Jean, 136
Tribute to the Angels (Doolittle), 70
Trilling, Lionel, 39, 53
  on modern literature as personal,
    175–76
  on rhetoric, 46

Ulysses (Joyce), 20
  African American response to,
    177–78
  stream-of-consciousness in,
    120–21
United States. *See* America
University of North Carolina, 137
Untermeyer, Louis, 86
urban imagery, 86–87
urbanization, 165–66
U.S.A. (Dos Passos), 46

Valediction To My Contemporaries
  (Gregory), 85
Vanderbilt University, 25, 142
Van Dyke, Henry, 155–56, 157
Van Gogh, Vincent, 16
Van Vechten, Carl, 128, 137–40
Verses For a Centennial (MacLeish),
  83
Victorianism, 159–60
visual arts, 16–18
Vorticism, 20

Wade, John Donald, 142
Walker, David, 129
Walls Do Not Fall, The (Doolittle),
  70
Walrond, Eric, 136, 138
Walsh, Ernest, 85
war. *See* World War I
Warren, Robert Penn, 142
  distrust of words, 47–48
  on industrialization, 25, 142
Waste Land, The (Eliot), 20, 21,
  allusion in, 79–80
  effect on William Carlos Williams,
    41
  illustrates human condition,
    80–81
  impact of, 72–73
  lack of plot in, 75–76
  modern city as setting in, 73–75
  musical sequence in, 76–77
  symbolism in, 77–78
  use of myth in, 78–79
  World War I influence in, 23
Watkins, Floyd, 44
Weston, Jessie L., 78–79
Wharton, Edith, 95
  distrust of rhetoric, 47
  literary movement in, 36–37
Whitehead, Alfred North, 49
Whitman, Walt, 69, 184, 186–87
Wilder, Thornton, 182
Williams, William Carlos, 17, 19, 37,
  58
  anti-intellectualism of, 41–42
  and Imagism, 20, 67–68
  philosophy of poetry, 21
  use of objectivism, 42–43
  on use of superfluous words,
    67–68
Wilson, Edmund, 151
Wilson, Woodrow, 46
Winesburg, Ohio (Anderson), 22, 39,
  183
Women in Love (Lawrence), 176
Woolf, Virginia, 31
World War I
  and African American migration,
    130–32
  and concrete language, 45
  influence of, 22–23, 118–19
    on Hemingway, 100–102
    on poetry, 82–83
  and use of rhetoric, 46–47

Young, Philip, 115
Young, Stark, 142
Young, Thomas Daniel, 25